The
Quotable
Quotations
Book

The Quotable Quotations Book

Compiled
by Alec Lewis

THOMAS Y. CROWELL, Publishers
New York   Established 1834

Acknowledgments to publishers and authors for permission to reprint copyrighted material begin on page 331.

U.S. Library of Congress Cataloging in Publication Data
Main entry under title:

The Quotable quotations book.
  1. Quotations, English. I. Lewis, Alec.
PN6081.Q58 1979   828'.9'1402   78-22461
ISBN 0-690-01489-9

80 81 82 83 10 9 8 7 6 5 4 3 2 1

For Lu, with love

INTRODUCTION

I began collecting statements on current topics in 1963 when I was writing speeches for a government official who liked to season his comments with quotations. Within weeks my collecting progressed from an act of self-defense to a fascination and finally to an addiction, and before long I realized that I had the makings of a book.

Over the years in which I have been preparing this book I have become increasingly aware of a number of questions, some unanswerable, that are related to what people have said. Among them are: Who really said it? Who said it first? What actually was said? How long will what they said be remembered? I should like to share with you just a few observations related to these questions.

Who really said it? We get a fair start by looking at the famous statement about winning being "the only thing" which is attributed to Vince Lombardi. The problem is that there's no record of Lombardi having said it, although he did express the thought less succinctly, as have a number of others. To find the exact words we have to go to a 1953 film, *Trouble Along the Way,* in which John Wayne played a football coach. The screenplay was by Melville Shavelson and Jack Rose, and the story was by Douglas Morrow and Robert Hardy Andrews. So it would appear the credit should go to one of them, but that raises a new and probably unanswerable question: Which one?

Outside the ring Muhammad Ali possibly is best known for his statements "I'm the greatest" and "float like a butterfly, sting like a bee." The fact is that he didn't originate either. The first was a saying he had learned from his father, and the second had been fed to him by his aide, Drew "Bundini" Brown.

In the social world, both the Duchess of Windsor and Mrs. William Paley are credited with the observation that "no woman can be too rich or too thin." But Truman Capote maintains it was he who first said it, on the "David Susskind Show" in 1958. It's more in his character and I believe him.

Duke Ellington and Fats Waller are credited with quite similar statements on the indefinability of jazz. The Ellington quotation is more familiar, but I think the one attributed to Waller is better. So that's the one I have put in this book.

In my file I have three statements by a Southwestern professor, all of them quotable, but also all of them lifted from others without credit. I have a complex sentence, excellent but stolen, that I found in the comments of a West Coast university president. My guess is that he didn't know of the theft, that the crime was committed and handed to him by a deft-fingered speech writer. I also have virtuoso sentences that have been lifted from Degas, Freud and Chesterton, and have been passed off as their own by a popular biographer, a popular psychologist and a popular clergyman. If I were interested I could gather volumes on the larceny of comedians. And for anyone who may care, Mussolini is reputed to have been one of history's most dedicated burglars of other people's words.

Who said it first? Although the thieving of words flourishes in some quarters, the fact that something has been said in much the same way by more than one person should not, in itself, suggest larceny. The human brain has not changed since long before the time of Aristotle, so it's not surprising that people frequently express the same thoughts from generation to generation, from culture to culture, even from neighborhood to neighborhood.

Lord Acton's commentary on the corruptibility of power is an observation that had been made earlier and generally better by Francis Bacon, Shakespeare, the elder William Pitt, Edmund Burke and Shelley, just to name some. And there is no doubt that each came to his opinion independently. The Lord Acton statement also is interesting for another reason which we will consider later.

On March 12, 1839, Charles Darwin wrote in his notebook: "It is difficult to believe in the dreadful but quiet war of organic beings going on [in] the peaceful woods & smiling fields." In 1969 J. A. Baker wrote much the same thing, and I see this as one more example of thoughtful and sensitive men observing the same condition and arriving at parallel conclusions. My only judgment is that Baker handled it better. You can read his statement on page 180 and make your own decision.

In 1922 George Santayana wrote *(Soliloquies in England):* "My atheism, like that of Spinoza, is true piety toward the universe and denies only gods fashioned by men in their own image, to be servants of their human interests." Seven years later Albert Einstein said (quoted in *Newsweek,* March 12, 1979): "I believe in Spinoza's God, who reveals himself in the orderly harmony of what exists, not in a God who concerns himself with the fates and notions of human beings." Can you imagine Einstein having to enter someone else's mind to find out what he should think?

Loren Eiseley has written (*The Unexpected Universe,* 1969): "Solutions to problems create problems." Two years earlier Russell Baker had said (interview in *Time,* January 19, 1967): "A solved problem creates two new problems, and the best prescription for happy living is not to solve any more problems than you have to." Both are original, yet basically the same. The only difference is that one draws this serious thought to an illogical conclusion.

In 1950 Clare Boothe Luce, introducing Eleanor Roosevelt at a dinner, said, "She is most famous for comforting the afflicted and afflicting the comfortable." In 1967 Bernice Fitz-Gibbon wrote (*Macy's, Gimbels and Me*), "A good ad should be like a good sermon: It must not only comfort the afflicted—it also must afflict the comfortable." It's possible that one influenced the other, but both make their points so I, for one, am not concerned.

Over the years I've noticed an increase in the published reports of wives having said about their husbands' retirements: "I married him for better or worse, but not for lunch." Someone had to say it first; my record goes back to a 1960 comment by Hazel Weiss after her husband, George, retired as general manager of the New York Yankees (George Weiss obituary, *New York Times,* August 14, 1972). As a side note, in this instance apparently the feeling was mutual, for soon afterward Weiss returned to activity as general manager of the Mets.

A number of people have said, "When you're young you always assume sex was invented the day you hit puberty," or words close to it. My records trace the saying to Professor John P. Roche of Brandeis University (quoted in *Newsweek,* February 20, 1967), but I don't know if he claims ownership. The observation that railroad stations were "the cathedrals of America" has been made by both Lucius Beebe and Rebecca West. The comment, "Most people who favor birth control have already been born," is not uncommon, and I'd run away from a debate on who said it first.

Finally there's a comment on New York: "It's unfortunate that a good many people in the city today mistake good manners for a sign of weakness, and that's a hell of a note." This was said by John Morgano, an officer of the New York Hotel and Motel Trades Council and former doorman at The Plaza (interview in the *Daily News,* March 22, 1970). About ten years earlier I heard my wife say the same thing in almost the same words. If you were to tell me you heard your Uncle Charley say it ten years before that, I would not be surprised.

What actually was said? Misquotations sometimes gain credence that threatens to obliterate what actually was said. Examples are the widely held belief that Emerson wrote "Consistency is the hobgoblin of little minds . . ." and that Lord Acton stated "Power corrupts . . ." Emerson actually wrote (*Self Reliance,* 1841), "A *foolish* consistency . . ."; Lord Acton's words were (letter to Bishop Mandell Creighton, April 5, 1887), "Power *tends* to corrupt . . ." The italics are mine to emphasize the changes these words bring to the meanings.

At least one misquotation is so deeply imbedded in our culture that it's almost synonymous with the flag. This is the statement attributed to Nathan Hale on the scaffold: "I regret that I have but one life to lose for my country." Frederick Mackenzie, a British captain who witnessed the hanging, had written in his diary that Hale had said, "It is the duty of every good officer to obey any orders given him by his commander-in-chief." In a Bicentennial lecture, Yale historian G. B. Warden said that the legendary quotation first came to print in an 1848 biography of Hale, and that the author probably took the thought from Joseph Addison's 1713 play, *Cato*.

Less serious and more fun are some misstatements that have been created by or attributed to inventive newspapermen. Leo Durocher probably is more famous for "Nice guys finish last" than for his record in baseball. But in his autobiography Durocher claims that the quotation is a sportswriter's distortion of his comment on Mel Ott's Giants: "Take a look at them. All nice guys. They'll finish last. Nice guys. Finish last." But Durocher is not displeased. He has written that "it has gotten me into Bartlett's *Quotations* . . . between John Betjeman and Wystan Hugh Auden. . . . Just who the hell were Betjeman and Auden anyway?"

Willie Sutton is best remembered for having said that he robbed banks "because that's where the money is." In his autobiography Sutton claims that he never said it, that the statement was created by a newspaper reporter. But when he wrote his autobiography, sensing where the money was, he gave it the title—you guessed it—*Where the Money Was.*

It is agreed that Thomas Edison said on his deathbed, "It is very beautiful over there," and for decades clergymen have been reciting it as evidence that Edison, an agnostic, had seen a preview of the life to come. Unfortunately those close to Edison report he merely was commenting on the autumn foliage seen from his window (*New York Times,* October 26, 1975).

W. C. Fields' "I Would Rather Be Living in Philadelphia," which I never have seen quoted correctly, is not an actual epitaph although many believe it to be. He wrote it for a feature collection of parody epitaphs that was published in the June 1925 issue of *Vanity Fair.* Dorothy Parker's "Excuse My Dust," which sometimes also is mistaken for a real epitaph, appeared in the same feature.

In my file I have three accounts of Charles de Gaulle's commentary on the problem of rallying a nation that demands so many different types of cheeses. One lists the number at 243, another at 246, the third at 265. In preparing this book, with scholarly objectivity I selected the quotation with the largest number.

How long will what they said be remembered? Anyone conjecturing on life expectancy for quotations should take a lesson in humility from the first edition of John Bartlett's *Familiar Quotations,* published in 1855. It had nothing from Chaucer, Dickens, Emerson, Hawthorne, Samuel Johnson, Melville, Thoreau, Shelley, Tocqueville or Whitman. La Rochefoucauld barely made it with one line; Keats got three lines. But space was given to a number of now buried names such as Christopher P. Cranch, Joshua Sylvester and Hekikory Taylor. This makes me tiptoe into the subject.

Some remarkably articulate and original people are writing and talking today. I think of Peter Ustinov who seems incapable of speaking an unquotable sentence, Gore Vidal even though he talks too much, Truman Capote playing the role of a mod Oscar Wilde, Norman Mailer who when he's good is very good, Donald Barr, Herbert Gold, Wilfrid Sheed, George Steiner, George F. Will and many others.

But durability is the question. My guess is that very few of the quotations in this or any current book will survive into the next century—although I do think this book will be looked into by a few researchers as long as binding and paper survive, only because of the living-it-now view it gives of our time.

Of course some quotations—I can't guess which—will survive for centuries. Certainly something will be remembered from each President just because he was president. I'm confident some of Winston Churchill will last as long as time, although I've noticed that certain of his statements are beginning to pale for those too young to feel in their guts the monumental crises of World War II.

Martin Luther King, Jr., elicits an emotional response now, but objectivity will come with time. Some of his words will diminish, but many will grow and they might not be the ones we know the best. Another possible survivor is Charles de Gaulle, who in this country hasn't yet emerged from the shadow of fashionable ridicule. At the top of my list is Albert Einstein. His statement (letter to Paul Ehrenfest, June 3, 1917) "Rejoice with your family in the beautiful land of life" is my favorite in this entire book.

This is an informal book in the sense that it is journalistic in concept and organization. Its subjects are for the present. Quotations within subjects have been selected for substance rather than for the prominence of people who said them. When leaders of contemporary thought make their points well, they are quoted. But when a cab driver, spot welder or street-smart kid does it better, the play goes to one of them.

My goal has been to stimulate, inform, amuse and sometimes antagonize. My guiding principle from the beginning has been: "If you

The Quotable Quotations Book

ABORTION also see BIRTH CONTROL

If men could get pregnant, abortion would be a sacrament.
WOMAN CAB DRIVER TO GLORIA STEINEM, Boston, 1971

Once you pass into the utilitarianism of abortion, where do you go?
Why do you kill an unborn child after six months and not old people
or not criminals or not just every second person in the world?
MSGR. VICTOR HEYLEN, speech to physicians, Brussels, 1967

ACCOUNTANTS/ACCOUNTING

When you make the mistake of adding the date to the right side of the
accounting statement, you must add it to the left side too.
ACCOUNTANTS' MAXIM

Did you ever hear of a kid playing accountant—even if he wanted to
be one?
JACKIE MASON, quoted in *Time*, Mar. 21, 1969

ACTORS/ACTING also see HOLLYWOOD; MOVIES; SHOW BIZ; THEATER

It took me a long time to discover that the key thing in acting is honesty. Once you know how to fake that, you've got it made.
ACTOR, quoted in Edmund Carpenter, *Oh, What a Blow That Phantom Gave Me!*, 1973

When you finally learn how to do it, you're too old for the good parts.
RUTH GORDON, quoted in Leonard Lyons' column, June 21, 1972

When they work, their *hours* are impossible and when they *don't*
work, *they* are impossible.
DR. RALPH R. GREENSON, interview in *TV Guide*, July 20, 1969

The only area where women have achieved equal status is in the profession of acting, and that is because *there* they are a necessity.
WILLIAM BAYER, *Breaking Through, Selling Out, Dropping Dead*,
1971

You're always a little disappointing in person because you can't be the edited essence of yourself.
>MEL BROOKS, interview in *New York Post*, Apr. 5, 1975

Poor dears, they have no consonants.
>DAME EDITH EVANS ON THE NEW STARS, quoted in *Newsweek*, Apr. 1, 1968

England produces the best fat actors.
>JIMMY CANNON, *Nobody Asked Me, But . . .*, Jack and Tom Cannon, eds., 1978

ADOLESCENCE also see CHILDHOOD; CHILDREN; YOUTH

At 14 you are still in most respects a dependent youth, in some respects a child. At 24 you are an adult. In between, extraordinary turbulences take place.
>DANIEL P. MOYNIHAN, quoted in *University*, Summer 1974

It confuses the sprouting adolescent to wake up every morning in a new body. It confuses the mother and father to find a new child every day in a familiar body.
>DONALD BARR, *New York Times*, Nov. 26, 1967

You can't get security from your parents because you're rebelling against them; you can't get it from your prejudices because you can't admit them.
>COLLEGE STUDENT, quoted in *Newsweek*, Apr. 3, 1967

At 3 A.M., I'm most scared about the future—then, when the thought of living becomes as scary as the thought of dying and being nineteen feels no different than being seven and a half.
>EDNA GOLDSMITH, Yale sophomore, *New York Times*, Jan. 29, 1975

Cute teen-agers exist only on television, I suspect. I know there are none in my neighborhood.
>ROBERT MACKENZIE, *TV Guide*, Jan. 27, 1979

I have no cure, only consolation: someone has passed this way before.
>STEFAN KANFER, *Time*, Feb. 7, 1972

A few years ago, adolescence was a phase; then it became a profession; now it is a new nationality.
>DONALD BARR, *Who Pushed Humpty Dumpty?*, 1971

They feel like men and women, look like men and women and have the knowledge that makes them feel powerful. But when you realize that they are not socially and emotionally mature, you discover that they are too powerful for their own good—too powerful for society's good.
ELIZABETH HALL, quoted in *Newsweek,* Apr. 24, 1972

If you reside in a state where you attain your legal majority while still in your teens, pretend that you don't. There isn't an adult alive who would want to be contractually bound by a decision he came to at the age of 19.
FRAN LEBOWITZ, *Newsweek,* Jan. 1, 1979

ADULTERY also see MARRIAGE

Adultery is a stimulant to men but a sedative to women.
MALCOLM DE CHAZAL, *Plastic Sense,* 1971

Sideways jumps (*Seitensprunge*)
GERMAN SLANG FOR ADULTERY

Ninety per cent of all Christians practice polygamy—only they don't call it that.
UTAH MORMON, quoted in *Newsweek,* Nov. 21, 1977

ADVERTISING also see TV: COMMERCIALS

Advertising is the lubricant for the free-enterprise system.
LEO-ARTHUR KELMENSON, speech to Soviet expatriates, Mar. 26, 1976

It is the greatest art form of the 20th century.
MARSHALL MCLUHAN, quoted in *Advertising Age,* Sept. 3, 1968

We grew up founding our dreams on the infinite promise of American advertising.
ZELDA FITZGERALD, *Save Me the Waltz,* 1932

In the ad biz, sincerity is a commodity bought and paid for like everything else.
Newsweek, June 19, 1967

A good ad should be like a good sermon: It must not only comfort the afflicted—it also must afflict the comfortable.
BERNICE FITZ-GIBBON, *Macy's, Gimbels and Me,* 1967

Those who most enjoy ads already own the products.
> EDMUND CARPENTER, *Oh, What a Blow That Phantom Gave Me!*, 1973

The guy you've really got to reach with your advertising is the copywriter for your chief rival's advertising agency. If you can terrorize him, you've got it licked.
> HOWARD L. GOSSAGE, interview in *Business Week,* Feb. 11, 1967

I start worrying about losing an account the minute I get it. The minute I sign the contract, I'm one step closer to losing it.
> HEAD OF AN AGENCY, quoted in Jerry Della Femina, *From Those Wonderful Folks Who Gave You Pearl Harbor,* 1970

AFRICA

Most people have a Tarzan view of Africa, as if there's something more savage about a spear than a howitzer.
> WARREN M. ROBBINS, interview in *Newsweek,* June 21, 1971

When God created Africa, he paused to add two finishing touches. One was the tsetse fly, to keep the white man away. The other was the palm tree, to give comfort if the tsetse fly failed.
> NIGERIAN BUSINESSMAN, quoted in *New York Times,* Nov. 8, 1976

When the missionaries arrived, the Africans had the land and the missionaries had the Bible. They taught us to pray with our eyes closed. When we opened them, they had the land and we had the Bible.
> JOMO KENYATTA, obituary in *Newsweek,* Sept. 4, 1978

Let it be. Let it find itself without outside interference. Let its people discover who they are.
> LAURENS VAN DER POST, interview in *New York Times,* July 16, 1978

AGING also see MIDDLE AGE; OLD AGE

In America, to look a couple of years younger than you actually are is not only an achievement for which you are to be congratulated, it is patriotic.
> CYNTHIA PROPPER SETON, *A Special and Curious Blessing,* 1968

You don't grow old gradually, or on purpose, the way you go downtown on a subway. It's more like finding yourself standing in the last station wondering how you got there.
ROBERT THOMAS ALLEN, *We Gave You the Electric Toothbrush,* 1971

Getting old in kids' country.
SHANA ALEXANDER ON AGING IN AMERICA, *Newsweek,* Nov. 11, 1974

No one sees the wolf at my side.
ANONYMOUS

I have everything now I had 20 years ago—except now it's all lower.
GYPSY ROSE LEE, quoted in *Newsweek,* Sept. 16, 1968

In our memories people we no longer see age gracefully.
GRAHAM GREENE, *The Honorary Consul,* 1973

How old would you be if you didn't know how old you was?
SATCHEL PAIGE, quoted in Garson Kanin, *It Takes Time to Become Young,* 1978

AIRPLANES also see TRANSPORTATION

Flight is the only truly new *sensation* that men have achieved in modern history.
JAMES DICKEY, *New York Times,* July 15, 1979

The really great visual experience today is to fly over a huge city and look down in the night. It's like a tremendous jubilant Christmas tree. You just feel life is worth living—when you come down you may have some doubts.
GYORGY KEPES, interview in *New York Times,* Dec. 26, 1969

There is no more nature . . . everything disappears. There remains a diagram—a map. Man, in short, looks through the eyes of God. And he perceives that God can have but an abstract view. This is not a good thing.
ALBERT CAMUS, *Notebooks 1942–1951,* 1966

There you are, up there, strapped in, trussed up, unable to affect your own destiny in any way. If the plane goes down, so do you. What a perfect place for God to get you.
ANONYMOUS, quoted in *New York Times,* Aug. 12, 1973

If God had intended us to fly he would never have given us railways.
MICHAEL FLANDERS, obituary in *New York Times,* Apr. 16, 1975

No. Crashing.
AMTRAK PASSENGER WHEN ASKED IF SHE WAS AFRAID OF FLYING, quoted
in *New York Times,* May 1, 1975

Flying in a plane from San Francisco to New York is nothing more
than a horizontal elevator ride.
HOWARD GOSSAGE, *Ramparts,* Apr. 1966

We developed the feeling on takeoff that Madison Square Garden was
rolling down the runway, and we were in it.
MELVIN DURSLAG ON THE 747, *Los Angeles Herald-Examiner,* 1970

I'd fly if you'd tell me what happens in the second hour on a plane
that doesn't happen in the first.
DUKE ELLINGTON, quoted in Leonard Lyons' column, Aug. 9, 1972

Red-eye express.
BUSINESSMAN'S NAME FOR LOS ANGELES-NEW YORK OVERNIGHT FLIGHT

Vomit comet.
CREW'S NAME FOR SAN JUAN-NEW YORK BUDGET FLIGHT

Isn't it good after an airplane trip to go home and look at some peach-
es on a plate.
FRANCIS PONGE, *Things,* 1971

ALCOHOL also see BEER

Through booze I met two Chief Justices, 50 world champs, six Presidents and DiMaggio and Babe Ruth.
TOOTS SHOR, *Quote,* Jan. 29, 1967

If a guy can't get drunk by midnight, he ain't trying.
TOOTS SHOR ON WORLD WAR II MIDNIGHT LIQUOR CURFEW, 1942

Other drugs tend to make you introspective, contemplative of your
own navel, whereas alcohol tends to make you contemplate other people's navels.
MORRIS CHAFETZ, quoted in Jack B. Weiner, *Drinking,* 1976

The life of the party almost always winds up in a corner with an overcoat over him.
> WILSON MIZNER, quoted in Richard O'Connor, *Rogue's Progress,* 1975

Drunks are rarely amusing unless they know some good songs and lose a lot at poker.
> KARYL ROOSEVELT, *New York Times,* Oct. 5, 1975

Alcohol could be called a false set of guts.
> BILL GLASS, *Stand Tall and Straight,* 1967

Alcoholism isn't a spectator sport. Eventually the whole family gets to play.
> JOYCE REBETA-BURDITT, *The Cracker Factory,* 1977

I wasn't considered as being an alcoholic. I just drank as a hobby.
> CHARLEY YOUNG, Bowery derelict, quoted in *Herald* (New York), Jan. 21, 1977

ALONENESS

People fighting their aloneness will do almost anything to avoid silence.
> MYRTLE BARKER, *I Am Only One,* 1966

I don't want to be alone. I want to be left alone.
> KATHARINE HEPBURN, interview in *TV Guide,* Dec. 15, 1973

AMBITION

I must keep aiming higher and higher—even though I know how silly it is.
> ARISTOTLE ONASSIS, quoted in *Newsweek,* Oct. 28, 1968

Avarice walks among us disguised as ambition.
> EZRA J. MISHAN, interview in Israel Shenker, *Words and Their Masters,* 1974

When I grow up I want to be a little boy.
> JOSEPH HELLER, *Something Happened,* 1974

AMERICA: SEEN BY THEM

The United States is the glory, jest, and terror of Mankind.
JAMES M. MINIFIE, Canadian, *The New Romans,* Al Purdy, ed., 1968

A world of its own.
MOHAMMED RIZA PAHLEVI, interview in *Newsweek,* Jan. 24, 1977

One comes to the United States—always, no matter how often—to see the future. It's what life in one's own country will be like five, ten, twenty years from now.
EHUD YONAY, Israeli, *New York Times,* Nov. 26, 1972

Instead of leading the world, America appears to have resolved to buy it.
THOMAS MANN, German, 1947, *Letters of Thomas Mann, 1889–1955,* Richard and Clara Winston, eds., 1971

Everyone is running to and fro, pressed by the stomach ache of business.
FREDERIC AUGUSTE BERTHOLDI, French sculptor of Statue of Liberty, letter to mother, June 12, 1871

In America, unhappiness about the rat race is part of the people's happiness.
RALF DAHRENDORF, German-born, quoted in *New York Times,* Oct. 15, 1976

The clear-desk system.
THOMAS MASARYK, president of Czechoslovakia, identifying America's greatest weakness, quoted in Hamilton Fish Armstrong, *Peace and Counterpeace,* 1971

I still believe the world would have been a better place if some of the American ideals of my youth had prevailed everywhere and, first of all, in the United States itself.
LUIGI BARZINI, Italian, *O America,* 1977

The weakness of American civilization, and perhaps the chief reason why it creates so much discontent, is that it is so curiously abstract. It is a bloodless extrapolation of a satisfying life. . . . You dine off the advertiser's "sizzling" and not the meat of the steak. Sex is discovered in manuals and not in bed. And as soon as a guaranteed egg substitute has been packaged and marketed, from a huge factory in New Jersey called "Old Mother Giles," then real white eggs will be even more sharply despised than brown eggs.
J. B. PRIESTLEY, English, *New Statesman,* Dec. 1971

I like going there for golf. America's one vast golf course today.
EDWARD, DUKE OF WINDSOR, quoted in *Newsweek,* Jan. 26, 1970

Is the U.S. a great power—or merely a large country?
EDITORIAL IN *Dong-A Ilbo,* South Korea, Feb. 1968

AMERICA: SEEN BY US

What makes America unique in our time is that confrontation with
the new is part of the daily American experience. For better or worse,
the rest of the world learns what is in store for it by observing what
happens in the United States.
ZBIGNIEW BRZEZINSKI, *Between Two Ages,* 1970

America where overnight success is both a legend and a major industry.
JOHN LEGGETT, *Ross and Tom,* 1974

An economic system prouder of the distribution of its products than of
the products themselves.
MURRAY KEMPTON, *New York Times,* Jan. 16, 1977

Off on a mountaintop on a vacation, we look back, and suddenly in the
distance the America we have left behind seems bizarre and surreal.
ARTHUR HERZOG, *The B.S. Factor,* 1973

So much of "official" American culture has been so cheaply optimistic
that we are likely almost by reflex to take pessimism as a measure of
seriousness.
ROBERT WARSHAW, quoted in *New York Times,* Sept. 22, 1972

To the intellectual, America's unforgivable sin is that it has revolutions without revolutionaries, and achieves the momentous in a mat-
ter-of-fact way.
ERIC HOFFER, "Reflections" (column), Feb. 9, 1968

America's dissidents are not committed to mental hospitals and sent
into exile; they thrive and prosper and buy a house in Nantucket and
take flyers in the commodities market.
TED MORGAN, *On Becoming American,* 1978

I'm very critical of the U.S., but get me outside the country and all of
a sudden I can't bring myself to say one nasty thing about the U.S.
SAUL ALINSKY

Those who find America an especially violent and oppressive country ("Amerika") have apparently never read the history of England or France, Germany or Russia, Indonesia or Burundi, Turkey or Uganda.
EUGENE D. GENOVESE, *New York Times,* June 18, 1978

We are a great country that overreached itself and is out of breath.
WALTER LIPPMANN, interview in *Washington Post Syndicate,* Oct. 23, 1971

Being a great power is no longer much fun.
DAVID SCHOENBAUM, *New York Times,* Oct. 28, 1973

As I see it, in this country—a land of the most persistent idealism and the blandest cynicism—the race is on between the decadence and its vitality.
ALISTAIR COOKE, *America,* 1973

I'll tell you what's wrong with the country! The women are polarized, the kids are polarized, the minorities are polarized, the hardhats are polarized, and nobody knows what polarized means.
JOSEPH SABO, cartoon, *Saturday Review,* May 1, 1976

AMERICANS: SEEN BY THEM

Punch in! Punch out! Eat quick!
TON THAT DINH, expatriate, former South Vietnamese general, interview in *New York Times,* Dec. 28, 1975

Better at having a love affair that lasts ten minutes than any other people in the world.
STEPHEN SPENDER, interview in *New York Post,* Apr. 26, 1975

One thinks of college girls working out their orgasm averages.
ANTHONY GLYN, *The British,* 1970

Americans are remorseless. They invite you to a party. You can't say, "I've got a splitting headache"—they'll send the doctor around.
V. S. PRITCHETT, interview in *New York Times,* May 22, 1977

Your chaps are either positive that they are always right about everything or positive they are always wrong. Neither attitude inspires much confidence.
AUSTRALIAN, quoted in *National Observer,* Aug. 4, 1969

Americans all have little lawns in front of their houses. Since they have no education naturally they get bored, so they spend Sunday cutting the grass.
PARIS–EAUBONNE COMMUTER, *Réalités,* from *Quote,* Oct. 8, 1967

Jesus Christ Lucky Strike God Damn Chesterfield SOB.
CHETNIK PASSWORD TO OSS AGENTS, YUGOSLAVIA, WORLD WAR II, quoted in Corey Ford, *Donovan of OSS,* 1970

AMERICANS: SEEN BY US

Although action is typical of the American style, thought and planning are not; it is considered heresy to state that some problems are not immediately or easily solvable.
DANIEL BELL, *Daedalus,* Summer 1967

One trouble with us Americans is that we're fixers rather than preventers.
GEN. JAMES DOOLITTLE, quoted in *Guideposts,* Mar. 1969

There are no second acts in American lives.
F. SCOTT FITZGERALD, *The Last Tycoon,* 1941

Losing is the great American sin.
JOHN TUNIS, quoted in *New York Times,* Mar. 20, 1977

Nothing is more difficult for Americans to understand than the possibility of tragedy.
HENRY A. KISSINGER, quoted in *New York Times,* Oct. 28, 1973

With our aptness for phrasemaking, we sometimes mesmerize ourselves into assuming that since we have cleverly labelled something, we have somehow magically solved the problem it presents.
LOUIS L. ALLEN, *Harvard Business Review,* Apr. 5, 1969

The American people can have anything they want; the trouble is they don't know what they want.
ATTRIBUTED TO EUGENE V. DEBS

Two hours is about as long as an American can wait for the close of a baseball game—or anything else, for that matter.
A. G. SPALDING, quoted in *New York Times,* Apr. 9, 1950

Only Americans have mastered the art of being prosperous though broke.
> KELLY FORDYCE, *Indianapolis Star,* May 25, 1969

The two-faced American dream—idealism and pragmatism.
> JACK KROLL, *Newsweek,* May 31, 1976

Historically the American people have always yearned mightily for leadership and have consistently mistrusted and maligned it whenever it appeared.
> SAMUEL B. GOULD, speech at Colgate University, Sept. 22, 1969

Sometimes it seems that we might have been happier if we had once had an aristocracy to blame everything on.
> ANATOLE BROYARD, *New York Times,* Apr. 12, 1972

We have always been people who dropped the past and then could not remember where it had been put.
> GLORIA EMERSON, *Winners and Losers,* 1977

We are game-playing, fun-loving creatures, we are the otters of the universe.
> RICHARD BACH, *Illusions,* 1977

We do have a zeal for laughter in most situations, give or take a dentist.
> JOSEPH HELLER, interview in *New York Times,* Sept. 10, 1968

ANIMALS also see DOGS; INSECTS

Animals don't know how old they are. They greet each day as young as they feel.
> DR. HARRY JOHNSON, *Business Management,* Nov. 1969

Wild animals and people have something in common; they love to look at each other.
> MAXINE A. ROCK, *Travel,* Feb. 1968

It's much easier to show compassion for animals. They are never wicked.
> HAILE SELASSIE I, EMPEROR OF ETHIOPIA, obituary in *Newsweek,* Sept. 8, 1975

They do not make me sick discussing their duty to God.
> WALT WHITMAN, in section later titled "Song of Myself," *Leaves of Grass,* 1855

ANTI-SEMITISM

Anti-Semitism is, unfortunately, not only a feeling which all gentiles at times feel, but also, and this is what matters, a feeling of which the majority of them are not ashamed.
> W. H. AUDEN, quoted in *Newsweek,* Nov. 13, 1972

Since my little daughter is only half-Jewish, would it be all right if she went in the pool only up to her waist?
> GROUCHO MARX, letter to country club after it barred his daughter as Jewish, obituary in *New York Times,* Aug. 20, 1977

What slavery and its aftermath achieved for the blacks, anti-Semitism did for the Jews: it kept the culture intact.
> JOSEPH PAPP, *New York Times,* Jan. 1, 1978

ANXIETY

Anxiety is the price that must be paid for boundless opportunity . . . and not everyone can handle it.
> TED MORGAN, *On Becoming American,* 1978

Anxiety is the dizziness of freedom.
> SØREN KIERKEGAARD, quoted in *New York Times,* Nov. 27, 1977

Man needs normal anxiety.
> DR. J. J. LOPEZ IBOR, speech at World Psychiatric Association Meeting, Dec. 1967

People use words like anxiety attacks as if anxiety is out there and attacks you.
> WAYNE W. DYER, interview in *New York Times,* June 5, 1977

APARTMENT

Without respect.
> WORKMAN ON HOW APARTMENTS ARE BUILT SO FAST, quoted in *New York Times*, July 3, 1973

Our apartment was much nicer before we moved in.
> JAMES R. WEST, quoted in *New York Post*, July 3, 1971

It seems each room is about a foot too small.
> DOUGLAS D. DONALD ON A MODERN APARTMENT, quoted in *New York Times*, Jan. 28, 1979

Except that the address is better, the terrace offers at a stiff price nothing more than the tenement fire escape offered for nothing.
> RICHARD J. WHALEN, *Fortune*, Sept. 1964

ARCHITECTURE also see CITY; HOUSES; SKYSCRAPERS

If I had to say which was telling the truth about society, a speech by a Minister of Housing or the actual building put up in his time, I should believe the building.
> LORD KENNETH CLARK, quoted in *Image*, June 1971

It is the art that has the greatest power to alter decisively and tangibly how we live and to modify steadily how we feel.
> JOHN FRASER, *Yale Review*, Winter 1970

The frightening thought that what you draw may become a building makes for reasoned lines.
> SAUL STEINBERG, quoted in *Newsweek*, Apr. 17, 1978

The postwar architecture is the accountants' revenge on the prewar businessmen's dreams.
> REM KOOLHAAS, *Delirious New York*, 1978

I'm not sure office buildings are even architecture. They're really a mathematical calculation, just three-dimensional investments.
> GORDON BUNSHAFT, quoted in *Fortune*, Feb. 1973

It is only air-conditioning which makes my architecture tolerable.
> PHILIP JOHNSON ON THE GLASS SKYSCRAPER, quoted in *New York Times*, May 22, 1977

ARISTOCRACY

I believe in aristocracy, though—if that is the right word, and if a democrat may use it. Not an aristocracy of power, based upon rank and influence, but an aristocracy of the sensitive, the considerate and the plucky. Its members are to be found in all nations and classes, and all through the ages, and there is a secret understanding between them when they meet. They represent the true human tradition, the one permanent victory of our queer race over cruelty and chaos.
    E. M. FORSTER, *Two Cheers for Democracy*, 1951

ARMY also see PENTAGON

The sergeant is the Army.
    DWIGHT D. EISENHOWER, quoted in *New York Times*, Dec. 24, 1972

The Army ain't as rough as the street.
    JUAN HERNANDEZ, recruit, quoted in *Newsweek*, Mar. 28, 1977

Very few people who come into the Army admit to being a combat infantryman by civilian profession.
    KEENE PETERSON ON THE ARMY CLASSIFICATION SYSTEM, Engineering Manpower Commission report, June 18, 1970

When I first went into the active Army, you could tell someone to move a chair across the room—now you have to tell him why.
    MAJ. ROBERT LEMBKE, quoted in *Newsweek*, Mar. 26, 1979

ART: CREATIVE PRODUCT also see PAINTING

Art is the community's medicine for the worst disease of the mind, the corruption of consciousness.
    R. G. COLLINGWOOD, *The Principles of Art*, 1955

Art is not a means by which we escape from life but a stratagem by which we conquer life's disorder.
    ALFRED BARR, JR., quoted in *Newsweek*, June 1, 1964

The twin curses of modern life are boredom and mindless episodic excitement. Life is poisoned by them and art is their antidote.
    HARRY S. BROUDY, *Music Educators' Journal*, Sept. 1969

AUTOBIOGRAPHY

Next to the writer of real estate advertisements, the autobiographer is the most suspect of prose artists.
Donal Henahan, *New York Times,* Feb. 11, 1977

Hiring someone to write your autobiography is like paying someone to take a bath for you.
Mae West, quoted in *Bookviews,* July 1978

The most tedious autobiographies I have ever read have been those written by performers and other members of the theatrical profession—who have been everywhere, met everyone, and understood nothing.
Sydney J. Harris, *Quote,* Aug. 28, 1977

AUTOMATION

If the body panel isn't where it's supposed to be, the welding robots will happily weld thin air.
Donald Hart, interview in *Newsweek,* Apr. 23, 1979

When the machines are high-priced or when only a mathematician can understand them, we use the two-dollar word *automation;* when the machine is an average-priced one that high-school students can understand, the one-dollar word *mechanization* is used; for low-priced machines any one can operate, we use the fifty-cent word *labor-saving.*
Donald A. and Eleanor C. Laird, *How to Get Along with Automation,* 1964

Automized and computerized industry requires more and more young men and women who have white-collar skills but behave with the docility expected of blue-collar workers.
Staughton Lynd, *Newsweek,* July 6, 1970

AUTOMOBILES also see TRANSPORTATION

The first thing an American does when he gets a little ahead is to buy an auto, and the second thing he does is to drive it over the horizon.
Walt A. Rostow to Soviet general at the Johnson-Kosygin Conference, Glassboro, N.J., June 23, 1967

Americans are broad-minded people. They'll accept the fact that a person can be an alcoholic, a dope fiend, a wife beater, and even a newspaperman, but if a man doesn't drive there's something wrong with him.
ART BUCHWALD, *Have I Ever Lied to You?*, 1968

The automobile is the woman in technological man's life; his mistress, wife and mother.
Kaiser News, no. 5, 1971

In most two-car families, the man drives the big new car to work, where it sits idle for nine hours, while the wife drives the old clunk—on and off, all day long. To her the clunk is a tool; to the man the car is a symbol in the company parking lot.
Kaiser News, no. 5, 1971

People don't come here to learn to drive. They come here to get a driver's license.
JACQUES RABINO, Parisian driving school owner, quoted in *Newsweek*, Oct. 20, 1969

There are no liberals behind steering wheels.
RUSSELL BAKER, *Poor Russell's Almanac*, 1972

Climbing into a hot car is like buckling on a pistol. It is the great equalizer.
HENRY GREGOR FELSEN, *To My Son—The Teen-Age Driver*, 1964

Cars are built for speed, and highways are built for speed. What is not built for speed is the human body.
TRANSPORTATION DEPARTMENT OFFICIAL, quoted in *Newsweek*, Aug. 9, 1976

Instead of bringing people together, the automobile actually tends to isolate or disperse them. Instead of walking or strolling, or sitting outside, the American roams in a car, his box, and he encounters other boxes, not people.
RALPH SLOVENKO, *New York Times*, Mar. 18, 1972

Think about all those people in automobiles, driving about with their debts.
ELIZABETH HARDWICK, interview in *New York Times*, Mar. 29, 1979

Who can tell what goes into a car today? The consumer won't know and the dealers get angry if you ask them.
RALPH NADER, speech at Mass Retailing Institute, May 11, 1970

The bumper's only use is a Braille device to help you park.
EUGENE BORDINAT, Ford vice president, quoted in *Road and Track,* Mar. 1970

My least favorite automobile commercial describes a new model as "Something to Believe In!"
ROBERT F. GOHEEN, *Foundation News,* Sept. 1971

AVERAGES also see STATISTICS

If a man stands with his right foot on a hot stove and his left foot in a freezer, some statisticians would assert that, on the average, he is comfortable.
ANONYMOUS, *Oral Hygiene,* Feb. 1967

That is like assuring the non-swimmer that he can safely walk across a river because its *average* depth is only four feet.
MILTON FRIEDMAN ON AVERAGES WITHOUT THEIR COMPONENTS, *Newsweek,* Jan. 10, 1972

AWARDS

I knew I had written a lot of nice papers about boranes, but I never actually knew that anyone read them.
WILLIAM NUNN LIPSCOMB, JR., 1976 Nobel laureate, chemistry, quoted in *New York Times,* Oct. 19, 1976

I'm especially pleased that someone from Philadelphia won. It's appropriate in the Bicentennial year and makes up in part for the Phillies not making it to the World Series.
BARUCH S. BLUMBERG, 1976 Nobel laureate, medicine, quoted in *New York Times,* Oct. 15, 1976

This medal, together with my American Express Card, will identify me worldwide—except at Bloomingdale's.
S. J. PERELMAN ON THE NATIONAL BOOK AWARD, Apr. 10, 1978

It is unthinkable for a Frenchman to arrive at middle age without having syphilis and the Cross of the Legion of Honor.
ATTRIBUTED TO ANDRÉ GIDE

It is taken rather seriously by those who have been awarded it.
ALFRED HITCHCOCK ON HIS LEGION OF HONOR AWARD, interview in *New York Post,* Apr. 9, 1976

In any case, let's eat breakfast.
ISAAC BASHEVIS SINGER TO HIS WIFE AFTER HEARING REPORT THAT HE WON THE NOBEL PRIZE FOR LITERATURE, quoted in *Newsweek,* Oct. 16, 1978

BABY

When we hear the baby laugh, it is the loveliest thing that can happen to us.
SIGMUND FREUD, quoted in Agnes M. McGlashan and Christopher J. Reeve, *Sigmund Freud,* 1970

A baby is an inestimable blessing and a bother.
MARK TWAIN, letter to Annie Webster, Sept. 1, 1876

BALLET

Dancers are like thoroughbreds, like Seabiscuit, strong, obedient; no matter how much weight is put on them, they run like mad and win.
GEORGE BALANCHINE, quoted in *Newsweek,* Jan. 13, 1969

As unnatural as dancing is, you have to find a natural way to do the unnatural.
GELSEY KIRKLAND, quoted in *Time,* May 1, 1978

That's a lot to see buggers jump.
NIGEL BRUCE ON THE PRICE OF BALLET TICKETS, quoted in Basil Rathbone, *In and Out of Character,* 1962

BANKS/BANKING

Our banking system grew up by accident; and whenever something happens by accident, it becomes a religion.
WALTER B. WRISTON, quoted in *Business Week,* Jan. 20, 1975

We don't issue loans to writers, artists, and tap dancers.
WHITE PLAINS, N.Y., BANKER, quoted in *New York Post,* Jan. 5, 1976

I've always found that a gambler's word is better than a banker's.
AL FARB, bail bondsman, interview in *Wall Street Journal,* Oct. 7, 1971

It is a rather pleasant experience to be alone in a bank at night.
WILLIE SUTTON, bank robber, quoted in *Newsweek,* Apr. 1, 1968

BASEBALL also see SPORTS

Baseball is a game of inches.
BRANCH RICKEY, *Quote,* July 31, 1966

Taking life 90 feet at a time.
ROGER ROSENBLATT, on "Special Edition," PBS, Apr. 5, 1979

There are only five things you can do in baseball—run, throw, catch, hit, and hit with power.
LEO DUROCHER, quoted in *Time,* July 16, 1973

You can't sit on a lead and run a few plays into the line and just kill the clock. You've got to throw the ball over the goddam plate and give the other man a chance.
EARL WEAVER, interview in *Time,* Apr. 30, 1973

Pitching is . . . the art of instilling fear.
SANDY KOUFAX, quoted in Robert E. Hood, *The Gashouse Gang,* 1976

I've got a right to knock down anybody holding a bat.
EARLY WYNN AFTER DUSTING HIS SON, quoted in Roger Kahn, *A Season in the Sun,* 1977

Baseball players are the weirdest of all. I think it's all that organ music.
PETER GENT, *Texas Celebrity Turkey Trot,* 1978

I don't think baseball could survive without all the statistical appurtenances involved in calculating pitching, hitting and fielding percentages. Some people could do without the games as long as they got the box scores.
JOHN M. CULKIN, *New York Times,* June 13, 1976

It also makes it easy for the generations to talk to one another.
JOEL OPPENHEIMER, *New York Times,* June 17, 1979

BEAUTIFUL PEOPLE also see CELEBRITIES

The Beautiful People, the celebrities, the presences, they just exist to be *there.*
MAURICE ZOLOTOW, *New York Times,* Dec. 29, 1968

One very clear impression I had of all the Beautiful People was their extreme prudence. It may be that they paid for their own airline tickets, but they paid for little else.
JAMES BRADY, *Superchic,* 1974

No woman can be too rich or too thin.
TRUMAN CAPOTE, "David Susskind Show," Metromedia, 1958

[They] all seemed to have nicknames like Dee Dee and Poo Poo.
JOHN CROSBY, *Party of the Year,* 1979

Except for the gigolos or fags or gigolo-fags, the men are as gray as can be. Anyone young or exciting is off breeding somewhere.
CAPPY BADRUTT, quoted in *Newsweek,* Aug. 27, 1973

BEAUTY

Beauty is a quality, not a form; a content, not an arrangement.
IRVING HOWE, *World of Our Fathers,* 1976

A 12-meter boat that can win a race is beautiful. She's doing what she was meant to do, and that's beautiful.
R. BUCKMINSTER FULLER, *Petroleum Today,* Fall 1968

It requires a certain kind of mind to see beauty in a hamburger bun.
RAY KROC, founder of McDonald's, *Grinding It Out,* 1977

I'm tired of all this nonsense about beauty being only skin-deep. That's deep enough. What do you want—an adorable pancreas?
JEAN KERR, *The Snake Has All the Lines,* 1960

BEER also see ALCOHOL

A moral species of beverage.
> BRITISH M.P., quoted in Michael Jackson, *The English Pub,* 1976

Beer is not a good cocktail-party drink, especially in a home where you don't know where the bathroom is.
> BILLY CARTER, interview in *Newsweek,* Nov. 14, 1977

Show me a nation whose national beverage is beer, and I'll show you an advanced toilet technology.
> MARK HAWKINS, *New York Times,* Sept. 25, 1977

BELIEF also see CONVICTIONS; IDEAS; PREJUDICES

Technological man can't believe in anything that can't be measured, taped, put in a computer.
> CLARE BOOTHE LUCE, interview in *Newsweek,* Nov. 26, 1973

Some people will believe anything if you whisper it to them.
> LOUIS B. NIZER, *Thinking on Your Feet,* 1940

One comes, finally, to believe whatever one repeats to one's self, whether the statement is true or false.
> NAPOLEON HILL, *Think and Grow Rich,* 1966

This man is dangerous; he believes what he says.
> ATTRIBUTED TO JOSEF GOEBBELS (ON ADOLF HITLER), in Helmut Heiber, *Goebbels,* 1972

BIBLE

I read the book of Job last night—I don't think God comes well out of it.
> VIRGINIA WOOLF, in letter to Lytton Strachey, *Letters of Virginia Woolf, 1911–1922,* Nigel Nicolson and Joanne Trautmann, eds., 1975

What a queer work the Bible is. Abraham (who is a pattern of all the virtues) twice over, when he is going abroad, says to his wife: "Sarah, my dear, you are a very good-looking person, and the King is very likely to fall in love with you. If he thinks I am your husband, he will put me to death, so as to be able to marry you, so you should travel as my sister, which you are, by the way." On each occasion the King does fall in love with her, takes her into his harem, and gets diseased in consequence, so he returns her to Abraham. Meanwhile, Abraham has a child by a maidservant, whom Sarah dismisses into the wilderness with the new-born infant, without Abraham objecting. Rum tale.
  BERTRAND RUSSELL, 1918 letter to Colette, *Autobiography 1914–1944,* 1968

God was more exciting then than He is now.
  CHILD AFTER HEARING BIBLE STORY, quoted in Gerald Kennedy, *The Seven Worlds of the Minister,* 1968

BILL OF RIGHTS

Can any one of you seriously say the Bill of Rights could get through Congress today? It wouldn't even get out of committee.
  F. LEE BAILEY, quoted in *Newsweek,* Apr. 17, 1967

BIRTH

Do you find the thought that you might never have been born (if it ever occurs to you) disturbing?
  MAX FRISCH, *Sketchbook 1966–1971,* 1974

When I was born, I owed twelve dollars.
  GEORGE S. KAUFMAN, quoted in Scott Meredith, *George S. Kaufman and His Friends,* 1974

BIRTH CONTROL also see ABORTION; POPULATION EXPLOSION

Birth control is as "unnatural" as a pocket handkerchief or false teeth.
  ARCHBISHOP OF YORK, quoted in Julian Huxley, *Memories,* 1971

A wide and easy road . . . toward conjugal infidelity and a general lowering of morality.
POPE PAUL VI, *Humanae Vitae,* 1968

Loop before you leap.
FAMILY-PLANNING SLOGAN, INDIA, quoted in Charlotte Y. Salisbury, *Asian Diary,* 1968

If my parents had been exposed to today's ideas of family planning, my brothers Win and David might not have made it.
JOHN D. ROCKEFELLER 3d, obituary in *Newsweek,* July 24, 1978

All you talk about is vaginas, vaginas, vaginas. I'm getting out of here.
JEANNETTE RANKIN TO MARGARET SANGER AT INTERNATIONAL BIRTH-CONTROL MEETING, NEW DELHI, quoted in Hannah Josephson, *Jeannette Rankin,* 1974

BIRTH CONTROL: THE PILL

The Pill came to market and changed the sexual and real-estate habits of millions; motel chains were created to serve them.
HERBERT GOLD, *New York Times,* Jan. 23, 1972

It makes it possible for the sexual woman to act like a sexual man.
DR. MARCUS CRAHAN, *Quote,* Nov. 19, 1967

It is in the interests of society to put the Pill into slot machines and to place cigarettes on prescription.
DR. MALCOLM POTTS, *Quote,* Mar. 22, 1970

When you take your pill/it's like a mine disaster./I think of all the people/lost inside you.
RICHARD BRAUTIGAN, *The Pill versus the Springhill Mine Disaster,* 1968

BISEXUALITY also see HOMOSEXUALITY

It's like being a mulatto. We take flak from both the straights and the gays.
SET DESIGNER, quoted in *New York Post,* Sept. 25, 1976

Like jello that has never set.
DR. NATALIE SHAINESS, quoted in *New York Post,* Sept. 25, 1976

It immediately doubles your chances for a date on Saturday night.
WOODY ALLEN, interview in *New York Times,* Dec. 1, 1975

BITTERNESS

Bitterness is a concept that is loaded with self-pity.
G. GORDON LIDDY ON RELEASE FROM WATERGATE PRISON SENTENCE,
"News," CBS-TV, Sept. 8, 1977

A man's embittered features are often only the petrified bewilderment
of a boy.
FRANZ KAFKA, quoted in Gustav Janouch, *Conversations with Kafka,*
1971

BLACKS also see GHETTOS; SLAVERY

It's always seemed to me that black people's grace has been with what
they do with language.
TONI MORRISON, interview in *New York Times,* Sept. 11, 1977

The black experience is 360 degrees. Love and sex are probably two of
them, but there are 358 more.
GILL SCOTT-HERON, interview in *Newsweek,* Feb. 10, 1975

What a horror it must be for a child to discover that his skin is the
wrong color.
SAM LEVENSON, *Everything but Money,* 1966

When blacks are unemployed, they are considered lazy and apathetic.
When whites are unemployed, it's considered a depression.
REV. JESSE JACKSON, quoted in *Time,* Apr. 6, 1970

We used to be "shiftless and lazy," now we're "fearsome and awe-
some." I think the black man should take pride in that.
JAMES EARL JONES, interview in *Newsweek,* Oct. 21, 1968

Something is dismally wrong with an America in which a white prostitute can buy a house where a black businessman can't.
REV. THEODORE M. HESBURGH, U.S. Civil Rights Commission hearing, 1970

I want to be the white man's brother, not his brother-in-law.
ATTRIBUTED TO MARTIN LUTHER KING, JR.

I don't want old people to run away from me because I'm young and black. Heck, half the time I'm just as scared as they are.
RICHARD SANTANA, high school student, quoted in *New York Times,* Apr. 22, 1977

When you meet an American Negro who's not a Methodist or a Baptist, some white man's been tampering with his religion.
BOOKER T. WASHINGTON, quoted in *New York Times,* Apr. 11, 1976

Black people are land people. They jived us into the cities.
JOHN A. WILLIAMS, *The Junior Bachelor Society,* 1976

White folks still in the lead.
LOUIS ARMSTRONG, quoted in *Reader's Digest,* Dec. 1971

BLINDNESS

To the blind everything is sudden.
APHORISM

The thing that hits you every day is when you wake up feeling rested and suddenly you realize you can't tell whether it's night or day. That's an awful feeling.
SAM HEYMAN, quoted in *New York Times,* Dec. 25, 1976

BLUE-COLLAR BLUES also see THE JOB

You get to the point where you stare at the rivets and to make the job mean something you start counting them like counting sheep. When you do that, you'd better watch out.
WILLIE SAUNDERS, riveter, quoted in *Newsweek,* May 17, 1971

They'll give better care to that machine than they will to you. If it breaks down, there's somebody out there to fix it right away. If I break down, I'm just pushed over to the other side till another man takes my place.
HARRY STALLINGS, spot welder, quoted in *New York Times,* Mar. 19, 1973

These are lives that travel very short arcs between minimal happiness and dull, undramatic misery. It is a culture without much variety.
GORDON BURNSIDE, *New York Times,* Sept. 30, 1973

BLUES see MUSIC: BLUES

THE BOMB

Within a hundred years of physical and chemical science man will
know what the atom is. It is my belief when science reaches this stage,
God will come down to earth with His big ring of keys and will say to
humanity, "Gentlemen, it is closing time."
> MARCELLIN BERTHELOT, French chemist, 1860, quoted in *New York
> Times,* Oct. 2, 1970

I am become death—the shatterer of worlds.
> PASSAGE FROM BHAGAVAD-GITA, Hindu sacred epic, which J. Robert
> Oppenheimer recited to himself at A-bomb test explosion, Alamo-
> gordo, N.M., July 16, 1945

Man has never before known himself in possession of a deadly sting,
which, when once used, results in his own certain death. Only some insects have.
> MAX FRANKEL, *New York Times,* Dec. 30, 1969

Kennedy said that if we had nuclear war we'd kill 300 million people
in the first hour. McNamara, who is a good businessman and likes to
save, says it would be only 200 million.
> NORMAN THOMAS, obituary in *New York Times,* Dec. 20, 1968

One of the questions which we have to ask ourselves as a country is
what in the name of God is strategic superiority? What do you do
with it?
> HENRY A. KISSINGER, quoted in *Newsweek,* July 15, 1974

The old checkerboard of strategy has run out of squares.
> *Newsweek,* Mar. 27, 1967

BOOKS also see LITERATURE; READING; WRITERS/WRITING

One swallows hard to see how quickly books age in these fast times.
> PAUL ZWEIG, *New York Times,* Nov. 28, 1976

Books come out so fast I can't even read their title pages.
> ALFRED A. KNOPF, interview in Israel Shenker, *Words and Their Mas-
> ters,* 1974

The oldest books are just out to those who have not read them.
ATTRIBUTED TO SAMUEL BUTLER

The best sellers on a list tend to cheat all other books.
ROBERT M. ZACHARY, quoted in *New York Times,* Mar. 5, 1978

The books that are talked about can be talked about just as well without being read.
SAMUEL McCHORD CROTHERS, quoted in *New York Times,* Apr. 13, 1967

I don't care what a person says—I'll look at his books and I'll know what he is.
SOL M. MALKIN, interview in Israel Shenker, *Words and Their Masters,* 1974

Chirpy textbooks.
JILL ROBINSON ON SELF-IMPROVEMENT BOOKS, *New York Times,* Sept. 12, 1977

BORES/BOREDOM

It is a sad truth that everyone is a bore to someone.
LLEWELLYN MILLER, *The Encylopedia of Etiquette,* 1968

Boredom, after all, is a form of criticism.
WILLIAM PHILLIPS, *A Sense of the Present,* 1967

The person who is bored in the modern world shows that he is in no full sense a member of it.
BRAND BLANSHARD, *The Uses of a Liberal Education,* Eugene Freeman, ed., 1974

Bored people, unless they sleep a lot, are cruel. It is no accident that boredom and cruelty are great preoccupations in our time.
RENATA ADLER, *Speedboat,* 1976

THE BOSS: FROM ABOVE

Don't tell me how hard you work. Tell me how much you get done.
JAMES J. LING, president, Ling-Temco-Vought, quoted in *Newsweek,* Oct. 9, 1967

Everything must be done immediately even if it doesn't have to be.
> LARRY KANE, president, Larry Kane, Inc., quoted in *New York Times*, Oct. 19, 1975

If you don't drive your business, you will be driven out of business.
> B. C. FORBES, publisher, quoted in *Forbes*, Apr. 1, 1974

I'm not hard to work with. I just like things done my way.
> GEORGE J. HECHT, chairman, *Parents'*, quoted in *New York Times*, Sept. 21, 1975

There's a little bit of the dictator in all of us. Fortunately, I was blessed with a disproportionately generous share.
> FREDRIC R. MANN, retired chairman, National Container Corp., quoted in *New York Times*, June 16, 1976

My name is on the building.
> HENRY FORD II, quoted in *Newsweek*, July 24, 1978

I have heard your views. They do not harmonize with mine. The decision is taken unanimously.
> CHARLES DE GAULLE, 1945, quoted in Jean-Raymond Tournoux, *Sons of France*, 1966

When I want to know what France thinks, I ask myself.
> DE GAULLE, *Sons of France*

Gentlemen, I've been thinking. Bull times zero is bull. Bull divided by zero is infinity bull. And I'm sick and tired of the bull you've been feeding me.
> HAROLD S. GENEEN, chairman, ITT, to staff, quoted in *New York Times*, Sept. 5, 1971

Dear, never forget one little point. It's my business. You just work here.
> ELIZABETH ARDEN TO HUSBAND, quoted in Alfred A. Lewis and Constance Woodworth, *Miss Elizabeth Arden*, 1972

If you're the chief executive you get more blame than you deserve, and you also get more credit than you deserve. If you want one, you've got to accept the other, too.
> K. T. KELLER, chairman, Chrysler Corp., obituary in *Newsweek*, Jan. 31, 1966

They tell me I often go out on a limb. Well, that's where I like to be.
> HENRY J. KAISER, chairman, Kaiser Industries, interview in *Los Angeles Times*, Aug. 19, 1959

Out of 25 guys there should be 15 who would run through a wall for you, two or three who don't like you at all, five who are indifferent and maybe three undecided. My job is to keep the last two groups from going the wrong way.

> BILLY MARTIN, N.Y. Yankees manager, quoted in *Newsweek,* July 12, 1976

I like my players to be married and in debt. That's the way you motivate them.

> ERNIE BANKS, minor league instructor for Chicago Cubs, quoted in *New York Times,* Apr. 11, 1976

The fine sticks. I reiterate that it will not be lifted. Please note the word "reiterate." I like it. Up to now, I have repeated and reasserted, but now I reiterate.

> MILLER HUGGINS, N.Y. Yankees manager, after fining Babe Ruth $5,000, 1925, quoted in *No Cheering in the Press Box,* Jerome Holtzman, ed., 1974

No! No! Young feller! Wait'll Sunday!

> CAPT. JOSIAH CLEVELAND, clipper-ship captain, on seeing a sailor pause to pull a splinter from his foot, 1866, quoted in Polly Burroughs, *Zeb,* 1972

THE BOSS: FROM BELOW

You'll never have a nervous breakdown, but you sure are a carrier.

> CO-WORKER TO FRED FRIENDLY, CBS News president, quoted in *Newsweek,* Mar. 27, 1972

Mr. Markel, I think you're a son of a bitch and I respect you.

> RESIGNING REPORTER TO LESTER MARKEL, *New York Times* Sunday editor, quoted in *New York Times,* June 11, 1972

His bite is worse than his bark.

> PRINCETON PROFESSOR ON DEPARTMENT CHAIRMAN, quoted in *Princeton Alumni Weekly,* May 13, 1969

He carves you up but leaves the skin around the body.

> FORD EXECUTIVE ON PHILIP CALDWELL, president, international operations, quoted in *New York Times,* Mar. 13, 1977

He's fair. He treats us all the same—like dogs.

> HENRY JORDAN, Green Bay Packers, on Vince Lombardi, quoted in Lombardi obituary, *New York Times,* Sept. 4, 1970

When he says, "Sit down," I don't even bother to look for a chair.
GREEN BAY PACKER ON VINCE LOMBARDI, quoted in *New York Times,*
Sept. 4, 1970

The Flamethrower.
EXECUTIVES' TERM FOR JOHN C. RICCARDO, chairman, Chrysler Corp.,
quoted in *Newsweek,* Nov. 13, 1978

The son of a bitch hasn't been born yet.
WYOMING RANCH FOREMAN WHEN ENGLISH VISITOR ASKED, "IS YOUR
MASTER AT HOME?" quoted in William H. Forbis, *The Cowboys,* 1973

THE BOSS: FROM THE SIDELINES

A 10,000-aspirin job.
JAPANESE TERM FOR EXECUTIVE RESPONSIBILITY, quoted in *Newsweek,*
Feb. 21, 1972

His quest for something new each month leads to widespread corporate premature ejaculation.
ROBERT TOWNSEND, *New York Times,* Apr. 30, 1973

The first-rate man will try to surround himself with his equals, or betters if possible. The second-rate man will surround himself with third-rate men. The third-rate man will surround himself with fifth-rate men.
ANDRÉ WEIL, quoted in *New York Times,* Mar. 16, 1973

We have yet to find a significant case where the company did not move in the direction of the chief executive's home.
KEN PATTON, N.Y.C. Economic Development Administrator, on corporate relocation, quoted in *New York Times,* Feb. 5, 1971

BOWLING also see SPORTS

The bowling alley is the poor man's country club.
SANFORD HANSELL, bowling center executive, quoted in *New York Times,* May 11, 1975

When I was a kid, I actually believed that wiping out the pin boy was the object of the game.
CHARLES ROSEN, *Have Jump Shot Will Travel,* 1975

BRAIN also see INTELLECT/INTELLIGENCE

Our most interesting undiscovered country.
CHRISTOPHER LEHMANN-HAUPT, *New York Times,* Feb. 14, 1975

The chief function of your body is to carry your brain around.
THOMAS A. EDISON, *Quote,* Nov. 27, 1966

The brain that doesn't feed itself, eats itself.
GORE VIDAL, interview in *New York Times,* June 18, 1978

The left hemisphere became the one to have if you were having only one.
HOWARD GARDNER, *The Shattered Mind,* 1975

Chairman Mao teaches us that if you wash your body, there is nothing wrong with washing your brains.
FAN TSEN-CHUNG, quoted in *Newsweek,* Mar. 26, 1973

BRAVERY

It is the perpetual dread of fear, the fear of fear, that shapes the face of a brave man.
GEORGES BERNANOS, *The Diary of a Country Priest,* 1937

It is believing in yourself, and that thing nobody can teach you. I have never heard of a University of Bravery.
EL CORDOBÉS (MANUEL BENÍTEZ PÉREZ), quoted in *Newsweek,* Mar. 22, 1971

If I ain't afraid of walkin' down a back alley in Harlem, I ain't afraid of you.
MUHAMMAD ALI, interview in Associated Press, Mar. 25, 1976

BREAKFAST see EATING: BREAKFAST

BREASTS

Look, a painter who has a feeling for breasts and buttocks is a saved man.
PIERRE AUGUSTE RENOIR

When the Skraelings came rushing toward her, she pulled one of her breasts out of her bodice and slapped it with her sword. The Skraelings were terrified at the sight and fled back to their boats and hastened away.
Eirek's Saga, tenth-century Norse tale

My breasts aren't actresses.
LIV ULLMANN ON NUDITY IN THE THEATER, quoted in *New York Times,* Dec. 22, 1974

BRITAIN/THE BRITISH also see LONDON

I have a feeling that this island is uninhabitable, and therefore people have tried to make it habitable by being reasonable with one another.
RALF DAHRENDORF, quoted in *New York Times,* Oct. 15, 1976

The hard truth is that as vulgarizers the British are, and always have been, incompetent. If they invent cheap gewgaws for people to take home as mementos of their improving visit to the Bard's shrine, they immediately salve their conscience by planting more flower gardens.
RICHARD D. ALTICK, *To Be in England,* 1969

The British capitalize on their accent when they don't want you to know what they're saying. But if you wake them up at 4 A.M., they speak perfect English, the same as we do.
HENRY A. KISSINGER, quoted in Leonard Lyons' column, Dec. 26, 1973

I'm convinced there's a small room in the attic of the Foreign Office where future diplomats are taught to stammer.
PETER USTINOV, interview in Israel Shenker, *Words and Their Masters,* 1974

The problem of economics in Britain is very much like that of sex in the United States. Both countries have an enormous difficulty in keeping it in perspective.
JOHN KENNETH GALBRAITH, quoted in *New York Times,* Dec. 18, 1966

It has been said with truth that the Labor Party has always been more Methodist than Marxist.
BERNARD LEVIN, *New York Times,* Apr. 21, 1968

It makes you want to cry; they are no longer a great power. All they've got are generals and admirals and bands.
GEN. GEORGE S. BROWN, quoted in *Newsweek,* Dec. 13, 1976

Remember that you are an Englishman, and have consequently won first prize in the lottery of life.
CECIL RHODES, quoted in *Bookviews,* Nov. 1977

England is knowing you will never be solvent.
JOHN WOOD, interview in *New York Post,* Sept. 24, 1977

The English think incompetence is the same thing as sincerity.
QUENTIN CRISP, quoted in *New York Times,* Jan. 30, 1977

In England everybody's in the inhibition business.
JOHN WOOD, interview in *Newsweek,* Mar. 13, 1978

We love clubs and mysteries and minor snobberies of all sorts—not so much because these bind us to our club mates but [because] of an unholy glee in keeping people out.
DAVID WATT, quoted in *New York Times,* July 17, 1973

When all is said, its atmosphere still contains fewer germs of aggression and brutality per cubic foot in a crowded bus, pub or queue than in any other country in which I have lived.
ARTHUR KOESTLER, quoted in *Newsweek,* Feb. 23, 1976

I love the courteous sound of the engines of the English cabs.
MEL BROOKS, interview in *New Yorker,* Oct. 30, 1978

A naturally aggressive people, the English have conscientiously tried to tame themselves, and many believe that the taming has gone too far.
ANTHONY BURGESS, *New York Times,* Jan. 28, 1973

FIERCE COMPETITION AT CHRYSANTHEMUM SHOW
Headline, *Times* (London), 1970

BUREAUCRACY/BUREAUCRATS

Bureaucratic function is sustained by fear of failure, as the church was once supported by the fear of damnation.
RICHARD N. GOODWIN, *The American Condition,* 1974

In government and out, there are vast realms of the bureaucracy dedicated to seeking more information, in perpetuity if need be, in order to avoid taking action.
MEG GREENFIELD, *Newsweek,* Dec. 18, 1978

Bureaucrats speak only of parts. It's as if you decide Picasso is good at legs, so you ask him to paint the legs. And since Matisse draws lovely heads, you get him to do the head. Then, when it's finished, you're astonished you've produced a mess!

> HENRY A. KISSINGER, quoted in *Newsweek,* Aug. 21, 1972

I have seen it happen more often than not that when one asks for choices one is always given three: two absurd ones and the preferred one. And the experienced bureaucrat, which I am slowly becoming, can usually tell the preferred one because it is almost always the one that is typed in the middle.

> HENRY A. KISSINGER, quoted in *New York Times,* Oct. 28, 1973

You start by saying no to requests. Then if you have to go to yes, okay. But if you start with yes, you can't go to no.

> MILDRED PERLMAN, N.Y. Civil Service Commission, interview in *New York Times,* Dec. 1, 1975

We need civil servants who are both servants and civil.

> EXECUTIVE, quoted in *Newsweek,* June 14, 1976

I can only assume that a "Do Not File" document is filed in a "Do Not File" file.

> SEN. FRANK CHURCH, Senate Intelligence Subcommittee hearing, 1975

Walt can write faster than I can read.

> JOHN F. KENNEDY ON THE FLOOD OF REPORTS FROM ADVISER WALT ROSTOW, in David Halberstam, *The Best and the Brightest,* 1972

How can I get out of Vietnam if I can't get the mail out of my own office?

> ROBERT F. KENNEDY, quoted in Jerry Bruno and Jeff Greenfield, *The Advance Man,* 1971

Genghis Khan conquered Asia with an army only half the size of New York City's civil service.

> EMANUEL SAVAS, quoted in *New York Times,* Oct. 8, 1972

BUSINESS/BUSINESSMEN

The only way to keep score in business is to add up how much money you make.

> HARRY B. HELMSLEY, chairman, Helmsley-Spear, interview in *New York Times,* Nov. 18, 1973

In business, the competition will bite you if you keep running; if you
stand still, they will swallow you.
> WILLIAM S. KNUDSEN, later chairman, General Motors, 1939

The business system is blessed with a built-in corrective, namely, that
one executive's mistakes become his competitors' assets.
> LEO CHERNE, speech at Chamber of Commerce conference, Jan. 31,
> 1967

In new business, if you engage in anything short of a direct assault on
the jugular vein, you're in the Mickey Mouse league.
> WILLIAM HOLDEN, advertising executive, interview in *Business Week,*
> Sept. 20, 1967

It's a combat zone.
> LEE IACOCCA, president, Ford Motor Co., quoted on "Henry Ford's
> America," PBS, Jan. 17, 1978

I want to talk with these people because they stay in power and you
change all the time.
> NIKITA S. KHRUSHCHEV TO ITALIAN GOVERNMENT OFFICIALS RE ITALY'S
> BUSINESS LEADERS, quoted in *Life,* Nov. 24, 1967

In management thirty years experience does not count for much if it
merely means ten times three of the same experience.
> NEIL J. MCKINNON, chairman, Canadian Imperial Bank of Com-
> merce, quoted in *Public Utilities Fortnightly,* Jan. 4, 1968

Businessmen tend to grow old early. They are committed to security
and stability. They won't rock the boat and won't gamble, denying the
future for a near-sighted present. They forget what made them successful in the first place.
> PETER C. GOLDMARK, CBS chief scientist, interview in *New York
> Times,* May 7, 1972

More frequently than not, an executive who gets along easily with others, who does not fight too hard for his position, who is willing to see
the point of view of the other fellow, especially if the other fellow is his
superior, gains a reputation of being constructive and cooperative.
And that he is. The question remains, what else is he?
> ELI GINZBERG, *What Makes an Executive?,* 1955

Whenever you're sitting across from some important person, always picture him sitting there in a suit of long red underwear. That's the way I always operated in business.
JOSEPH P. KENNEDY, quoted in Lawrence F. O'Brien, *No Final Victories,* 1974

BUSYBODIES

Right now I get the sense that there are more people trying to rearrange the thinking of other people than ever before. They don't want to rearrange their own thinking.
SAMUEL LUBELL, speech at City College of New York, Apr. 25, 1971

The passion for setting people right is in itself an afflictive disease.
MARIANNE MOORE, obituary in *New York Times,* Feb. 6, 1972

CALIFORNIA also see LOS ANGELES; SAN FRANCISCO

California stretches out on the west coast of America like a centerfold from Playboy.
"SONG AT TWILIGHT," PBS, Jan. 21, 1977

Sunny nutland.
EDWIN DIAMOND, on "Special Edition," PBS, June 11, 1979

"Are you still married?" is more courteous than rude an inquiry of someone you've not seen for a week or two.
RALPH KEYES ON SOUTHERN CALIFORNIA, *Newsweek,* Oct. 13, 1975

California audiences applaud whenever a musician hesitates long enough to turn a page.
LEONARD MICHAELS, *New York Times,* Oct. 26, 1975

Living in California adds ten years to a man's life. And those extra ten years I'd like to spend in New York.
HARRY RUBY, quoted in Leonard Lyons' column, Feb. 26, 1974

CAPITALISM also see COMMUNISM; PROFIT; SOCIALISM

It has been the first to show what man's activity can bring about. It has accomplished wonders far surpassing Egyptian pyramids, Roman aqueducts, and Gothic cathedrals.
KARL MARX, *Manifesto of the Communist Party,* 1848

On my visits to America I discovered that the old Marxist dictum, "From each according to his abilities, to each according to his needs," was probably more in force in America, that holy of holies of capitalism, than in any other country in the world.
FELIX HOUPHOUET-BOIGNY, president, Ivory Coast, quoted in *Newsweek,* Aug. 9, 1965

Capitalism equals love of money in my view, and we didn't start out that way. We started out with a love of individual enterprise.
ERIC SLOANE, *The Spirits of '76,* 1973

Under capitalism man exploits man. Under communism, it's just the opposite.
MOSCOW STREET JOKE, quoted in Hedrick Smith, *The Russians,* 1976

CAPITAL PUNISHMENT

Those who assert that capital punishment is wrong because the state should not itself take on the guilt of murder completely miss the point. For by failing to take the life of those who murder their fellow men, the state becomes a passive accessory after the fact.
NETTIE LEEF, *New York Times,* July 30, 1975

I believe capital punishment to be an appropriate remedy for anyone who does *me* injury, but under no other circumstances.
F. LEE BAILEY, *Quote,* Feb. 13, 1977

Have you noticed that right-to-life people are always in favor of capital punishment?
GORE VIDAL, "Dick Cavett Show," PBS, Apr. 10, 1979

CARTOONS

If it's big, hit it.
BILL MAULDIN, quoted in *Newsweek,* Jan. 22, 1979

A cartoon, if it's good, has to be unfair.
JOHN B. OAKES, quoted in *Newsweek,* June 16, 1970

CATHOLICISM also see THE CHURCHES; RELIGION

The great achievement of the Catholic Church lay in harmonising, civilising the deepest impulses of ordinary, ignorant people.
LORD KENNETH CLARK, *Civilisation,* 1970

All the steam in the world could not, like the Virgin, build Chartres.
HENRY ADAMS, *Mont St. Michel and Chartres,* 1905

We tell the public that the Pope is infallible and we give him absolute power—and then we in the Curia make sure he can never use it.
ITALIAN CARDINAL, quoted in *New York Times,* June 3, 1979

Why shouldn't we have a foreign Pope? After all, St. Peter was one.
ROME CAB DRIVER, quoted in *Time,* Oct. 30, 1978

CELEBRITIES also see BEAUTIFUL PEOPLE; FAME; GLORY

Somebody who is known for being known.
STUDS TERKEL, "Dick Cavett Show," PBS, June 9, 1978

To some people all celebrities have equal value.
DICK CAVETT, "Dick Cavett Show," PBS, June 9, 1978

Celebrities in general are chosen, like the Calendar of Saints, to meet certain needs: thus, Frank Sinatra is the patron celebrity of comebacks, Liza Minnelli of daughters, Jackie Onassis of curious marriages.
WILFRID SHEED, *Muhammad Ali,* 1975

To be a celebrity in America is to be forgiven everything.
MARY MCGRORY, quoted in *New York Times,* Feb. 1, 1976

I'm famous. That's my job.
JERRY RUBIN, *Growing (Up) at 37,* 1976

You have a lot of friends who love you dearly and you don't know who they are.
SHELLEY WINTERS, interview in *New York Times,* June 18, 1976

CENTRAL INTELLIGENCE AGENCY see CIA

CENTURY: SIXTEENTH

All is pell-mell, confounded, nothing goes as it should.
Louis Le Roy, 1575, quoted in *New York Times,* Nov. 10, 1975

CENTURY: SEVENTEENTH

The life of man, solitary, poor, nasty, brutish and short.
Thomas Hobbes, *Leviathan,* 1651

CENTURY: EIGHTEENTH

An age pregnant with the most gigantic yearnings and shaken by the convulsions resulting from the death of old empires.
Henry Fuseli (Johann Heinrich Fuessli) on the day the Bastille was stormed, quoted in *New York Times,* July 8, 1975

Nothing worth noting.
Louis XVI in diary that same day, quoted in *New York Times,* Dec. 31, 1974

CENTURY: NINETEENTH also see SLAVERY

Invention was seen as a profession for the ambitious, just as, say, corporate management is today.
John Brooks, *New York Times,* Feb. 25, 1979

It saw the wholesale application of industrialization and technology on such a scale that the conditions of life for the first time in history were altered so profoundly as to create a sense of discontinuity with the past.
Hans Aarsleff, *University* (Princeton), Winter 1972

It is an age of shocks; a discipline so strong, so manifold, so rapid, and so whirling that only when it is at an end, if then, can I comprehend it.
William Gladstone, *The Nineteenth Century,* Asa Briggs, ed., 1970

The future is to me a blank. I cannot at all guess what is coming.
GLADSTONE, as the century was ending, *The Nineteenth Century*

CENTURY: TWENTIETH also see DECADES; MODERN TIMES

The horror of the twentieth century is the size of each event, and the paucity of its reverberation.
NORMAN MAILER, *Of a Fire on the Moon,* 1970

✓The noise of things collapsing is so loud that we are taking the prodigious step from the nineteenth century to the twenty-first without a moment of calm in which we can see where we are going.
BRUCE CATTON, *Waiting for the Morning Train,* 1972

Too direful to contemplate—that is to say, like all the other centuries.
THORNTON WILDER, *Theophilus North,* 1973

Future archeologists specializing in our culture will divide the twentieth century into two groups called Beercan Culture I (tin) and II (aluminum).
LUCIEN BRUSH, quoted in *University* (Princeton), Winter 1969–1970

From the Protestant ethic to the psychedelic bazaar.
DANIEL BELL, *The Cultural Contradictions of Capitalism,* 1976

I am ashamed of my century/for being so entertaining/but I have to smile.
FRANK O'HARA, "Naphtha," *Lunch Poems,* 1964

CHAMPIONS

Being a champion means proving you are champion whenever proof seems required.
MICHAEL WOOD, *New York Times,* July 27, 1975

You have to be able to get up off the floor when you can't.
JACK DEMPSEY, quoted on "ABC News," ABC-TV, July 26, 1975

People refer to you as the world champion. Then they refer to you as the ex-world champion. All carry on as usual.
GRAHAM HILL, quoted in *Newsweek,* Nov. 18, 1968

CHANGE also see PROGRESS

When you start dealing with real change you are talking about inter-fering with those who are in possession of something.
CARL B. STOKES, *Promise of Power*, 1973

There is no way to make people like change. You can only make them feel less threatened by it.
FREDERICK O'R. HAYES, N.Y.C. budget director, quoted in *Fortune*, Mar. 1969

Careful consideration is the best known defense against change.
JOHN C. BURTON, interview in *New York Times*, June 25, 1972

The calamity of modern existence is that the world changes so fast that there is little likelihood that the old will continue to remain very much wiser than the young.
SEYMOUR L. HALLECK, *Christian Herald*, May 1969

Young people reflect social change most radically because they are partly its products.
HERBERT HENDIN, *The Age of Sensation*, 1975

How come nothing's like it was until it's gone?
WILL MASTIN, quoted in Sammy Davis, Jr., *Yes, I Can!*, 1965

CHASTITY see SEX

CHESS

Chess is life.
BOBBY FISCHER, quoted in Alexander Cockburn, *Idle Passion*, 1975

Chess is a surrogate life.
BURT HOCHBERG, letter to *New York Times*, Nov. 17, 1974

A play substitute for the art of war.
ERNEST JONES

Men who play at the grandmaster level are, almost without exception, strange and unpleasant.
D. KEITH MANO, *New York Times*, Oct. 13, 1974

I like the moment when I break a man's ego.
BOBBY FISCHER, quoted in *Newsweek,* July 31, 1972

CHICAGO

The muscular look, the modern look of Chicago.
DAVID MITCHELL, interview in *New York,* May 15, 1978

A town with a Queen Anne front and a Mary Ann back.
PAUL H. DOUGLAS, quoted in *New York Times,* May 29, 1977

Chicago is not the most corrupt American city; it's the most theatrically corrupt.
STUDS TERKEL, "Dick Cavett Show," PBS, June 9, 1978

A real goddam crazy place! Nobody's safe on the streets!
LUCKY LUCIANO, quoted in John Kobler, *Capone,* 1971

CHILDHOOD also see ADOLESCENCE; CHILDREN; YOUTH

That great Cathedral space which was childhood.
VIRGINIA WOOLF, *Moments of Being,* 1976

The child's life goes on for what seems to him long years in a single street of his town or in his city block.
SHERWOOD ANDERSON, *Sherwood Anderson's Memoirs,* Ray Lewis White, ed., 1969

Childhood is frequently a solemn business for those inside it.
GEORGE F. WILL, *Newsweek,* Dec. 11, 1978

Childhood is the country that produces the most nostalgic, contentious and opinionated exiles.
RICHARD EDER, *New York Times,* June 16, 1973

The experiences of the first three years of life are almost entirely lost to us, and when we attempt to enter into a small child's world, we come as foreigners who have forgotten the landscape and no longer speak the native tongue.
SELMA FRAIBERG, *The Magic Years,* 1968

I used to believe that the people on TV could see *me*.
SONIA O. LISKER, *I Used To,* 1977

How can I run away when I don't know where I am?
NATASHA LAING, 6, quoted in R. D. Laing, *Conversations with Adam and Natasha,* 1977

CHILDREN also see FAMILY; FATHERS; MOTHERS; PARENTS

In a secular age, children have become the last sacred objects.
JOSEPH EPSTEIN, *Divorced in America,* 1974

Children are gleeful barbarians.
JOSEPH MORGENSTERN, *Newsweek,* Jan. 1, 1968

Childish innocence is cruel, heedless and free of the hypocrisies in which adults indulge to make life endurable and society viable.
KENNETH CRAWFORD, *Newsweek,* May 19, 1969

Some parents . . . say it is toy guns that make boys warlike. . . . But give a boy a rubber duck and he will seize its neck like the butt of a pistol and shout "Bang!"
GEORGE F. WILL, *Newsweek,* Dec. 11, 1978

Children . . . are forever staring into mirrors and getting everything all wrong.
ANNE ROIPHE, *New York Times,* Nov. 19, 1978

Everywhere I go, kids walk around not with books under their arms, but with radios up against their heads. Children can't read or write, but they can memorize whole albums.
REV. JESSE JACKSON, quoted in *Newsweek,* June 26, 1977

Being built closer to the floor, they can dust the baseboards in half the time.
LOIS GOULD, *Not Responsible for Personal Articles,* 1978

The future occupation of all moppets is to be skilled consumers.
DAVID RIESMAN, quoted in Martha Weinman Lear, *The Child Worshipers,* 1963

My theory is that children are the grown-ups. They are very calculating by nature. . . . I went to Macy's to see Santa Claus and to listen to the kids. . . . It was like a business convention at the Statler Hilton.
RICHARD LINDNER, interview in *Newsweek*, May 23, 1977

If Booth Tarkington were to write *Seventeen* today, he would have to call it *Twelve*.
ARTHUR PEARL, *Quote*, July 2, 1967

CHINA / THE CHINESE

The Chinese, from the highest to the lowest, have an imperturbable quiet dignity, which is usually not destroyed even by a European education.
BERTRAND RUSSELL, *The Problem of China*, 1922

The Chinese has a profound sense of history, a chronology that precedes him and moves into the future through his children.
SOL SANDERS, *A Sense of Asia*, 1969

The trouble with Chinese history is that there is altogether too much of it.
AMERICAN MISSIONARY, quoted in *Newsweek*, Feb. 21, 1972

CHRIST

Christ died for all men—not just the ones you know and like.
CATHOLIC TEXTBOOK

If Jesus were to come to-day, people would not even crucify him. They would ask him to dinner, and hear what he had to say, and make fun of it.
THOMAS CARLYLE, quoted in D. A. Wilson, *Carlyle at His Zenith*, 1927

Every age, it seems, tries to fit Jesus to its own enthusiasms. In the 1920's many called him a social reformer. In the 1960's some of the foremost historians decided he was a violent revolutionary.
PIERSON PARKER, *New York Times*, July 22, 1973

That moderate democrat.
> ALEKSANDR PUSHKIN, quoted in Henri Troyat, *Pushkin,* 1970

CHRISTIANITY

The Christian ideal has not been tried and found wanting; it has been found difficult and left untried.
> G. K. CHESTERTON, *What's Wrong with the World,* 1910

The white Christian church never raised to the heights of Christ. It stayed within the limits of culture.
> REV. JESSE JACKSON, "McNeil/Lehrer Report," PBS, Mar. 10, 1977

I once taught a college course where I asked the class, "Is there an absolute external morality?" And I was astonished to discover that, without exception, every Catholic student said yes, and every Protestant student said no.
> ROBERT PIRSIG, *New York Times,* June 8, 1975

THE CHURCHES also see CATHOLICISM; RELIGION

It takes a brave man to stand up and admit he goes to church.
> JERRY KRAMER, Green Bay Packers, quoting his mother who is quoting Roy Rogers, *Instant Replay,* Dick Schaap, ed., 1968

The place of the church is not to change society, but to change men and women who will then do the changing of society.
> REV. DANIEL A. POLING, obituary in *New York Times,* Feb. 8, 1968

The Church always arrives on the scene a little breathless and a little late.
> REV. BERNARD J. F. LONERGAN, S.J., speech at St. Leo College, Apr. 18, 1970

The real trouble with the Church is that we have so many good people with great convictions about little things. They slow us down.
> HENRY KNOX SHERRILL, quoted in Rita Snowden, *The Time of Our Lives,* 1966

The church must be relevant and stop answering questions that no one is asking.
> T. CECIL MYERS, *Thunder on the Mountain,* 1965

We do not want churches. They will teach us to quarrel about God.
CHIEF JOSEPH OF NEZ PERCÉS, quoted in Dee Brown, *Bury My Heart at Wounded Knee*, 1971

CIA

There are no rules in such a game. Hitherto acceptable norms of human conduct do not apply.
HOOVER COMMISSION REPORT ON THE INTELLIGENCE COMMUNITY, July 4, 1954

It's the wrong game for a great nation.
JOHN STOCKWELL, ex-CIA agent, *In Search of Enemies*, 1978

While our citizens may take pride in the solid front of high morality that our nation presents, they can also sleep more easily at night from knowing that behind this front we are in fact capable of matching the Soviets perfidy for perfidy.
MILES COPELAND, ex-CIA agent, *The Game of Nations*, 1970

I don't think the intelligence reports are all that hot. Some days I get more out of the *New York Times*.
JOHN F. KENNEDY

CIGARETTES

We cannot accept the attitude that everyone should be left to smoke—and then given a heart transplant at 65.
DR. PHILIP R. LEE, assistant secretary, HEW, quoted in *Newsweek*, Jan. 22, 1968

Smoking shortens your life by eight years. I love watching pro football on television. If I smoke, I'll miss 350 games.
TONY CURTIS ON WHY HE QUIT, interview in *Sports Illustrated*, Jan. 19, 1970

Notice! If You Put Your Cigarette in Your Plate, Please Notify the Waitress and She Will Gladly Serve Your Food In an Ashtray.
SIGN IN COLORADO RESTAURANT, quoted in Jane Howard, *A Different Woman*, 1973

CIRCUS

The circus is the only spectacle I know that, while you watch it, gives the quality of a truly happy dream.
ATTRIBUTED TO ERNEST HEMINGWAY

Acrobats have always been, & will always remain, the only truly and honestly miraculous things.
E. E. CUMMINGS, *Selected Letters of E. E. Cummings*, F. W. Dupee and George Stade, eds., 1969

CITY also see SUBURBS; SUBWAYS; TOWNS, SMALL

An idea, a song, a discovery, an invention, may be born anywhere. But if it is to be communicated, if it is to be tested and compared and appreciated, then someone has always carried it to the city.
MAX WAYS, speech to The Conference Board, Nov. 28, 1967

I can't even enjoy a blade of grass unless I know there's a subway handy.
FRANK O'HARA, *Meditations in an Emergency*, 1957

I've heard it said that the American city lacks everything from which no profit is possible.
WILFRED OWEN, interview in *New York Times*, June 3, 1970

Where people are encouraged to be good consumers and to want goods but are themselves unwanted goods.
JOSEPH MORGENSTERN, *Newsweek*, May 18, 1970

Places where the mountains are gone.
APPALACHIAN NATIVE, quoted in Robert Coles, *The South Goes North*, 1971

A natural territory for the psychopath with histrionic gifts.
JONATHAN RABAN, *Soft City*, 1974

I hate to say it, but crime is an overhead you have to pay if you want to live in the city.
GEORGE MOSCONE, San Francisco mayor, quoted in *Newsweek*, Dec. 20, 1976

Every morning we gather in the Mayor's office to pray for money and we face Washington.
> ASSISTANT TO DETROIT MAYOR, quoted in *Time*, Mar. 13, 1972

The outcome of the cities will depend on the race between the automobile and the elevator, and anyone who bets on the elevator is crazy.
> FRANK LLOYD WRIGHT, quoted on "The Chrome-Plated Nightmare," PBS, May 27, 1974

CIVIL SERVICE see BUREAUCRACY/BUREAUCRATS

CIVILIZATION also see MODERN TIMES

Look into almost any field of practical endeavor and we will find accurate data going back only a century or two. Civilization has just begun.
> ARTHUR E. MORGAN, *Observations*, 1968

As a historian, you have to be conscious of the fact that every civilization that has ever existed has ultimately collapsed.
> HENRY A. KISSINGER, interview in *New York Times*, Oct. 13, 1974

The basic problem is that our civilization, which is a civilization of machines, can teach man everything except how to be a man.
> ANDRÉ MALRAUX, interview in *New York Times*, Oct. 22, 1968

Past civilizations have been destroyed by barbarians from outside, but we are doing this job ourselves.
> MALCOLM MUGGERIDGE, speech at Edinburgh International Festival, Aug. 24, 1969

Can we ever recover from the titanic humorlessness of our civilization?
> THOMAS MERTON, obituary in *New York Times*, Dec. 11, 1968

It would be a good idea.
> MOHANDAS K. GANDHI ON WESTERN CIVILIZATION, quoted in *New York Times*, Apr. 4, 1976

CLASS: SOCIAL also see **SERVANTS; STANDARD OF LIVING**

A duchess will be a duchess in a bath towel. It's all a matter of style.
CAROL LAWRENCE, quoted in *TV Guide*, May 17, 1969

My soul is all for moving to a classless society. But with my heart and with my guts I lament the passing of class.
LOUIS MACNEICE, *The Poetry of the Thirties*, A. T. Tolley, ed., 1976

The closer the distance between the lower and middle class, the more militant and aggressive and assertive the lower class becomes.
ELLIOTT LUBY, interview, Associated Press, Mar. 11, 1968

Is a certified public accountant upper lower middle class or lower upper middle class?
CHARLES MERRILL SMITH, *Instant Status*, 1972

CLUBS

A club is not a club unless you can keep somebody out.
ANONYMOUS

Clubs do not exist so much to kill time as to abolish it.
JOHN RUSSELL, *New York Times*, Aug. 11, 1975

You say you haven't got a club, young feller? Where the devil do you relieve yourself, then?
LAURENCE MEYNELL, *Burlington Square*, 1975

COCKTAIL PARTIES

They have all the trappings of fellowship, but none of the substance.
ROBERT FARRAR CAPON, *The Supper of the Lamb*, 1970

A hundred standing people smiling and talking to one another, nodding like gooney birds.
WILLIAM COLE, *New York Times*, Dec. 3, 1972

A device for paying off obligations to people you don't want to invite to dinner.
CHARLES MERRILL SMITH, *Instant Status*, 1972

COLLECTORS/COLLECTING

You never own a coin. You only have life tenancy on it. You hold it, study it, appreciate it. It goes on to others after you to do the same.
EDWARD JANIS, speech to American Numismatic Association, Aug. 25, 1976

The thrill is knowing you have a piece of paper some famous person actually touched. And for a few seconds his mind was thinking about that signature.
HERMAN DARVICK, interview in *New York Times,* May 21, 1976

A button collector is probably the only living creature who can name every losing Vice Presidential candidate.
ROBERT ROUSE, quoted in *Newsweek,* Aug. 26, 1974

I collect barbed wire because I collect barbed wire.
R. L. CHAPMAN, quoted in *New York Times,* May 4, 1971

If an individual collects anything long enough, it will eventually have some value.
DR. ALFRED C. KINSEY, quoted in Wardell B. Pomeroy, *Dr. Kinsey and the Institute for Sex Research,* 1972

COLLEGES/UNIVERSITIES also see EDUCATION; SCHOOLS; TEACHERS/TEACHING

A place to learn how to learn.
HENRY M. WRISTON, *New York Times,* June 11, 1975

As long as intelligence is better than stupidity, knowledge than ignorance, and virtue than vice, no university can be run except on an elitist basis.
JOHN R. SILBER, *New York Times,* Sept. 1, 1976

A university must give its priority to the numerically small but historically significant band of men and women who believe the worth and dignity of knowledge does not depend solely upon its current usefulness.
KINGMAN BREWSTER, speech to American Association for the Advancement of Science, Boston, Dec. 30, 1969

There is only one justification for universities, as distinguished from trade schools. They must be centers of criticism.
ROBERT M. HUTCHINS

The university is simply the canary in the coal mine. It is the most sensitive barometer of social change.
JAMES PERKINS, quoted in *Newsweek,* June 15, 1970

The use of a university is to make young gentlemen as unlike their fathers as possible.
WOODROW WILSON, 1909

College is always on the road to somewhere else.
TOM ROBBINS, interview in *Bookviews,* Feb. 1978

A society that thinks the choice between ways of living is just a choice between equally eligible "life-styles" turns universities into academic cafeterias offering junk food for the mind.
GEORGE F. WILL, *Newsweek,* May 29, 1978

The average college student is a very badly programmed computer.
JOHN WILKINSON, *John Wilkinson on the Quantitative Society,* 1964

How do you go about becoming a 17-year-old philosopher king when thoughts of screwing keep interrupting your reveries of the nature of man?
CAREY WINFREY, *Starts and Finishes,* 1975

Fifty per cent of what I know today will be obsolete in five years, but I don't know which half.
JAMES R. HICKMAN, medical student, quoted in *Newsweek,* May 27, 1968

Campus agitators are rarely, if ever, students or faculty from the scientific disciplines; they tend to come out of the social sciences, which are relatively inexact in their researches, and the humanities, which are and should be preoccupied with unanswerable questions.
SAMUEL B. GOULD, speech at Colgate University, Sept. 22, 1969

I find the three major administrative problems on a campus are sex for the students, athletics for the alumni and parking for the faculty.
CLARK KERR, quoted in *New York Times,* Nov. 17, 1958

COLUMNISTS also see NEWS/NEWSPAPERS

If you lose your temper at a newspaper columnist, he'll get rich or famous or both.
JAMES C. HAGERTY, EISENHOWER'S PRESS SECRETARY, AFTER LOSING HIS TEMPER AT ART BUCHWALD, quoted in *New York Times,* Mar. 17, 1968

The Democrats seem to be pleased if some columnists are on their side; Republicans, indignant if not all of them are.
BEN H. BAGDIKIAN, *Columbia Journalism Review,* Fall 1964

COMEDY/COMEDIANS also see HUMOR/HUMORISTS; LAUGHTER; SATIRE; TRAGEDY; WIT

Comedy is criticism.
LOUIS KRONENBERGER, *The Thread of Laughter,* 1952

Comedy is a man in trouble.
JERRY LEWIS, interview in *Newsweek,* Dec. 25, 1972

Most comedy is at least partly cruel, which is why we like it so much, and most comedy writers of intelligence have let some disenchantment with humanity filter through their work.
PETER S. PRESCOTT, *Soundings,* 1972

Any good comedy has its basis in tragedy. It is a hair's breadth removed—not the tragedy of death, but the abiding one of life.
S. N. BEHRMAN, obituary in *Newsweek,* Sept. 24, 1973

Tragedy can be turned into comedy by sitting down.
DOROTHY L. SAYERS, *The Unpleasantness at the Bellona Club,* 1928

There's something secondary about comedy. Comedy teases a problem, it pokes fun at it, but it never really confronts it.
WOODY ALLEN, interview in *Newsweek,* June 23, 1975

Unless you have a curious mind, you cannot be a comedian.
JOEY BISHOP, *The Great Comedians Talk About Comedy,* Larry Wilde, ed., 1968

COMMITTEES/CONFERENCES

Creativity always dies a quick death in rooms that house conference tables.
BRUCE HERSCHENSOHN, *New York Times,* Apr. 2, 1975

The most likely place to have your idea pocket picked is at a meeting. . . . Here an idea becomes public property the moment it hits the air waves.
JANE TRAHEY, *Jane Trahey on Women and Power,* 1977

When a committee flies the Atlantic, let me know.
EXECUTIVE WHEN TOLD LINDBERGH HAD JUST FLOWN THE ATLANTIC "ALL BY HIMSELF," quoted in *Look,* Apr. 4, 1967

THE COMMON PEOPLE

I entertained them with banners.
CHARLES DE GAULLE, quoted in André Malraux, *Felled Oaks,* 1972

No one is so dangerous as a respectable person with a sense of outrage. Once aroused, a square can easily turn into a skinhead.
EDITORIAL, *New Statesman,* Sept. 1969

You better watch out. The common man is standing up and some day he's going to elect a policeman President of the United States.
ERIC HOFFER, interview in *Newsweek,* Oct. 6, 1969

COMMON SENSE

If a man has common sense, he has all the sense there is.
SAM RAYBURN, quoted on "Washington Week in Review," PBS, Dec. 7, 1973

If common sense were as unerring as calculus, as some suggest, I don't understand why so many mistakes are made so often by so many people.
GARY H. WINKEL, interview in *New York Times,* Apr. 3, 1971

COMMUNISM also see CAPITALISM; SOCIALISM

It is incredible how many insights one obtains when viewing a ruling Communist party as a company of merchant adventurers lodged in the body of a backward country.

ERIC HOFFER, *Working and Thinking on the Waterfront,* 1969

It is a good philosophy, but a bad political system.

MILOVAN DJILAS, *Princeton Alumni Weekly,* Feb. 4, 1969

I don't like Communism because it hands out wealth through rationing books.

BRIG. GEN. OMAR TORRIJOS HERRERA, Chief of Government, Panama, quoted in *New York Times,* Sept. 7, 1977

It did not offer an answer to the question: why should a man be good?

JAYA PRAKASH NARAYAN, quoted in *New York Times,* Jan. 26, 1977

Under Communism everyone must have a job. But there is no requirement to work.

WARSAW RESIDENT, quoted in *New York Times,* Aug. 15, 1976

The cold war of rhetoric between communism and capitalism has killed no soldiers, but the air is full of the small corpses of words that once were alive: democracy, freedom, liberation.

DONALD HALL, *New York Times,* May 7, 1967

What is called Communism in backward countries is hunger becoming articulate.

LORD BOYD ORR, obituary in *Newsweek,* May 5, 1971

In the third year of Soviet rule in America you will no longer chew gum!

LEON TROTSKY, "If America Should Go Communist," *Liberty,* Mar. 23, 1935

COMMUTERS/COMMUTING

They stand like infantry at dawn waiting to be shipped to the front.

ALEX SHOUMATOFF, *Westchester,* 1979

Shot out like so much puffed rice.

WILLIAM A. EMERSON, Jr., *Newsweek,* Dec. 29, 1975

Like being pecked to death by a duck.
> LONG ISLAND COMMUTER, quoted in *Newsweek,* Feb. 17, 1969

If you can do four years on the New Haven, you won't even notice it when you crack up.
> CONNECTICUT COMMUTER, quoted in *New York,* Apr. 29, 1968

COMPETITION

Do you know the first thing I do every day? I read the *New York Times* obituary page, because maybe a pianist has died somewhere.
> LEOPOLD GODOWSKY, quoted in *New York Times,* Feb. 15, 1977

My rule on honorary degrees has been to always have one more than Arthur Schlesinger, Jr.
> JOHN KENNETH GALBRAITH, *Ambassador's Journal,* 1969

I had a better year than he did.
> BABE RUTH, in 1930, when told that Herbert Hoover made less than the $80,000 Ruth was holding out for, quoted in *Newsweek,* Aug. 13, 1973

COMPOSERS see MUSIC: COMPOSERS

COMPUTERS

All a computer does is tell a *consistent* story: a consistent truth or, if the programmer's guesses are unlucky, a consistent fiction.
> PAUL A. SAMUELSON, *Newsweek,* Oct. 4, 1971

They can rattle off the Manhattan telephone directory unerringly time after time, which no human can do, but they cannot begin to distinguish one face from another, as babies can do.
> LEE DEMBART, *New York Times,* May 8, 1977

Anyone who wishes to persuade a computer to work for him must explain his problem to the computer in precise detail. Before he can explain the problem, he must understand it thoroughly himself.
> JOHN LEAR, *Saturday Review,* Nov. 1, 1969

A computer does not substitute for judgment any more than a pencil substitutes for literacy. But writing without a pencil is no particular advantage.
ROBERT S. McNAMARA, *The Essence of Security,* 1968

The first time a person gets a screwdriver, he's going to go around the house tightening all the screws, whether they need it or not. There's no reason a computer will not be similarly abused.
THEODORE K. RABB, quoted in *Princeton Alumni Weekly,* Oct. 14, 1971

It would take one hundred clerks working for one hundred years to make a mistake as monumental as a single computer can make in one thousandth of a second.
Dental Economics, Nov. 1968

Policy makers speak of huge machine systems as being responsible for maintaining international peace. (Who gave these systems that responsibility? To whom do we complain should they fail?)
JOSEPH WEIZENBAUM, *New York Times,* May 28, 1972

There is no worse mess than a computer mess.
IBM EXECUTIVE, quoted in *New York Times,* Jan. 30, 1977

In addition to hardware, which is the computer, and software, which is the program, computer scientists have lately begun talking about "wetware," which is the human brain.
LEE DEMBART, *New York Times,* May 8, 1977

In the future, you're going to get computers as prizes in breakfast cereals. You'll throw them out because your house will be littered with them.
ROBERT LUCKY, interview in *Newsweek,* June 4, 1979

CONFERENCES see COMMITTEES/CONFERENCES

CONFORMISTS/CONFORMITY

Every society honors its live conformists and its dead troublemakers.
MIGNON McLAUGHLIN, *The Neurotic's Notebook,* 1963

Where all think alike, no one thinks very much.
ATTRIBUTED TO WALTER LIPPMANN

"The common good" is the most common argument politicians use for coercing individuals to conform to social custom.
PERRY LONDON, *Columbia Forum,* Spring 1972

Woe to him inside a nonconformist clique who does not conform with nonconformity.
ERIC HOFFER, *Reflections on the Human Condition,* 1973

CONFUSION

I am not confused. I'm just well mixed.
ROBERT FROST, quoted in *Wall Street Journal,* Aug. 5, 1969

Anybody who isn't confused isn't well informed.
ANONYMOUS

Sometimes I wonder, and then I don't know.
JOHN L. SULLIVAN

CONGRESS

It is an institution designed only to react, not to plan or lead.
JIMMY BRESLIN, *How the Good Guys Finally Won,* 1975

The one power that Congress has is the power of the purse.
WILLIAM PROXMIRE, speech at Chamber of Commerce conference, Washington, Jan. 31, 1967

It is said that the titles of most bills in Congress are like the titles of Marx Brothers movies (*Duck Soup, Animal Crackers*): they do not tell much about the contents.
GEORGE F. WILL, *Newsweek,* Oct. 3, 1977

There is rarely political risk in supporting the President and rarely political advantage in disagreement—unless and until a particular policy appears a failure.
NICHOLAS DEB. KATZENBACH, *New York Times,* Feb. 18, 1973

It is Congress that voters mistrust, not their own congressmen.
PETER GOLDMAN, *Newsweek,* Nov. 6, 1978

Nobody ever deported a senator.
ATTRIBUTED TO LUCKY LUCIANO

Congress is generously sprinkled with vaudevillians who would never have made the Palace.
ANONYMOUS

What can you expect from that zoo?
JOHN F. KENNEDY, quoted in *US News & World Report,* July 22, 1968

We had better seats for *Hello Dolly.*
ATTRIBUTED TO ROBERT F. KENNEDY WHEN SHOWN HIS SEAT AS A FRESHMAN SENATOR, Jan. 5, 1965

CONSCIENCE

Conscience is nothing but other people inside you.
LUIGI PIRANDELLO, *Each in His Own Way* (drama), 1923

Commit a crime and the world is made of passing policemen.
JEB STUART MAGRUDER, *An American Life,* 1974

A conscience cannot prevent sin. It only prevents you from enjoying it.
HARRY HERSHFIELD, obituary in *New York Post,* Dec. 16, 1974

I cannot and will not cut my conscience to fit this year's fashions.
LILLIAN HELLMAN, letter to House Un-American Activities Committee, 1952

CONSERVATION/CONSERVATIONISTS also see EARTH; NATURE

All of us understand the put-and-take of checking accounts, but few understand the careful accounts of deposits and withdrawals that nature keeps.
ALFRED BESTER, *Holiday,* June 1966

Everything is connected to everything else.
BARRY COMMONER, *New Yorker,* Sept. 22, 1972

Don't dismiss our extermination of passenger pigeons and Carolina parakeets by saying that extinction had always gone on. Evolution of new species used to occur too.
DANIEL L. MCKINLEY, *New York Times,* July 18, 1971

Over the long haul of life on this planet, it is the ecologists, and not the bookkeepers of business, who are the ultimate accountants.
STEWART L. UDALL, speech to Congress of Optimum Population and Environment, June 9, 1970

Ecology is boring for the same reason that destruction is fun.
DON DE LILLO, quoted in *New York Times,* July 14, 1974

We've got a program to invent a new name for ecology, so we can keep it alive after it's been talked to death. We're thinking of calling it politics.
HARVEY WHEELER, quoted in *Newsweek,* Jan. 26, 1970

CONSERVATION: MINING

Mining is like a search-and-destroy mission.
STEWART L. UDALL, *1976—Agenda for Tomorrow,* 1968

It's hard not to chuckle. The white man is doing to other white men what the white man once did to the Indian.
DEWITT DILLON, Crow Indian, on strip mining, quoted in *Newsweek,* Oct. 9, 1972

CONSERVATIVES also see LIBERALS/LIBERALISM; RADICALS

Conservatives don't have a very optimistic view of human nature.
NICHOLAS WAHL, quoted in *New York Post,* June 15, 1974

They define themselves in terms of what they oppose.
GEORGE F. WILL, *Newsweek,* Sept. 30, 1974

Somehow liberals have been unable to acquire from life what conservatives seem to be endowed with at birth; namely, a healthy skepticism of the powers of government agencies to do good.
DANIEL P. MOYNIHAN, quoted in *New York Post,* May 14, 1969

One might say that the only difference between old-school liberals and conservatives is that the former would destroy the market through public means and the latter through private means.
    THEODORE J. LOWI, *The End of Liberalism,* 1969

The central shortcoming of conservatives is the failure to retrieve their wounded.
    WHITTAKER CHAMBERS, quoted in *New York Times,* Aug. 2, 1973

Do you know what a conservative is? That's a liberal who got mugged the night before.
    FRANK RIZZO, Philadelphia mayor, quoted in *Newsweek,* Dec. 18, 1972

I've got money so I'm a Conservative.
    LORD THOMSON of FLEET, obituary in *New York Times,* Aug. 5, 1976

CONSUMERS

In the jungle of the market place, the intelligent buyer must be alert to every commercial sound, to every snapping of a selling twig, to every rustle that may signal the uprising arm holding the knife pointed toward the jugular vein.
    DEXTER MASTERS, *The Intelligent Buyer and the Telltale Seller,* 1966

The American consumer is not notable for his imagination and does not know what he "wants."
    ANDREW HACKER, *New York Times,* June 14, 1966

CONTRADICTION

If there were no contradictions and no struggle, there would be no world, no process, no life, and there would be nothing at all.
    MAO ZEDONG, obituary in *New York Times,* Sept. 10, 1976

Do I contradict myself? / Very well, then, I contradict myself.
    WALT WHITMAN, in section later titled "Song of Myself," *Leaves of Grass,* 1855

CONVERSATION

How odd it is that people can hardly be in a room together before they know what to talk about. The same on the telephone or in the street! They greet one another and then at once know what to talk about.
MAX FRISCH, *Sketchbook 1966–1971*, 1974

Beware of the man who will not engage in idle conversation; he is planning to steal your walking stick or water your stock.
WILLIAM A. EMERSON, Jr., quoted in *Newsweek*, Oct. 29, 1973

The word, even the most contradictory word, preserves contact—it is silence which isolates.
THOMAS MANN, *The Magic Mountain*, 1924

CONVICTIONS also see BELIEF; IDEAS; PREJUDICES

The difference between a conviction and a prejudice is that you can explain a conviction without getting angry.
ANONYMOUS

Nearly all our disasters come of a few fools having the "courage of their convictions."
COVENTRY PATMORE, *The Rod, the Root and the Flower*, 1895

COOKING also see EATING; FOOD

If you can organize your kitchen, you can organize your life.
DR. LOUIS PARRISH, *Cooking as Therapy*, 1975

Watch everything on the stove the way you would watch a piece of toast.
DINTY MOORE, quoted in *Newsweek*, Aug. 20, 1973

You just put things in hot water and take them out again after a little while.
FRENCH CHEF ON ENGLISH COOKING, quoted in Arthur Hawkins, *Who Needs a Cookbook*, 1968

Murder is commoner among cooks than among members of any other profession.
W. H. AUDEN, *Forewords and Afterwords*, 1973

CORPORATIONS also see ORGANIZATIONS

The large corporation, though still primarily a private economic entity, has such vast social impact (where it locates, whom it hires, what technology it pursues) that it has become a public trust with a communal constituency.
STEPHEN B. SHEPARD, *New York Times,* Feb. 25, 1974

The men who run modern international corporations are the first in history with the organization, the technology, the money, and the ideology to make a credible try at managing the world as an integrated unit. By making ordinary business decisions, the managers . . . now have more power than most sovereign governments to determine where people will live; what work they will do, if any; what they will eat, drink and wear; what sorts of knowledge, schools and universities they will encourage; and what kind of society their children will inherit.
RICHARD J. BARNET AND RONALD MÜLLER, *Global Reach,* 1975

Corporations, especially the large and complex ones with which we have to live, now appear to possess some of the qualities of nation states—including, perhaps, an alarming capacity to insulate their members from the moral consequences of their actions.
PAUL EDDY, ELAINE POTTER AND BRUCE PAGE, *Destination Disaster,* 1976

They usually do not much care what society's rules are so long as the rules are clear.
GEORGE F. WILL, *Newsweek,* Feb. 19, 1979

Aggressive is not a pleasant word. Yet it's the highest form of praise in a corporate job-performance review.
ANONYMOUS

Armies and corporations alike have ways of sweetening the news as it ascends the hierarchy of command.
ROBERT L. HEILBRONER AND OTHERS, *In the Name of Profit,* 1972

Too much agreement, from too narrow a group, makes for decisions that don't work.
HARLAN CLEVELAND, *The Future Executive,* 1972

COSMETICS

The best thing is to look natural, but it takes makeup to look natural.
CALVIN KLEIN, *New York Times,* Mar. 6, 1977

The sexual-industrial complex.
FRANCINE DU PLESSIX GRAY ON THE COSMETICS INDUSTRY, *New York Times,* Jan. 15, 1978

COUNTERCULTURE

The counter-culture was really a supermarket, with counters labelled drugs, Marx, rock, Zen and love.
PETE HAMILL, *New York Times,* Nov. 30, 1975

The cult is simply an extension of the idea that everyone's supreme aim in life is self-fulfillment and happiness and that one is entitled to wreck marriage, children and certainly one's own health and sanity in pursuit of this.
STEPHEN SPENDER, *Partisan Review,* Spring 1972

COUNTRIES: COMPARISONS

All countries hate their immediate neighbors and like the next but one.
CHARLES ISSAWI, *Columbia Forum,* Spring 1970

When a Frenchman slips away from a party early, without telling the host, he says he is taking English leave. An Englishman who sneaks away calls it French leave.
LONDON DISPATCH, *New York Times,* Aug. 15, 1976

In America only the successful writer is important, in France all writers are important, in England no writer is important, and in Australia you have to explain what a writer is.
GEOFFREY COTTRELL, *New York Journal-American,* Sept. 22, 1961

COURTS see also LAW; LAWYERS

A defendant is entitled to a fair trial but not a perfect one.
U.S. SUPREME COURT, *Lutwak v. U.S.,* 1953

This is not a court of love, of compassion, but a court of law.
DANIEL COBURN, N.J. attorney, quoted in *Newsweek,* Nov. 3, 1975

This case proves that our justice system works—if you have the money and the influence to go all the way.
ROBERT ARUM, when Supreme Court reversed Muhammad Ali's conviction for draft evasion, quoted in *New York Times,* Sept. 28, 1975

In America, an acquittal doesn't mean you're innocent, it means you beat the rap. My clients lose even when they win.
F. LEE BAILEY, speech to Bar Association of N.Y., Mar. 4, 1972

CREATIVITY

The essence of the creative act is to see the familiar as strange.
Kaiser News, no. 3, 1967

A capacity for childlike wonder, carried into adult life, typifies the creative person.
Kaiser News, no. 3, 1967

The creative person is unique in that during the initial stages he prefers the chaotic and disorderly and tends to reject what has already been systemized.
RALPH J. HALLMAN, *Journal of Humanistic Psychology,* Fall 1966

The intellect has little to do on the road to discovery. There comes a leap in consciousness, call it intuition or what you will, and the solution comes to you and you don't know how or why.
ALBERT EINSTEIN, quoted in *Forbes,* Sept. 15, 1974

The only trade at which the novice and apprentice earn nothing while they learn is the creative trade.
W. G. ROGERS, *Ladies Bountiful,* 1968

A first-rate soup is more creative than a second-rate painting.
ABRAHAM MASLOW, *Personality Symposium #1, 1950,* W. Wolff, ed.

Highly creative people are often off their rockers.
STANLEY HOFFMANN, quoted in *New York Post,* June 15, 1974

CRIME also see FORGERY; GANGSTERS; PRISONS; STEALING

In the war on crime the bad guys are ahead.
THOMAS PLATE, *Crime Pays!,* 1975

The biggest obstacle to solving some of the more heinous crimes is their senselessness—in some crimes there just isn't a motive.
EDWIN T. DREHER, N.Y.C. deputy police chief, interview in *New York Post,* Jan. 12, 1976

A good deal of criminal activity is motivated not by aggression, but by desire to relieve boredom, to create excitement, to call attention to oneself.
THOMAS SZASZ, *Heresies,* 1976

Organized crime will put a man in the White House some day, and he won't know it until they hand him the bill.
POLITICAL SCIENTIST, quoted in Donald R. Cressey, *Theft of the Nation,* 1969

CRITICISM: ARTISTIC

In the arts, the critic is the only independent source of information. The rest is advertising.
PAULINE KAEL, quoted in *Newsweek,* Dec. 24, 1973

Criticism functions for democratic societies as conversation functioned for aristocratic societies.
HILTON KRAMER, quoted in *Newsweek,* Dec. 24, 1973

Criticism is a luxury product: You [the publisher] have to support a man to spend a month or two months producing something that will be read by very few people.
WILFRID SHEED, interview in *New York Times,* Jan. 21, 1979

It is unfortunate that more and more we confuse the function of criticism with being a sort of racing tip sheet. If you work for the mass media you're going to be used as a market report, a Good Housekeeping Seal of Approval.
CLIVE BARNES, quoted in *Newsweek,* Dec. 24, 1973

The temptation is tremendous to say that you like what you think you ought to like and don't like what you think you oughtn't to like.
ARNOLD BENNETT, *Arnold Bennett: The Evening Standard Years,* Andrew Mylett, ed., 1974

You will never learn art criticism until you have had relations with the ice man.
DR. ALBERT C. BARNES TO WOMAN CRITIC WHO HAD RIDICULED HIS ART COLLECTION, quoted in *New York Times,* Mar. 24, 1974

It is better, given the choice, to have friends.
ELIZABETH BISHOP, explaining her refusal to write criticism, quoted in *Newsweek,* Jan. 31, 1977

CRITICISM: PERSONAL

You criticize a newsman and he starts yelling: "First Amendment! Spiro Agnew!" You criticize a college professor and he starts yelling: "Academic Freedom! Anti-intellectualism!"
MOLLY IVINS, *New York Times,* Sept. 7, 1975

They have vilified me, they have crucified me, yes, they have even criticized me.
RICHARD J. DALEY, *Quotations from Mayor Daley,* Peter Yessne, comp., 1969

It takes a rare person to want to hear what he doesn't want to hear.
DICK CAVETT, "Dick Cavett Show," PBS, Feb. 27, 1978

CROWDS

The crowd is the soul of the future in the body of the past.
ANONYMOUS

A crowd has the mind of a woman.
"ADAM SMITH" (GEORGE GOODMAN), *The Money Game,* 1968

The crowd always wants to grow.
ELIAS CANETTI, *Crowds and Power,* 1979

Crowds are the most lonely thing of all.
L. S. LOWRY, quoted in *Newsweek,* Jan. 2, 1967

One precept of crowd photography—and politics—is that people tend to wave whatever is put into their hands.
Newsweek, Dec. 9, 1968

CULTURE see SOCIETY: THE CULTURE

CULTURE, POP see POP CULTURE

CURIOSITY

I think, at a child's birth, if a mother could ask a fairy godmother to endow it with the most useful gift, that gift would be curiosity.
ELEANOR ROOSEVELT, quoted in *Today's Health,* from *Quote,* Oct. 2, 1966

People say: idle curiosity. The one thing that curiosity cannot be is idle.
LEO ROSTEN, "David Susskind Show," Metromedia, Feb. 19, 1978

Good questions outrank easy answers.
PAUL A. SAMUELSON, *Newsweek,* Aug. 21, 1978

A man should go on living if only to satisfy his curiosity.
JEWISH PROVERB

DAYDREAMS also see DREAMERS/REALISTS

Most of us have a B movie running in our heads most of the time.
DR. ALEXANDER ROGAWSKI, quoted in *Time,* Oct. 3, 1977

The chief advantage of the uninterrupted daydream is its absence of risk.
DR. FRITZ REDLICH, quoted in *New York Times,* Sept. 24, 1967

DEATH also see LIFE; SUICIDE

A dying man needs to die as a sleepy man needs to sleep, and there comes a time when it is wrong, as well as useless, to resist.
STEWART ALSOP, *Stay of Execution,* 1973

Death is simply un-American. Its inevitability is an affront to our inalienable rights to "life, liberty, and the pursuit of happiness."
DAVID HENDIN, *Death as a Fact of Life,* 1973

Untimely deaths seem common—but I don't remember hearing of a timely one.
FRANK A. CLARK, *Quote*, Oct. 30, 1977

It's not that I'm afraid to die. I just don't want to be there when it happens.
WOODY ALLEN, interview in *Newsweek*, June 23, 1975

Out here we don't care for it.
SOL WURTZEL, Hollywood executive, quoted in S. N. Behrman, *People in a Diary*, 1972

Think of death as a pie in the face from God.
JERRY BELSON, *The End* (film), 1978

This one-to-a-customer experience.
JULIAN MOYNIHAN, *New York Times*, Oct. 10, 1976

That extraordinary day after one's funeral.
GEORGE STEINER, "Tower of Babel," PBS, Nov. 9, 1977

DECADE: 1900-1909

At the turn of the century everyone still hoped for the best; only benighted souls or disturbed minds furtively suspected the worst.
LEWIS MUMFORD, *My Works and Days*, 1979

A simpler time when a man followed his father's trade, when families stuck together, when neighborhoods counted, when everyone knew what church you belonged to, what ward you lived in and what saloon you patronized.
FRANK MAIER, *Newsweek*, Jan. 3, 1976

There was a lot of sexual fainting.
E. L. DOCTOROW, *Ragtime*, 1975

I am goddam tired of listening to all this babble for reform. America is a hell of a success.
JOSEPH G. CANNON, speaker, House of Representatives

DECADE: 1910-1919 see WORLD WAR I

DECADE: 1920-1929

A tense truce in a war that began in 1914 and ended in 1945.
HAMILTON FISH ARMSTRONG, quoted in *Newsweek,* June 28, 1971

It was an era paralyzed by sophistication.
ALDOUS HUXLEY, quoted by Alistair Cooke, PBS, Feb. 18, 1973

The first self-conscious youth generation in America.
PAUL FUSSELL, *New York Times,* Apr. 24, 1977

In the 1920's it was legs. My God, women hadn't shown their legs for 2,000 years.
ROBERT RILEY, interview in *New York Times,* Dec. 12, 1973

I'm runnin' wild;/I've lost control.
JOE GREY AND LEO WOOD, "Runnin' Wild," 1922 song

No era ever vanished so suddenly, so completely, as the twenties.
DAVID DEMPSEY, *New York Times,* Feb. 15, 1970

DECADE: 1930-1939 also see THE DEPRESSION: ECONOMIC

Gentlemen, in the little moment that remains to us between the crisis and the catastrophe, we might as well take a glass of champagne.
FRENCH AMBASSADOR PAUL CLAUDEL AT WASHINGTON PARTY CELEBRATING HOOVER MORATORIUM ON WAR DEBTS, 1931, quoted in Claude Cockburn, *The Devil's Decade,* 1973

It was in Spain that men learned that one can be right and yet be beaten, that force can vanquish spirit, that there are times when courage is not its own recompense.
ALBERT CAMUS, quoted in *Newsweek,* Oct. 13, 1975

We are barbarians. We want to be barbarians. It is an honorable title.
ADOLF HITLER, quoted in "The Life of Adolf Hitler," PBS, Dec. 12, 1974

I'm wobbling about all over the place.
BRITISH PRIME MINISTER NEVILLE CHAMBERLAIN WHEN SIMULTANEOUS-
LY ADVISED TO STAND UP TO HITLER AND TO CAPITULATE, Munich Con-
ference, 1938, *The Diaries of Sir Alexander Cadogan, 1938–1945,*
David Dilks, ed., 1972

A low dishonest decade.
W. H. AUDEN, "September 1, 1939," *Another Time,* 1940

DECADE: 1940-1949 see THE BOMB; THE HOLOCAUST;
WORLD WAR II

DECADE: 1950-1959

Circled by fury, we were the unfurious; surrounded by passion, we
were the dispassionate.
GERALD CLARKE, *Time,* June 29, 1970

The post-war binge of pretentious motherhood.
GEORGE GILDER, *Sexual Suicide,* 1973

They had no Hemingway or Mauldin because as a group they did
nothing that could be romanticized or caricatured.
ROBERT KIELY, *New York Times,* Apr. 23, 1972

The Russians launched Sputnik and we launched the Edsel.
RICHARD FREEDMAN, *New York Times,* Mar. 5, 1978

Eisenhower sat on his ass and we were a thousand times better off.
ERIC HOFFER, interview in *People,* Jan. 16, 1978

DECADE: 1960-1969 also see ASTRONAUTS; HIPPIES;
MOONLANDING; VIETNAM; ZEN

America started the sixties thinking it could save the world and ended
them wondering whether it could save face.
JAMES RESTON, *New York Times,* Dec. 30, 1969

When Utopia was proclaimed to be a matter of will power.
FLORA LEWIS, *New York Times,* Mar. 27, 1975

Before anyone noticed it, liberalism was mortgaging its future by sending military missions to an obscure Southeast Asian capital called Saigon.
JOHN CHAMBERLAIN, *Wall Street Journal*, July 3, 1974

From Vietnam I learned to despise my countrymen, my government, and the entire English-speaking world, with its history of genocide and international conquest. I was a normal kid.
RAYMOND MUNGO, *Famous Long Ago*, 1970

The first parent-financed revolt.
ALASDAIR MACINTYRE, *Herbert Marcuse*, 1970

Some of these kids don't know what country this is. They think it's Bolivia.
IRVING KRISTOL, *New York Times*, Apr. 12, 1970

When everybody seemed to dislike everybody.
DONALD BARR, interview in *New York Times*, Jan. 19, 1975

Any man who is willing to exchange his life for mine can do so.
JOHN F. KENNEDY, quoted in Jim Bishop, *The Day That Kennedy Was Shot*, 1968

America returns to its ancient demons.
CHARLES DE GAULLE ON THE KENNEDY ASSASSINATION, quoted in Jean-Raymond Tournoux, *Intimate Biography*, 1973

Ease with sex and difficulties with love.
SARA DAVIDSON, *Loose Change*, 1977

The poor wouldn't be caught dead wearing the clothes their affluent counterparts were buying in order to look like the poor.
ROGER RICKLEFS, *Wall Street Journal*, Dec. 22, 1976

We thought we could change a mammoth government by wearing flowers and holding hands.
GRACE WING SLICK, quoted in *Newsweek*, Feb. 23, 1976

We were marching since we were babies and all we did was make Jane Fonda famous.
ROBERT PATRICK, *Kennedy's Children* (drama), 1976

After 1965, dissent became conformity, the straights became oddballs.
STEVEN B. ROBERTS, *New York Times*, Oct. 3, 1976

DECADE: 1970-1979 also see ENERGY CRISIS; MEDITA-
TION KICK; VIETNAM; WATERGATE

In the summer of 1970, many young people discovered what their elders already knew, that the tragedy of the world is that it is run by human beings.
DR. WILLARD DALRYMPLE, *University* (Princeton), Winter 1973

It's a sad thing, a very sad thing when a nation like this one has to
creep into a new decade with its tail between its legs.
THOMAS J. WATSON, JR., speech to Bond Club, N.Y.C., Jan. 7, 1970

We're living in a kind of pallid emotional time, we're so jaded we've
almost managed to make sex boring, when somebody new approaches
you, you're afraid you're being approached according to page 136.
COLLEEN DEWHURST, interview in *New York Times,* Feb. 17, 1974

Women my age can't remember the names of half the men we've slept
with since we were 17.
GRADUATE STUDENT, quoted in *New York Times,* Oct. 2, 1977

For both sexes in this society, caring deeply for anyone is becoming
synonymous with losing. . . . They *envy* machines.
HERBERT HENDIN, *The Age of Sensation,* 1975

Our problem is that we have no reference points. All our traditions are
crumbling. Look at the Catholic Church. The only people who want to
get married today are Catholic priests.
MORTIMER FEINBERG, quoted in *Business Week,* Mar. 10, 1975

For the first time in the history of our country a majority of our people believe that the next five years will be worse than the past five
years.
JIMMY CARTER, TV speech, July 15, 1979

Whatever happened to the fun in our future?
GEORGE F. WILL, *Newsweek,* July 9, 1979

DECIMALS see MATHEMATICS

DEFENSE DEPARTMENT see PENTAGON

DEMOCRACY also see EQUALITY; LIBERTY; POLITICS

Democracy, like any noncoercive relationship, rests on a shared understanding of limits.
ELIZABETH DREW, *Washington Journal,* 1975

Compromise is a noble word that sums up democracy.
SAUL ALINSKY

Democracy begins with a free discussion of our sins.
W. H. AUDEN, quoted on "Bill Moyers' Journal," PBS, June 5, 1973

No democracy is possible without friction.
NICHOLAS VON HOFFMANN, *Make-Believe Presidents,* 1978

It's a lot of people pulling together who hate each other's guts.
"CALUCCI'S DEPARTMENT," CBS-TV, Sept. 8, 1973

Democracy is the most difficult of all forms of government, since it requires the widest spread of intelligence, and we forgot to make ourselves intelligent when we made ourselves sovereign.
WILL AND ARIEL DURANT, *The Lessons of History,* 1968

Democracy is not merely an electoral parade, but is a sincere effort to keep in step with the slowest soldier in the battalion.
GIUSEPPE PREZZOLINI, *Machiavelli,* introduction to Italian edition, 1927

Policies are rarely made in a democracy; they emerge.
GARTH L. MANGUM, *Annals of American Academy of Political and Social Science,* Sept. 1969

The weakness of democracy—the reason why Karl Marx and others must be laughing in their graves—is precisely that it's about winning votes. No government can afford to have a survival strategy because that means losing votes.
ANDREW KNIGHT, *Newsweek,* Jan. 13, 1975

The reason democracy doesn't work is that, while bribing of individual voters is illegal, the bribing of whole classes of voters is not.
Dublin Opinion, from *Quote,* Oct. 29, 1967

Democracy is shaking my nerves to pieces.
HENRY ADAMS, *Democracy,* 1880

Democracy may not prove in the long run to be as efficient as other forms of government, but it has one saving grace: it allows us to know and say that it isn't.
BILL MOYERS, *Newsweek,* June 3, 1975

So Two Cheers for Democracy: one because it admits variety and two because it permits criticism. Two cheers are quite enough: there is no occasion to give three. Only Love, the Beloved Republic, deserves that.
E. M. FORSTER, *Two Cheers for Democracy,* 1951

DEMOCRATS/DEMOCRATIC PARTY also see REPUBLI-CANS/REPUBLICAN PARTY

The Democratic Party is not one—but two—political parties with the same name. They unite only once every two years—to wage political campaigns.
ATTRIBUTED TO DWIGHT D. EISENHOWER

You can never underestimate the ability of the Democrats to wet their finger and hold it to the wind.
RONALD REAGAN, quoted in *Newsweek,* July 10, 1978

Have you ever tried to split sawdust?
EUGENE J. MCCARTHY, when accused of splitting the party, *Quote,* May 19, 1968

Listening to Democrats complain about inflation is like listening to germs complain about disease.
SPIRO AGNEW, quoted in *Newsweek,* July 20, 1970

There are only six Democrats in all of Hinsdale County and you, you son of a bitch, you ate five of them.
ATTRIBUTED TO COLORADO JUDGE SENTENCING ALFRED E. PACKER FOR CANNIBALIZING FIVE MEMBERS OF PROSPECTING PARTY, 1874, quoted in *Newsweek,* Aug. 22, 1977

THE DEPRESSION: ECONOMIC also see DECADE: 1930-1939

There's a lot of nostalgia for the Depression, though obviously by people who didn't live through it.
HILTON KRAMER, *New York Times,* Dec. 26, 1972

Liquidate labor, liquidate stocks, liquidate farmers.
ANDREW MELLON, Treasury Secretary, to President Herbert Hoover, quoted in *Wall Street Journal*, Dec. 2, 1974

My life on the farm during the Great Depression more nearly resembled farm life of fully 2,000 years ago than farm life today.
JIMMY CARTER, *Why Not the Best?*, 1975

I don't know. I'm not depressed. I can pot out any time I want.
19-YEAR-OLD WHEN ASKED WHAT THE DEPRESSION WAS, quoted in Studs Terkel, *Hard Times*, 1970

DEPRESSION: EMOTION

Depression is our epidemic emotional illness.
WEBSTER SCHOTT, *New York Times*, Mar. 16, 1975

Depression is a form of self-inflicted punishment for the commission of sins—real or imagined.
ANONYMOUS, *Go to Health*, Bobbie Savitz, ed., 1973

The black dog.
WINSTON CHURCHILL ON HIS DEPRESSIONS, quoted in *Newsweek*, Dec. 26, 1977

Depressed people are very good at plodding along.
DR. LEONARD SIMON, interview in *New York Post*, Apr. 23, 1977

THE DEVIL

A perfidious and astute charmer who manages to insinuate himself into us by way of the senses, of fantasy, of concupiscence, of utopian logic, of disorderly social contacts.
POPE PAUL VI, speech to papal audience, Nov. 1972

Say what you will about the devil, he's a hustler.
KIN HUBBARD (FRANK MCKINNEY HUBBARD), quoted in *Forbes*, Apr. 1, 1974

DIARIES

A continuing confrontation with oneself in the midst of life.
IRA PROGOFF, quoted in Tristine Rainer, *The New Diary,* 1978

I must write it all out, at any cost. Writing is thinking. It is more than living, for it is being conscious of living.
ANNE MORROW LINDBERGH, *Locked Rooms and Open Doors,* 1974

The born diarists are the snails of life: they are secretive and enclosed in their shells.
V. S. PRITCHETT, *New York Times,* Nov. 26, 1967

DICTATORSHIP

Strong thumbs, no fingers.
CHARLES E. LINDBLOM, *Politics and Markets,* 1977

Everything not Forbidden is Compulsory.
T. H. WHITE, *The Book of Merlyn,* 1977

Only tyranny refuses the risk of movement and offers the perfection of a fearful immobility, even in the name of morality.
ANDRÉ MALRAUX, quoted in *New York Times,* Dec. 12, 1976

A dog is a dog except when he is facing you. Then he is Mr. Dog.
HAITIAN FARMER, quoted in *Newsweek,* June 27, 1966

No regime which depends for its existence on authoritarian power is going to reform itself to death.
GADDIS SMITH, *New York Times,* Feb. 25, 1968

DINNER see EATING: DINNER

DIPLOMACY also see FOREIGN POLICY; STATE DEPARTMENT

The art of restraining power.
HENRY A. KISSINGER, quoted in *New York Times,* Oct. 28, 1973

Diplomacy is frequently the art of making a good impression unexpectedly.
DIPLOMATIC AXIOM

I live by my principles. My first principle is expediency.
STATESMAN, quoted in Leonard Lyons' column, Dec. 15, 1971

Do you think when two representatives holding diametrically opposing views get together and shake hands, the contradictions between our systems will simply melt away? What kind of a daydream is that?
NIKITA S. KHRUSHCHEV, on summit diplomacy, *Khrushchev Remembers,* 1974

You mustn't make yourself appear ridiculous by addressing someone as comrade when he should be called citizen, or citizen when he should be called mister.
KABET TSHIBANGU, Zäire, quoted in *New York Times,* Aug. 28, 1975

Sometimes you have to go through the motions. Sometimes the motions are more important than the substance.
AMERICAN DIPLOMAT, quoted in *Newsweek,* Mar. 24, 1975

DISCIPLINE

Though discipline and freedom seem antithetical, each without the other destroys itself.
DONALD BARR, *Who Pushed Humpty Dumpty?,* 1971

Discipline is the basis of a satisfying life, but discipline is out of style.
KATHARINE HEPBURN, interview in *TV Guide,* Dec. 15, 1973

DISCO see MUSIC: DISCO

DISLIKE also see HATRED

The tragedy of disliking a fellow is that we want everyone else to dislike him, too.
FRANK A. CLARK, *Quote,* Feb. 13, 1977

If this little girl gets better, I'll never dislike anybody again in my life—except two guys.
TOOTS SHOR'S PRAYER WHEN HIS DAUGHTER WAS NEAR DEATH, quoted in *New York Times,* Dec. 24, 1976

DISORDER also see ORDER; PLAN/PLANNERS; RANDOM-NESS

It is the loose ends with which men hang themselves.
ZELDA FITZGERALD, quoted in *New York Times,* Aug. 13, 1967

I think you have to be willing to settle for the messiness of experience. That may be what we mean by life.
DANIEL J. BOORSTIN, interview in *New York Post,* May 1, 1972

DIVORCE also see MARRIAGE, SECOND

Though many, whose church forbids it, believe divorce is sin, it may be said that aside from these groups, two marriages with a divorce are thought normal; among the rich, three are normal; and in Hollywood four are normal.
EDMUND WILSON, *The Cold War and the Income Tax,* 1963

Moving from marriage to divorce is like traveling to a foreign country. Few of us are eager for the journey; few can afford the fare; and few know how to cope en route or what to expect when we arrive.
ELEANOR DIENSTAG, *Psychology Today,* Mar. 1977

What the hell, if you get divorced the chances are you'll end up with somebody else's castoff. What's so great about that?
ANONYMOUS, quoted in E. E. LeMaster, *Blue-Collar Aristocrats,* 1975

DOCTORS also see HEALTH; HOSPITALS; MEDICAL CARE; SICKNESS

Doctors overawe us with their power over life and death and their un-intelligible handwriting.
DAVID HAPGOOD, *New York Times,* Jan. 26, 1975

Once someone has chosen to fall ill, he has to apply for the role of patient: he auditions for the part by reciting his complaints as vividly and convincingly as he can.
> JONATHAN MILLER, on the patient-doctor relationship, *The Body in Question,* 1979

I always have to laugh when the AMA claims that doctors have no special powers over people. How many people can tell you to take off your clothes and you'll do it?
> DR. ROBERT S. MENDELSOHN, *Confessions of a Medical Heretic,* 1979

If you have more surgeons, you'll get more surgery. If you have more internists, you'll get more lab tests.
> DR. JOHN WENNBERG, quoted in *Newsweek,* May 28, 1979

Doctors are difficult people to live with because nobody ever says no to them.
> DIVORCED WIFE OF PHYSICIAN, quoted in *New York Times,* Oct. 27, 1976

DOGS also see ANIMALS

A dog is the only thing on this earth that loves you more than he loves himself.
> JOSH BILLINGS, *Affurisms,* 1865

The dog who meets with a good master is the happier of the two.
> MAURICE MAETERLINCK, *Our Friend the Dog,* 1905

If dogs could talk, perhaps we would find it as hard to get along with them as we do with people.
> KAREL ČAPEK, quoted in *New York Times,* May 14, 1967

Anybody who doesn't know what soap tastes like never washed a dog.
> FRANKLIN P. JONES, *Quote,* May 15, 1977

What are you supposed to do, rent them a motel room?
> MRS. DONALD ORR, on Stanfield, Ore., ordinance forbidding "animals to engage in sex in public view," quoted in Cleveland Amory's column, July 3, 1975

DREAMERS/REALISTS also see DAYDREAMS

"Realistic people" who pursue "practical aims" are rarely as realistic and practical, in the long run of life, as the dreamers who pursue their dreams.
HANS SELYE, *The Stress of Life,* 1956

The dreamer is the realist of today. The realist climbs on the shoulders of the dreamer and makes a lot of noise, but he's really behind the procession.
MAURICE LAVANOUX, quoted in *New York Times,* Sept. 2, 1972

Like all dreamers, I confused disenchantment with truth.
JEAN-PAUL SARTRE, *The Words,* 1964

DREAMS also see SLEEP

A way to discharge built-up pressure—to go safely and quietly insane each night.
EDWIN DIAMOND, *New York Times,* Feb. 12, 1967

So flowerlike is it in its candor and veracity that it makes us blush for the deceitfulness of our lives.
CARL G. JUNG, quoted in Joseph Campbell, *The Mythic Image,* 1975

Too soft a bed tends to make people dream which is unhealthy and weakening.
How Girls Can Help Their Country, Girl Scout Manual, 1913

If a man could pass through Paradise in a dream, and have a flower presented to him as a pledge that his soul had really been there, and if he found that flower in his hand when he awoke— Ay! and what then?
SAMUEL TAYLOR COLERIDGE, *Anima Poetae,* 1895

DRUGS: ADDICTIVE

This society seems to have swallowed the notion that there is a chemical solution for all problems, including the problem of how to spend one's spare time.
DR. JOEL FORT, quoted in *New York Times,* Mar. 10, 1969

If God can be found through any drug, God is not worthy of being God.
MEHERE BABA, *Quote,* Sept. 17, 1967

The children "turned on" by marijuana, cocaine (now common), LSD, or methadone are like radios tuned to nothing, they play the noise of their own tubes.
DONALD BARR, *Who Pushed Humpty Dumpty?,* 1971

Drug users play upon their own fantasies. So does everybody else, but drug users don't care whether anybody is listening.
GÜNTER GRASS, interview in *New York Times,* Mar. 19, 1970

If drugs are the answer, what's the question?
ANONYMOUS MOTTO

Every time I give a check to an addict, I say to myself, "I just paid for a fix." But I also say, "I just kept someone from being robbed."
WELFARE WORKER, quoted in *New York Times,* Mar. 19, 1972

Junkies all wear hats, if they have hats.
WILLIAM S. BURROUGHS, *Junky,* 1963

A major error of the current drug classification system is that it treats alcohol and nicotine—two of the most harmful drugs—essentially as nondrugs.
EDWARD M. BRECHER, *Licit and Illicit Drugs,* 1972

Death is the greatest kick for all./That's why they save it for the last.
GRAFFITO, Los Angeles

DRUGS: LSD

LSD is, if you like, a psychiatric X-ray. With LSD you have no greater vision of the universe than you did before. It no more expands your consciousness than an X-ray expands your lungs when you see them on the screen. All you do is get a better look.
DR. MARVIN ZIPORYN, quoted in *Kaiser News,* no. 6, 1966

It makes you take yourself too seriously, a symptom of madness.
CHARLES W. SLACK, letter to *New York Times,* Sept. 22, 1974

Any idiot knows that you don't take LSD above the ground floor.
TIMOTHY LEARY, interview in *New York Times,* Aug. 6, 1967

DRUGS: MARIJUANA

There isn't any evidence that people are any smarter or more beautiful or wiser taking pot, but there's a lot of evidence that they feel that way.

KENNETH KENISTON, quoted in *Newsweek*, July 24, 1967

It's not to solve problems, just to giggle.

STUDENT, quoted in *Time*, Sept. 26, 1969

Cigarettes give you cancer, heart trouble and everything else. But pot has a built-in safety device; three cigarettes and you gotta pass out.

JACQUELINE SUSANN

Make it legal and the cigarette companies will come in and put filter tips on your pot and vitamins and menthol in your pot. No. I say keep it criminal.

NORMAN MAILER, interview in *Wall Street Journal*, May 2, 1969

By the time we grow up all the Senators and Congressmen will have smoked grass.

STUDENT, quoted in *New York Post*, Feb. 18, 1969

DRUGS: PHARMACEUTICAL

Modern medicine has made drugs highly legitimate, something to be taken casually and not only during moments of acute and certified stress. Our children, far from being in revolt against an older generation, may in fact be acknowledging how influential a model that older generation was.

WILLIAM SIMON AND JOHN H. GAGNON, quoted in *Time*, Sept. 26, 1969

The pharmaceutical industry is redefining and relabeling as medicinal problems calling for drug intervention a wide range of human behaviors which, in the past, have been viewed as falling within the bounds of the normal trials and tribulations of human existence.

DRS. HENRY L. LENNARD, LEON J. EPSTEIN AND DONALD C. RANSOM, *Mystification and Drug Misuse*, 1971

That great American tabernacle, the medicine cabinet.

PETER FASOLINO, *Newsweek*, June 13, 1977

DUBLIN also see IRELAND

Filled with people hating each other for the love of God.
MICHAEL CAMPBELL, *Nothing Doing,* 1970

Scribal implements are venerated—there are Pen Shops in Dublin, as there are stores in New York consecrated to the Grand Piano.
HUGH KENNER, *New York Times,* May 23, 1976

The town is as full as ever of "characters" all created by each other.
WILFRID SHEED, *New York Times,* Aug. 1, 1971

Remember, whoever you meet in this fair city, you'll hear a lot of rubbish.
BARRISTER IN O'CONNELL STREET BAR, quoted in Richard Howard Brown, *I Am of Ireland,* 1974

EARTH also see CONSERVATION/CONSERVATIONISTS; NATURE

A tiny raft in the enormous, empty night.
ARCHIBALD MACLEISH, quoted in *New York Times,* Apr. 19, 1970

Earth provides enough to satisfy every man's need, but not every man's greed.
MOHANDAS K. GANDHI, quoted in E. F. Schumacher, *Small Is Beautiful,* 1973

Now there is one outstanding important fact regarding Spaceship Earth, and that is that no instruction book came with it.
R. BUCKMINSTER FULLER, quoted in *New York Times,* Aug. 8, 1971

EATING also see COOKING; FOOD

People are the only animals who eat themselves to death.
AMERICAN MEDICAL ASSOCIATION ADVERTISEMENT, June 1971

Man is the only animal, I believe, who pretends he is thinking of other things while he is eating.
ROBERT LYND, *New York Times,* Nov. 26, 1967

EATING: BREAKFAST

It takes some skill to spoil a breakfast—even the English can't do it.
JOHN KENNETH GALBRAITH, *Ambassador's Journal,* 1969

If you have to work before breakfast, get your breakfast first.
JOSH BILLINGS, *Civil War Humor,* Doris Benardete, ed., 1963

All happiness depends on a leisurely breakfast.
JOHN GUNTHER, obituary in *Newsweek,* June 8, 1970

EATING: DINNER

The first want of man is his dinner, and the second is his girl.
JOHN ADAMS, quoted in James David Barbar, *The Presidential Character,* 1972

A dinner invitation, once accepted, is a sacred obligation. If you die before the dinner takes place, your executor must attend.
WARD MCALLISTER, *Society as I Have Found It,* 1890

The social dinner is of medieval inefficiency.
JEAN-JACQUES SERVAN-SCHREIBER, *New York Times,* May 19, 1968

ECCENTRICITY

An age is great in art and every other way in proportion to the eccentrics who thrive in that time. . . . The trouble with this era is that there is very little eccentricity.
GEORGE FRAZIER, quoted in *Time,* Feb. 25, 1974

Sure, I'm eccentric. If you're poor, you're only crazy.
LOUIS J. SCHWEITZER, obituary in *New York Times,* Sept. 21, 1971

ECOLOGY see CONSERVATION/CONSERVATIONISTS

ECONOMICS/ECONOMISTS

Once demystified, the dismal science is nothing less than the study of power.
RICHARD J. BARNET, *New York Times,* Sept. 16, 1973

Economics is about the cost of our appetites.
> GEORGE F. WILL, *Newsweek,* Feb. 23, 1976

A body of occasionally useful truisms.
> R. H. TAWNEY, quoted in Ross Terrill, *R. H. Tawney and His Times,* 1973

I have been gradually coming under the conviction, disturbing for a professional theorist, that there is no such thing as economics.
> KENNETH E. BOULDING, quoted in Leonard Silk, *The Economists,* 1976

There must be someone in this Administration who could explain it to me, but I probably wouldn't understand it. There must be a book I could read, but I probably wouldn't understand that either.
> WARREN G. HARDING, quoted in *Newsweek,* Feb. 24, 1975

To me, this is a kind of sad profession, although it is the one profession where you can gain great eminence without ever being right.
> GEORGE MEANY, speech to Society of American Business Writers, May 1975

We have crystal balls but they're no good.
> ALFRED KAHN, "MacNeil/Lehrer Report," PBS, Mar. 23, 1979

Can't someone bring me a one-handed economist?
> HARRY S. TRUMAN, after hearing an "on one hand . . . on the other hand" analysis by Edwin G. Nourse, quoted in Nourse obituary, *New York Times,* Apr. 10, 1974

Economists should make recommendations, politicians should carry them out. That's the way it should be. But the way things are going now, the politicians make the recommendations and the economists are merely called in to justify them.
> PIERRE RINFRET, quoted in *Forbes,* Dec. 1967

If economists could manage to get themselves thought of as humble, competent people, like dentists, that would be splendid.
> ATTRIBUTED TO JOHN MAYNARD KEYNES

THE ECONOMY

The American economy is the eighth wonder of the world, and the ninth is the economic ignorance of the American people.
> BURTON CRANE, quoted in *Public Relations Journal,* Mar. 1964

We have become to some extent, I think, economic hypochondriacs. You get a wiggle in a statistic . . . and everyone runs to get the thermometer.
PAUL W. McCRACKEN, quoted in *Newsweek,* Feb. 3, 1969

The time will never come when everybody is richer than everybody else.
C. E. AYRES, *The Guaranteed Income,* Robert Theobald, ed., 1966

EDUCATION also see COLLEGES/UNIVERSITIES; SCHOOLS; TEACHERS/TEACHING

Education is learning what you didn't even know you didn't know.
DANIEL J. BOORSTIN, *Democracy and Its Discontents,* 1974

Education is to get where you can start to learn.
GEORGE AIKEN, quoted in *New York Times,* Jan. 29, 1967

If you work hard and intelligently, you should be able to detect when a man is talking rot, and that, in my view, is the main, if not the sole, purpose of education.
OXFORD PROFESSOR, quoted in *Newsweek,* Feb. 6, 1978

Can't someone just want to learn the poems of Pushkin because he loves them?
KAREL VAN HET REVE, on education for relevance, quoted in *New York Times,* May 21, 1976

It is in fact a part of the function of education to help us to escape— not from our own time, for we are bound by that—but from the intellectual and emotional limitations of our own time.
T. S. ELIOT, obituary in *New York Times,* Jan. 5, 1965

At the moment, to be an educated man or woman doesn't mean anything. It may mean that you know all about urban this or rural that. But there is no common denominator.
HENRY ROSOVSKY, quoted in *Newsweek,* May 15, 1978

I would suggest that the B.A. be issued on paper which deteriorates in five years.
WILLIAM HABER, quoted in *Public Relations Journal,* Nov. 1965

Men without education are condemned to live as outsiders—outside the twentieth century, foreigners in their own land.
> ROBERT F. KENNEDY, *Bulletin of Atomic Scientists,* from *Quote,* Jan. 15, 1967

I missed being an elevator boy by just about that much, when my mother reached up and made me go back to school after laying out for two years.
> LYNDON B. JOHNSON, quoted in Eric F. Goldman, *The Tragedy of Lyndon B. Johnson,* 1969

A good education is the next best thing to a pushy mother.
> CHARLES SCHULZ, *Peanuts,* Oct. 5, 1976

EFFICIENCY

Efficiency is intelligent laziness.
> ARNOLD H. GLASGOW, quoted in *Reader's Digest,* June 1974

The worst enemy of life, freedom and the common decencies is total anarchy; their second worst enemy is total efficiency.
> ALDOUS HUXLEY, *Tomorrow and Tomorrow and Tomorrow,* 1956

ELECTIONS see POLITICS: THE ELECTION

EMOTION

The energy that actually shapes the world springs from emotions—racial pride, leader worship, religious beliefs, love of war.
> GEORGE ORWELL, quoted in *New York Times,* Aug. 11, 1968

Anyone who says he is not emotional is not getting what he should out of life.
> EZER WEIZMAN, quoted in *Time,* Oct. 30, 1978

EMPLOYEES see BLUE-COLLAR BLUES; THE BOSS: FROM BELOW; THE JOB

ENEMIES also see FRIENDS

Brothers and sisters, friends and enemies: I just can't believe that everyone in here is a friend and I don't want to leave anybody out.
MALCOLM X, speaking at Harlem rally, quoted in *Columbia Forum,* Spring 1966

Friends may come and go, but enemies accumulate.
ANONYMOUS

The enemy of my enemy is my friend.
ARAB PROVERB

To bless thine enemy is a good way to satisfy thy vanity.
JORGE LUIS BORGES, *In Praise of Darkness,* 1974

One's life is one's enemy.
ROBERT PINSKY, *Sadness and Happiness,* 1975

We have met the enemy and they is us.
WALT KELLY, *Pogo* antipollution poster, 1970

ENERGY CRISIS also see OPEC

Considering the prices we've been paying, we haven't been wasteful [of energy] at all. We've simply been using it according to the way it's been valued in the marketplace.
BERNARD GELB, quoted in *Newsweek,* Apr. 18, 1977

Industrial mankind can be likened to . . . irresponsible tenants in a rented house. . . . We've been burning up the furniture, woodwork and food supplies to keep the place warm because we've been too irresponsible and lazy to figure out how to work the central heating.
HENRY KING STANFORD, speech at scientific conference, Dec. 1976

If the energy crisis forces us to diminish automobile use in the cities, stops us from building highways and covering the country with concrete and asphalt, forces us to rehabilitate the railroads, causes us to invest in mass transportation and limits the waste of electrical energy, one can only assume that the Arab nations and the big oil companies have united to save the American Republic.
JOHN KENNETH GALBRAITH, quoted in *Newsweek,* Dec. 31, 1973

Popeye is running out of cheap spinach.
PETER G. PETERSON, Secretary of Commerce, quoted in *Newsweek,* Jan. 22, 1973

ENGINEERS

When the weight of the paperwork equals the weight of the equipment, the project is complete.
ENGINEERS' MAXIM

In the old Met, when an elevator got stuck, a little man appeared who went bump! bump! bump! And lo, the elevator worked. Now comes a Harvard engineer . . . and he investigates.
RUDOLF BING ON THE NEW METROPOLITAN OPERA HOUSE, interview in *Wall Street Journal,* Mar. 2, 1972

ENGLAND/THE ENGLISH see BRITAIN/THE BRITISH

ENVIRONMENT: PHYSICAL see CONSERVATION/CONSERVATIONISTS

ENVIRONMENT: SOCIAL see SOCIETY: THE CULTURE

EQUALITY also see DEMOCRACY; LIBERTY

Liberty without equality is a name of noble sound and squalid result.
L. T. HOBHOUSE, quoted in *Columbia Forum,* Spring 1972

No man who says *I'm as good as you* believes it. He would not say so if he did. The St. Bernard never says it to the toy dog, nor the scholar to the dunce, not the employable to the bum, nor the pretty woman to the plain. The claim of equality, outside the strictly political field, is made only by those who feel themselves to be in some way inferior.
C. S. LEWIS, *The Screwtape Letters,* 1942

Nature has never read the Declaration of Independence. It continues to make us unequal.
WILL DURANT, *New York Daily News,* May 3, 1970

Before God we are relatively all equally wise—equally foolish.
ALBERT EINSTEIN, *Cosmic Religion with Other Opinions,* 1931

ETHNICITY see MELTING POT

EUROPE

It is easier to feel sorry for Europe than to pity ourselves. They copy our unborn bourgeoisie; we mimic their dead revolutionaries. We yearn for their past; they simulate our future.
> CHARLES NEWMAN, *A Child's History of America,* 1973

Europeanization gone to America and returned to Europe as Americanization is now complete.
> STEPHEN SPENDER, *Partisan Review,* Spring 1972

In the thirties people who supported Communism thought it would work and people who supported Fascism thought it would work. Now nobody believes anything will work.
> LOUIS HEREN, English journalist, quoted in *New York Times,* Mar. 23, 1975

EVIL also see GUILT; SIN

I always said to people that society consists of two forces fighting one another, good and evil. There's talent on both sides, but there's more talent on the side of evil. Make no mistake. They hire the best brains, the best people.
> ALEX ROSE, New York Liberal Party leader, obituary in *New York Post,* Dec. 28, 1976

You're mistaken if you think wrongdoers are always unhappy. The really professional evil-doers love it. They're as happy as larks in the sky. . . . The unhappy ones are only the guilty amateurs and the neurotics.
> MURIEL SPARK, *Territorial Rights,* 1979

Evil is unspectacular and always human/And shares our bed and eats at our own table.
> W. H. AUDEN, "Herman Melville," in *Another Time,* 1940

EXPATRIATES

Exchanging a relevant malaise for an irrelevant one.
> ANATOLE BROYARD, *New York Times,* Jan. 28, 1974

Happy to pay the price, if they were even aware of it, of living where nothing happening around them would be really any of their business, ever again.
ELEANOR CLARK, *Rome and a Villa,* 1952

In my waking hours in London I saw myself as Joel McCrea in *Foreign Correspondent,* wearing a double-breasted trench coat and hiding in windmills. I finally realized I was Perelman from Providence, Rhode Island.
S. J. PERELMAN, interview in Israel Shenker, *Words and Their Masters,* 1974

EXPERTS

Our faith has gone from God to experts.
ROBERT PENN WARREN, "Bill Moyers' Journal," PBS, Apr. 9, 1976

I am not supposed to be an expert in every field. I am supposed to be an expert in picking experts.
MOSHE DAYAN, quoted in *Newsweek,* Dec. 21, 1970

I'm sure if the world should blow itself up, the last audible voice to be heard would be that of an expert saying it couldn't be done.
PETER USTINOV, interview in *TV Guide,* Nov. 18, 1966

American art experts secretly yearn to be knighted by the Queen— that's why they talk that way.
CHARLES CHRISTOPHER MARK, "Special Edition," PBS, New York, June 23, 1979

On the subject of wild mushrooms, it is easy to tell who is an expert and who is not: The expert is the one who is still alive.
DONAL HENAHAN, *New York Times,* Oct. 22, 1966

FACTS

A fact, it seems to me, is a great thing—a sentence printed, if not by God, then at least by the devil.
THOMAS CARLYLE, letter to Ralph Waldo Emerson, 1836

Facts are never neutral; they are impregnated with value judgments.
PETER GAY, *Style in History,* 1974

Because of the high place we accord sheer fact in our world, it is assumed that anyone who states a fact (even without passing judgment on it) is, therefore, in favor of it.
JACQUES ELLUL, *Propaganda,* 1965

How can I when they're all around me?
E. M. FORSTER WHEN TOLD TO "FACE THE FACTS," quoted in *New York Times,* Oct. 10, 1971

FAILURE also see LOSING; MAKING IT; SUCCESS

Some people spend their lives failing and never notice.
JUDITH ROSSNER, *Attachments,* 1977

Never give a man up until he has failed at something he likes.
LEWIS E. LAWES, Sing Sing warden, quoted in *Little Gazette,* Oct. 1969

The failure is to be 40 and not to have tried.
BEATRICE COLEN, interview in *Image,* Jan. 1974

He who fails has no friends.
TURKISH PROVERB

FAIRNESS

Fair play with others is primarily not blaming them for anything that is wrong with us.
ERIC HOFFER, *Working and Thinking on the Waterfront,* 1969

We should first be fair. Then, if there's something to spare, we may be clever.
RAYMOND MOLEY, obituary in *Newsweek,* Mar. 3, 1975

FAITH see BELIEF; RELIGION

FALLIBILITY

Babe Ruth struck out 1,330 times.
GRAFFITO, N.Y.C., 1977

It must be the awareness of human fallibility which we all carry within us that makes the man without error so obnoxious to us.
ROBERT GOHEEN, quoted in *Newsweek,* June 23, 1969

FAME also see CELEBRITY; GLORY; NOTORIETY

The tragedy of being famous is that you must devote so much time to being famous.
PABLO PICASSO, quoted in Leonard Lyons' column, Apr. 10, 1973

When people have heard of you, favorably or not, they change.
JOHN STEINBECK, quoted in *Newsweek,* Oct. 25, 1976

People like me to sound like a lot of big cannons.
MAO ZEDONG, quoted in Richard M. Nixon, *RN,* 1978

Fame has its advantages. Anything you do gets used. Society places no obstacles.
JOHN CAGE, *M Writings '67-'72,* 1973

A friend recently said, "Just imagine *not* being famous—what would happen?" And all of a sudden I saw the face of a passer-by on the street and the oddest feeling came over me.
GLORIA SWANSON, interview in *Image,* Nov. 1971

Everywhere I go, I'm being honored and I don't really deserve it. It makes me scared. Is my plane going to blow up?
MUHAMMAD ALI AT HARLEM TRIBUTE, Apr. 14, 1979

My fan mail is enormous. Everyone is under six.
ALEXANDER CALDER, quoted in *New York Times,* Aug. 6, 1976

FAMILY also see CHILDREN; FATHERS; MOTHERS; PARENTS

Having a family is like having a bowling alley installed in your brain.
MARTIN MULL, quoted in *Newsweek,* Apr. 3, 1978

We're the ultimate nuclear family, and sometimes I feel as if someone is trying to split the atom.
GEORGIA HOUSER, quoted in *Newsweek,* May 15, 1978

Families are pleasant, but in business they're a pain in the neck.
JEAN FERNIOT, quoted in *New York Times,* May 19, 1968

The kinship of family is all shot to hell, and it had to be. You can't have a mobile labor force if you have to take grandmother and grandfather along.
DR. JAMES A. PETERSON, quoted in *Business Week,* July 8, 1972

FANATICISM

A fanatic is a man that does what he thinks th' Lord wud do if He knew the facts iv the case.
FINLEY PETER DUNNE, *Mr. Dooley's Opinions,* 1900

Scratch a fanatic and you find a wound that never healed.
WILLIAM NORTH JAYME, interview in *Newsweek,* May 12, 1973

Great fanatics can no longer arise. They are swamped by distractions.
JOHN UPDIKE, *The Coup,* 1978

FARMS/FARMERS

We plant millions of acres and gather only 0.1 per cent of the energy of the sun. What is a farm? It's really an incredibly inefficient light trap.
ARTHUR C. CLARKE, interview in *Forbes,* Apr. 15, 1967

I've seen farmers who can't read and farmers who can't write, but I've never seen a farmer who can't figure.
FORREST HILL, quoted in *Kaiser News,* no. 1, 1968

Some say you shouldn't prune except at the right time of the year. I generally do it when the saw is sharp.
GEORGE AIKEN, quoted in *New York Times,* Jan. 29, 1967

No city can offer any excitement comparable to what happens when there is a new pure-bred calf.
LOUIS BROMFIELD, quoted in *New York Times,* May 19, 1974

I would like to die in my henhouse.
MARY ADAMS, farm widow, quoted in John Baskin, *New Burlington,* 1976

FASHION also see NEW; OLD

Fashion is the business that turns mystique into blue-chip stocks, obsolescence into dollars, and a hemline revolution into profit.
EDITH RAYMOND LOCKE, fashion editor, quoted in *Stores,* May 1970

Art on your back or in your home or personal life—that's fashion.
GEORGE BAYLIS, interview in *New York Times,* Sept. 16, 1973

Fashion is fun; it's a game that rouses passions, that intrigues; it's entertainment of an extremely exciting kind, but it's not an art.
JOHN FAIRCHILD, interview in *Réalités* (Paris), Apr. 1970

Fashion has a perverse truth of its own. It's in no way influenced by people outside it. When Chanel made clothing that looked poor—the kind of clothes you could ride the subway in—it certainly wasn't created for people who actually rode the subways.
CECIL BEATON, interview in *New York Times,* Dec. 19, 1971

The same costume will be indecent 10 years before its time, smart in its time, dowdy one year after its time, ridiculous 20 years after its time, quaint 50 years after its time, romantic 100 years after its time and beautiful 150 years after its time.
JAMES LAVER, quoted in *Newsweek,* Mar. 16, 1970

In difficult times fashion is always outrageous.
ELSA SCHIAPARELLI, quoted in *Newsweek,* Mar. 29, 1971

The climate of opinion that generates long skirts is not a socially liberal one.
WILLIAM L. O'NEILL, quoted in *Newsweek,* Mar. 16, 1970

A dress has no meaning unless it makes a man want to take it off.
FRANÇOISE SAGAN, quoted in *Observer* (London), Dec. 14, 1969

Men and women with time on their hands, and money in their pockets, will dress like peacocks and behave like sparrows.
J. H. PLUMB, *New York Times,* Nov. 13, 1966

Before you go out, always take off something you've put on, because you probably are wearing too much.
ANITA COLBY, quoted in *Cosmopolitan,* Apr. 1968

If fashion isn't worn by everybody, then it is only eccentricity.
GABRIELLE CHANEL, quoted in Edmonde Charles-Roux, *Chanel,* 1975

When I started at least women dressed to please men. Now they dress to astonish one another.
CHANEL, Charles-Roux, *Chanel*

Why do women pay attention to fashion? Because we all wear clothes, that's why.
JUNE WEIR, quoted in *New York Times,* Aug. 15, 1976

FATHERS also see **CHILDREN; FAMILY; MOTHERS; PARENTS**

A father is a banker provided by nature.
FRENCH PROVERB

How sad that men would base an entire civilization on the principle of paternity, upon the legal ownership and presumed responsibility for children, and then never really get to know their sons and daughters very well.
PHYLLIS CHESLER, *About Men,* 1978

FATNESS/THINNESS

The reason fat people are happy is that the nerves are well protected.
LUCIANO PAVAROTTI, interview in *Newsweek,* Mar. 5, 1973

Who ever heard of fat men heading a riot, or herding together in turbulent mobs?
WASHINGTON IRVING, *Knickerbocker's History of New York,* 1809

The fertile inventors and narrators and genre painters have all been rather burly genial fellows. . . . The gut of a round fat man, like G. K. Chesterton, may be as much as forty feet long. The gut of a thin man, like myself, may be as little as eighteen feet long and weigh less than half of what the Chesterton intestine weighs. It would obviously be miraculous if this physical difference were not correlated with a mental difference.
ALDOUS HUXLEY, *Letters of Aldous Huxley,* Grover Smith, ed., 1970

It's much easier nowadays to place a black person on a job than somebody who's fat.
KAY SNOW, employment agent, quoted in *New York Times,* Mar. 31, 1975

Imprisoned in every fat man a thin one is wildly signalling to be let out.
CYRIL CONNOLLY, *The Unquiet Grave*, 1951

Except in special cases, obesity is a voluntary illness.
HENRY M. WRISTON, *New York Times*, May 23, 1976

Attributing overweight to overeating is hardly more illuminating than ascribing alcohol to alcoholism.
DR. JEAN MAYER, speech at Columbia University, Dec. 26, 1973

FBI

The FBI is filled with Fordham graduates keeping tabs on Harvard men in the State Department.
DANIEL P. MOYNIHAN, quoted in *Newsweek*, Oct. 4, 1971

The people who have made you frantic by watching you are just as frantic about who is watching them.
WARREN HINCKLE, *New York Times*, July 13, 1975

FEAR also see RISKS; SECURITY

I fear Allah, thunderstorms and bad airplane rides.
MUHAMMAD ALI, quoted in *Newsweek*, Nov. 11, 1974

No sir, I fear not death. I fear only sleep. I want to know what is happening to me.
CHARLES DE GAULLE REFUSING ANESTHESIA FOR SURGERY, quoted in David Schoenbrun, *The Three Lives of Charles de Gaulle*, 1966

I found out a long time ago that no matter how scared you are, you're a damned sight safer if nobody knows it.
JOHN L. McCLELLAN, quoted in *New York Times*, Oct. 8, 1967

There is no one on this earth who is not twisted by fear and insecurity.
DORIS LESSING, *A Small Personal Voice*, 1974

I've developed a new philosophy. I only dread one day at a time.
CHARLES SCHULZ, *Peanuts*

FEDERAL BUREAU OF INVESTIGATION see FBI

FOLK MUSIC see MUSIC: FOLK

FOOD also see COOKING; EATING

An Englishman teaching an American about food is like the blind leading the one-eyed.
A. J. LIEBLING, quoted by Alistair Cooke, "Masterpiece Theatre," PBS, Oct. 20, 1974

In the selection of seafood you won't go wrong if you stick to things the other fish won't eat.
CHARLES MERRILL SMITH, *Instant Status,* 1972

Safety experts agree that it is necessary to wait a week before going into the water after eating a hot knish.
TOM BUCKLEY, *New York Times,* June 9, 1976

Bagels are made with love and a little cement.
SHOP SIGN, N.Y.C.

The greatest cure for a batting slump ever invented.
BABE RUTH ON SCALLIONS, quoted in Leo Durocher, *Nice Guys Finish Last,* 1975

FOOTBALL also see SPORTS

The object of football is not to annihilate the other team, but to advance the ball.
CLARK SHAUGHNESSY, Stanford University coach, obituary in *New York Times,* May 16, 1970

Football is not a contact sport. It's a collision sport. Dancing is a good example of a contact sport.
DUFFY DAUGHERTY, Michigan State University coach, *Quote,* Aug. 27, 1967

It is committee meetings, called huddles, separated by outbursts of violence.
GEORGE F. WILL, *Newsweek,* Sept. 6, 1976

A game that requires the constant conjuring of animosity.
VINCE LOMBARDI, quoted in *New York Times,* Dec. 10, 1967

In football, the contract is either you hurt the opponent or he hurts you. The coach must have his men feeling that they not only can kill, but that they should kill.
DR. CHESTER M. PIERCE, quoted in *Physician and Sportsmedicine,* May 1977

To see some of our best-educated boys spending the afternoon knocking each other down, while thousands cheer them on, hardly gives a picture of a peace-loving nation.
LYNDON B. JOHNSON, quoted in *New York Times,* Dec. 10, 1967

This isn't nuclear physics, it's a game. How smart do you really have to be?
TERRY BRADSHAW, Pittsburgh Steelers, interview in *Newsweek,* Jan. 22, 1979

If it's the ultimate, how come they're playing it again next year?
DUANE THOMAS, Dallas Cowboys, when reporter called the Superbowl "the ultimate game," quoted in *Newsweek,* Aug. 30, 1971

FOOTNOTES

Scholarly barbed-wire.
EDMUND WILSON, quoted in *Princeton Alumni Weekly,* Dec. 4, 1973

Let's make up a footnote. Nobody will ever know.
FREDERICK A. POTTLE, while editing the private papers of James Boswell, quoted in *New York Times,* July 25, 1976

FOREIGN AID

Instead of The Ugly Americans we should be labelled The Childish Americans, who think that by sharing a half-licked lollypop in our favorite democratic flavor we can make people love us.
GRACE NIES FLETCHER, *In Quest of the Least Coin,* 1969

I feel the happiest when I can light my American cigarettes with Soviet matches.
MOHAMMAD DAUD KHAN, president of Afghanistan, quoted in *Newsweek,* July 30, 1973

The Russians can give you arms, but only the United States can give you a solution.
ANWAR EL-SADAT, quoted in *Newsweek,* Jan. 13, 1975

FOREIGN POLICY also see DIPLOMACY; STATE DEPARTMENT

No nation has friends—only interests.
CHARLES DE GAULLE, quoted in *US News & World Report,* Sept. 19, 1966

In the nuclear age, it is no longer possible to assume that by patient accumulation of marginal advantage one can ultimately destroy one's opponent. All foreign policy has to start with that insight.
HENRY A. KISSINGER, quoted in *Newsweek,* June 12, 1972

Governments are quite familiar with the process of sending inaccurate messages to each other.
DEAN RUSK, *Quote,* Sept. 11, 1966

Nations... continually engage in acts that, if committed by thee or me against hostile neighbors, would land us in the slammer for life with no chance for parole.
STANLEY ELLIN, *New York Times,* Oct. 17, 1976

We cannot, when it comes to dealings between governments, assign moral values the same significance we give them in personal life.
GEORGE F. KENNAN, *Realities of American Foreign Policy,* 1954

Expediency is a good quality in a statesman. These high-principled men who rule the world and ruin it are men who won't be expedient, won't compromise.
WALTER LIPPMANN, interview in *Washington Post* Syndicate, Oct. 23, 1971

Foreign policy is the only field of endeavor where a man gets promoted for being wrong.
ARTHUR M. SCHLESINGER, JR., quoted in *New York Times,* Dec. 18, 1966

The poets say things are not what they seem. The great trouble is sometimes they are what they seem. And the question is are they or aren't they what they seem. That is what makes government, and particularly foreign affairs, an art and not a science.
DEAN ACHESON, "A Conversation with Dean Acheson," CBS-TV, Sept. 28, 1969

I see little hope for a peaceful world until men are excluded from the realm of foreign policy altogether and all decisions concerning international relations are reserved for women, preferably married ones.
W. H. AUDEN, obituary in *Newsweek*, Oct. 8, 1973

I'll never get credit for anything I do in foreign policy because I didn't go to Harvard.
LYNDON B. JOHNSON, obituary in *Newsweek*, Feb. 5, 1973

FORGERY also see CRIME

It's kind of nerve-racking, really. You have to be on your toes so much of the time. It's kind of like selling, you have to keep smiling all the time. You know, you have to sell as much as anything else. After a while your face gets tired.
CHECK FORGER, quoted in Bruce Jackson, *A Thief's Primer*, 1969

It is often said in art circles that there are about 600 original Corot paintings, 3,000 of which are in the United States.
THOMAS W. LEAVITT, museum director, quoted in *New York Times*, Nov. 9, 1976

I love forgeries! I love the forger's mentality!
THOMAS HOVING, museum director, interview in *New Yorker*, May 20, 1967

FRANCE/THE FRENCH also see PARIS

The most verbal nation on the face of the earth, where language is the Muzak of the mind.
JOSEPH MORGENSTERN, *Newsweek*, Apr. 15, 1968

In France art is often politics conducted by other means.
MARK STEVENS, *Newsweek*, Feb. 7, 1977

When the French mount the barricades, the atmosphere is likely to become festive.
WILLIAM BARRETT, *New York Times*, Feb. 11, 1979

It's impossible in normal times to rally a nation that has 265 kinds of cheese.
CHARLES DE GAULLE, quoted in *Newsweek*, Nov. 13, 1967

The Frenchman has his heart on the left and his pocketbook on the right, and at election time he votes his pocketbook.
FRENCH AXIOM

Much of French history is simply Paris history presented as a *fait accompli* to the provinces.
SANCHE DE GRAMONT, *The French*, 1969

France needs a common denominator.
ANTOINE DE SAINT-EXUPÉRY, quoted in Curtis Cate, *Antoine de Saint-Exupéry*, 1970

Avarice is the predominant French characteristic because of long peasant history.
JEAN-PAUL ARON, quoted in *Newsweek*, Nov. 22, 1976

They have often accepted death but rarely taxes as the burden of patriotism.
DAVID SCHOENBRUN, *New York Times*, Dec. 22, 1968

Though one Frenchman, meeting another, will never ask directly what the other did during the war, that will be the first thing he will try to find out.
CLYDE H. FARNSWORTH, *New York Times*, Feb. 20, 1973

The French do not go to priests, doctors, or psychiatrists, to talk over their problems. They sit over a cup of coffee or a glass of wine and talk to each other.
ERIC SEVAREID, "Town Meeting of the World," CBS-TV, Mar. 1, 1966

FREEDOM

Freedom is always and exclusively freedom for the one who thinks differently.
ATTRIBUTED TO ROSA LUXEMBURG

Freedom . . . is nothing more than an opportunity to discipline ourselves, rather than to be disciplined by others.
THOMAS A. MURPHY, speech to Associated Industries of N.Y., Sept. 24, 1976

Freedom is truly a short blanket that, if it covers one part of the body, leaves some other part out in the cold.
GUIDO PIOVENE, *In Search of Europe*, 1975

Once you think you've found freedom—someone else builds a prison round it. You can't get out. All you can do is furnish it as attractively as possible.
PETER USTINOV, interview in North American Newspaper Alliance, Oct. 3, 1968

If everything would be permitted to me, I would feel lost in this abyss of freedom.
IGOR STRAVINSKY, quoted at Yale University Oral History Project in American Music, June 1, 1976

When the freedom they wished for most was freedom from responsibility, then Athens ceased to be free and was never free again.
EDITH HAMILTON, *Reader's Digest,* Mar. 1959

FREE SPEECH also see PROTEST

However pernicious an opinion may seem, we depend for its correction not on the consciences of judges and juries but on the competition of other ideas.
SUPREME COURT JUSTICE LEWIS F. POWELL, 1974

The sound of tireless voices is the price we pay for the right to hear the music of our own opinions.
ADLAI STEVENSON, quoted in *Princeton Alumni Weekly,* Aug. 12, 1971

Anyone can speak at Smith College who does not break the furniture.
WILLIAM NEILSON, Smith College president, quoted in *Princeton Alumni Weekly,* Aug. 12, 1971

THE FRENCH see FRANCE/THE FRENCH

FREUD/FREUDIANS see PSYCHOANALYSIS/PSYCHO-THERAPIES

FRIENDS also see ENEMIES

A friendship is ultimately a more interesting exploration than a love affair, because it lacks the spur of sex and, one presumes, is forged in a cooler furnace.
JOE FLAHERTY, *New York Times,* Dec. 17, 1978

Friendship is a very taxing and arduous form of leisure activity.
MORTIMER ADLER, "Bill Moyers' Journal," PBS, Mar. 22, 1979

Sooner or later you've heard what all your best friends have to say.
Then comes the tolerance of real love.
NED ROREM, *Commentary,* Nov. 1966

Your friend will argue with you.
ALEKSANDR I. SOLZHENITSYN, quoted in *Newsweek,* July 28, 1975

Men kick friendship around like a football, but it doesn't seem to
crack. Women treat it like glass and it goes to pieces.
ANNE MORROW LINDBERGH, *Locked Rooms and Open Doors,* 1974

Why was it that everyone seemed to have more friends when they
were kids than when they were adults?
RICHARD PRICE, *Ladies' Man,* 1978

I like people who complicate my life, but I always seem to pick the
wrong ones.
CALVIN KLEIN, interview in *Newsweek,* May 8, 1978

THE FUTURE also see HINDSIGHT; THE PAST

You will always underestimate the future.
ATTRIBUTED TO CHARLES F. KETTERING

It takes only a year or two for the exaggerations to come true. Nothing will remain in the next ten years. Or there will be twice as much of
it.
WARREN G. BENNIS, *Technology Review,* Apr. 1966

We are entering a very radical world of discontinuities.
EUGENE CAFIERO, president, Chrysler Corp., interview in *Newsweek,*
July 21, 1975

What is clear is that the revolution of rising expectations, which has
been one of the chief features of Western society in the past 25 years,
is being transformed into a *revolution of rising entitlements* for the
next 25.
DANIEL BELL, *The Cultural Contradictions of Capitalism,* 1976

I would feel more optimistic about a bright future for man if he spent
less time proving that he can outwit Nature and more time tasting her
sweetness and respecting her seniority.
E. B. WHITE, *Essays of E. B. White,* 1977

The East Wind is prevailing over the West Wind.
MAO ZEDONG, 1957, obituary in *Newsweek,* Sept. 20, 1976

The handwriting on the wall may be a forgery.
RALPH HODGSON, quoted in *New York Times,* Oct. 22, 1972

The future is an opaque mirror. Anyone who tries to look into it sees
nothing but the dim outlines of an old and worried face.
JIM BISHOP, *Quote,* Feb. 5, 1967

GAMBLERS/GAMBLING also see THE HORSES; POKER

A real gambler is the type of guy you abuse him and throw him out
the window, and a minute later he's knocking on the door asking for
the price on the Celtics game.
BOOKIE, quoted in *Newsweek,* Apr. 10, 1972

When you're betting, you can get high on the air conditioning.
NORTON PEPPIS, quoted in *Newsweek,* Mar. 10, 1972

When I lose a football game, my wife knows I've got to be alone. But
when I win, I jump on her like a fumble.
NORTON PEPPIS, quoted in *Newsweek,* Sept. 23, 1974

In pressure games, always bet against the Dallas Cowboys, the San
Francisco Giants and Germany.
GAMBLERS' MAXIM, quoted in *Newsweek,* June 21, 1971

GANGSTERS also see CRIME

I am like any other man. All I do is supply a demand.
ATTRIBUTED TO AL CAPONE

I've killed no one that in the first place didn't deserve killing.
MICKEY COHEN, obituary in Associated Press, July 30, 1976

Don't worry, we only kill each other.
BUGSY SIEGEL TO CONTRACTOR BUILDING CASINO FOR HIM, quoted in
New York Times, Aug. 20, 1972

GENERAL MOTORS also see CORPORATIONS

America is a company town, and the company is General Motors.
ANONYMOUS

The history of General Motors over the past 50 years is far more important than the history of Switzerland or Holland.
ANTONY JAY, *Management and Machiavelli,* 1968

General Motors could buy Delaware if DuPont were willing to sell it.
RALPH NADER, *Corporate Power in America,* 1973

GENERATION GAP

Our society has become more segregated by age than any previous society in history to a degree that is becoming intolerable to all concerned.
SISTER MARY DOROTHY ANN, BVM, *Catholic World,* 1966

What's happening now is an immigration in time, with people over 40 the migrants into the present age, and the children born in it the natives.
MARGARET MEAD, *Culture and Commitment,* 1970

Even very recently, the elders could say: "You know I have been young and *you* never have been old." But today's young people can reply: "You have never been young in the world I am young in, and you never can be . . ." This break between generations is wholly new: it is planetary and universal.
MEAD, *Culture and Commitment*

I call the older generation depression-scarred and the younger generation prosperity-scarred.
WALTER E. HOADLEY, *Forbes,* Mar. 15, 1966

There's only a difference in memories, that's all.
W. H. AUDEN, interview in *New York Times,* Oct. 19, 1971

It is never easy to explain to a later generation the achievements of an earlier one in shattering an unacceptable status quo, because these achievements in turn have become a status quo beyond which it wishes to advance.
FRANK FREIDEL, *New York Times,* Feb. 1, 1970

The generation gap is just another way of saying that the younger generation makes overt what is covert in the older generation; the child expresses openly what the parent represses.
ERIK ERIKSON, quoted in J. Anthony Lukas, *Don't Shoot—We Are Your Children,* 1971

We have taken the attitudinal temperature of the young so often that perhaps we have forgotten what normal is supposed to be.
J. HOWARD LAERI, speech in Birmingham, Ala., Apr. 21, 1967

GENEROSITY

Generous people are rarely mentally ill people.
DR. KARL MENNINGER, quoted in *Reader's Digest,* Nov. 1970

We'd all like a reputation for generosity, and we'd all like to buy it cheap.
MIGNON McLAUGHLIN, *The Neurotic's Notebook,* 1963

GENITALS

Men do consider that their penis is a fantastic object.
SUSANNA AGNELLI, *We Always Wore Sailor Suits,* 1975

The man's most masculine part is also the most easily intimidated.
ROBERT MUSIL, quoted in George F. Gilder, *Sexual Suicide,* 1973

Embryologically speaking, it is correct to say that the penis is an exaggerated clitoris.
DR. MARY JANE SHERFEY, *The Nature and Evolution of Female Sexuality,* 1972

The genitals themselves have not undergone the development of the rest of the human form in the direction of beauty.
SIGMUND FREUD, quoted in Bernard Rudofsky, *The Unfashionable Human Body,* 1971

GENIUS also see TALENT

Every man of genius sees the world at a different angle from his fellows.
HAVELOCK ELLIS, quoted in *Columbia Forum,* Winter 1969

Evidently one characteristic of genius is to search for relevance in the apparently commonplace and frivolous.
DAVID ELKIND, *New York Times,* May 26, 1968

A man possesses talent; genius possesses the man.
ISAAC STERN, "Previn and the Pittsburgh," PBS, Apr. 23, 1978

Genius is a spiritual greed.
V. S. PRITCHETT, *The Mythmakers,* 1979

Give me a condor's quill! Give me Vesuvius's crater for an inkstand!
HERMAN MELVILLE, *Moby-Dick,* 1851

When I am finished painting, I paint again for relaxation.
PABLO PICASSO, quoted in Françoise Gilot, *Life with Picasso,* 1964

I don't know why God or gods, or whoever it was, selected me to be the vessel. Believe me, this is not humility, false modesty; it is simply amazement.
WILLIAM FAULKNER, letter to Joan Williams, 1953, *Selected Letters of William Faulkner,* Joseph Blotner, ed., 1977

The average underdeveloped mind thinks that any genius is weird.
EDWARD J. DALY, interview in *Newsweek,* Apr. 23, 1979

Before I was a genius, I was a drudge.
IGNACE PADEREWSKI, quoted in *Writer's Digest,* Apr. 1967

GERMANS/GERMANY

People without nuances.
JOSEPH GOEBBELS, *The Secret Conferences of Dr. Goebbels,* Willi A. Boelcke, ed., 1970

I've never met a relaxed German.
HEINRICH BÖLL, quoted in *Time,* May 21, 1973

How can you expect the Germans to revolt when they don't even dare walk on the grass?
JOSEPH STALIN, quoted in *Newsweek,* Sept. 13, 1965

As soon as six or seven Germans arrived in any place they founded a choir or singing group almost as quickly as they built a brewery.
RICHARD O'CONNOR, *The German-Americans,* 1968

When you start a sentence in German, you have to know in the beginning what the end will be.
OTTO FRIEDRICH, *Before the Deluge,* 1972

GHETTOS also see BLACKS

The section of the niggers where a nickel costs a dime.
LANGSTON HUGHES, quoted in *Vital Speeches,* Sept. 15, 1970

Six blocks of cruelty.
NTOZAKE SHANGE, *For Colored Girls Who Have Considered Suicide* (drama), 1975

It's a kind of concentration camp, and not many people survive it.
JAMES BALDWIN, *A Rap on Race,* 1971

You mustn't forget that the key feature of living in an oppressed condition is the assassination of all hope.
LIVINGSTON WINGATE, quoted in *Newsweek,* Apr. 19, 1971

You can view our communities as war-torn areas. And our people as those who view the police and other authorities as occupying forces.
ARTHUR BARNES, interview in *New York Post,* Aug. 14, 1975

Living in a frustrating, stress-inducing environment like a ghetto every day of your life makes many people walking powder kegs. There's a pent-up rage that isn't ventilated elsewhere; when something happens to trigger that rage, it can be murderous.
DR. LAMAURICE GARDNER, quoted in *Newsweek,* Jan. 1, 1973

Form is everything in the ghetto and substance is nothing—it's not what you say, man, it's how you lay it down that counts.
REGINALD BRAGONIER, JR., *New York Times,* Sept. 7, 1975

GLORY also see FAME; NOTORIETY

Glory gives herself only to those who have always dreamed of her.
CHARLES DE GAULLE, quoted in *Little Gazette,* Oct. 1969

The paths of glory lead but to the grave, but so do all other paths.
GEORGE F. WILL, *Newsweek,* June 27, 1977

GOD also see RELIGION

Yes, God is a verb.
R. BUCKMINSTER FULLER, *No More Secondhand God,* 1963

I believe in God, only I spell it Nature.
FRANK LLOYD WRIGHT, *Quote,* Aug. 14, 1966

I believe the wrong God is temporarily running the world and that the true God has gone under.
ANTHONY BURGESS, introduction to his translation of *Cyrano de Bergerac,* 1971

Someday after mastering the winds, the waves, the tides and gravity, we shall harness for God the energies of Love, and then, for the second time in the history of the world, man will discover fire.
PIERRE TEILHARD DE CHARDIN, quoted, Nobel Symposium, Stockholm, Sept. 17, 1969

We treat God as the police treat a man when he has been arrested; whatever He does will be used in evidence against him.
C. S. LEWIS, *Essays on Theology and Ethics,* Walter Hooper, ed., 1970

God Is Back—And Boy Is He Mad.
CALIFORNIA BUMPER STICKER, quoted in *Bookviews,* Mar. 1978

God lives in a box all week and comes out on Sunday in funny clothes to talk about money.
SEAN MICHAELS, 5, quoted in *Enquirer,* 1973

Your Arms Too Short to Box with God.
TITLE OF GOSPEL MUSICAL BY ALEX BRADFORD, 1977

GOLD

The world is a pleasanter place when there are low gold prices. Low gold prices signify trust and friendship.
HENRY JARECKI, bullion dealer, quoted in *Newsweek,* Jan. 13, 1975

If all men were rational, all politicians honest and we had a world central bank issuing a single currency that was universally acceptable, then gold would drop to $20 an ounce—and be overvalued at that.
ANDRÉ SHARON, gold analyst, quoted in *Newsweek,* Dec. 16, 1974

GOLF also see SPORTS

Golf is a kind of outdoor billiards, with manual dexterity and proper mental approach at a premium.
BOBBY RIGGS, *Court Hustler,* 1973

You don't know what pressure is until you play for five bucks with only two in your pocket.
LEE TREVINO, interview in *Newsweek,* May 5, 1971

If there is any larceny in a man, golf will bring it out.
PAUL GALLICO, quoted in *New York Times,* Mar. 6, 1977

GOVERNMENT

Government is nothing but who collects the money and how do they spend it.
GORE VIDAL, "David Susskind Show," Metromedia, Mar. 27, 1977

In government the budget is the message.
I. F. STONE, *Polemics and Prophecies 1967–70,* 1970

The only way a government can provide anything to anybody is if they first take it away from somebody else. The government is capable of providing nothing but control. That is its only purpose.
SIMON L. MILLER, JR., *Once Upon a Time,* 1974

In government the sin of pride manifests itself in the recurring delusion that *things are under control.*
GEORGE F. WILL, *Newsweek,* Feb. 7, 1977

The national motto, *E pluribus unum,* simply does not apply to relations among federal agencies.
BERNARD J. FRIEDEN AND MARSHALL KAPLAN, *The Politics of Neglect,* 1975

Two characteristics of government are that it cannot do anything quickly, and that it never knows when to quit.
GEORGE STIGLER, quoted in *New York Times,* July 27, 1975

We don't solve problems so much as we *colonize* them. First comes the problem, then come the "pilot projects" and the speeches and the legislation . . . and then the consultants and bureaucrats and the contractors and subcontractors . . . and the next thing you know there is a settlement the size of Virginia living on it.
MEG GREENFIELD, *Newsweek,* Jan. 30, 1978

Anyone who thinks he will be happy and prosperous with the government looking after him should take a close look at the American Indian.
ANONYMOUS, *Nation's Business,* Apr. 1967

GRANDPARENTS also see FAMILY

Why do grandparents and grandchildren get along so well together? Perhaps the best answer is the one I heard from a psychiatrist recently: "Because they have a common enemy—the parents."
SYDNEY J. HARRIS, *Leaving the Surface,* 1968

A grandmother will rush you to a hospital if you scrath your finger. They are seriesly disturbed about grems.
SMALL BOY, quoted in Lee Parr McGrath and Joan Scobey, *What Is a Grandmother,* 1970

She's a good lady. I don't think she knows all our names. She calls us all, "Dear."
ONE OF ROSE KENNEDY'S 29 GRANDCHILDREN, quoted in *Look,* Mar. 5, 1979

GREED

Greed. That's what makes the world go round. Greed. It's what makes some people successful. It's what makes some actors stars, and the rest just actors. Greed is the difference.
LEE SHUBERT, quoted in Jerry Stagg, *The Brothers Shubert*, 1968

Even those who appear to take nothing seriously take their greed or vanity seriously.
DR. MICHAEL MACCOBY, interview in *New York Times*, Jan. 1, 1969

I know him [greed]. He's a good old son of a bitch.
BILLY CARTER, interview in *Newsweek*, Nov. 14, 1977

GUILT also see EVIL; SIN

Guilt is a guardian of our goodness.
DR. WILLARD GAYLIN, *Atlantic Monthly*, Jan. 1979

Guilt is what civilizes.
PHILLIP LOPATE, *Confessions of Summer*, 1979

No one should ever have a guilt feeling about his thoughts.
THEODOR REIK, obituary in *Newsweek*, Jan. 12, 1970

You can get used to anything if you have to, even to feeling perpetually guilty.
GOLDA MEIR, on her inattention to her children, *My Life*, 1975

GUNS

The ultimate purpose of making a gun is to fire it.
ERICH FROMM, interview in *New York Times*, Dec. 15, 1973

The deep emotional layers of our personality simply do not register the fact that the cocking of a forefinger to release a shot tears the entrails of another man.
KONRAD LORENZ, quoted in *Time*, July 28, 1967

Guns are made of enduring metal. They outlive their owners. They go on about their business.
ROY MEADOR, *New York Times*, July 30, 1976

HAIR

When you've got gray hair, every move you make seems "young" and "spry," instead of just being normally active. It's like you're getting a new talent. So I dyed my hair gray when I was about twenty-three or twenty-four.
> ANDY WARHOL, *The Philosophy of Andy Warhol (From A to B and Back Again)*, 1975

If you suddenly get a flash of blinding insight and decide you're different from everyone else, the first person you've got to convince is yourself. So you let your hair grow. Later on, after you've convinced yourself, you get it cut.
> PRINCETON STUDENT, quoted in *Princeton Alumni Weekly*, June 6, 1967

Any man over 30 with long hair looks like his mother.
> ORSON WELLES, quoted in *Newsweek*, July 30, 1973

I could never get my hair past the wind-tunnel test.
> RUSSELL BAKER, interview in Israel Shenker, *Words and Their Masters*, 1974

Think of the many loving ways in which advertisements refer to scalp hair—satiny, glowing, shimmering, breathing, living. Living indeed! It is as dead as rope.
> DR. WILLIAM MONTAGNA, *New York Times*, May 9, 1967

HANDWRITING

Every man has one thing he can do better than anyone else—and usually it's reading his own handwriting.
> G. NORMAN COLLIE, *Education Digest*, Apr. 1967

People often do the best handwriting of their entire lives in grades 4 to 6.
> FRANCES GOFORTH AND C. W. HUNNICUT, *Today's Education*, Feb. 1970

You are a lucky voman I do not speak my signature to you.
> OTTO PREMINGER TO FAN WHO COMPLAINED ABOUT HIS ILLEGIBLE AUTOGRAPH, quoted in Earl Wilson's column, May 24, 1975

HAPPINESS

The end for which we all more or less strive is happiness. Our differences in behavior are due to our different notions of what happiness is.
LOUISE ROPES LOOMIS, introduction, Aristotle's *On Man in the Universe,* Classics Club ed., 1971

It is the very pursuit of happiness that thwarts happiness.
VIKTOR E. FRANKL, *The Unconscious God,* 1975

Everything exists in limited quantity—even happiness.
PABLO PICASSO, quoted in Françoise Gilot, *Life with Picasso,* 1964

The people who think they are happy should rummage through their dreams.
EDWARD DAHLBERG, *New York Times,* Jan. 15, 1967

Happiness? Come, what should I do with it?
COLETTE, quoted in Dorothea Straus, *Showcases,* 1974

Nobody's really happy about anything. You're *interested.*
"DR. SEUSS" (THEODOR GEISEL), interview in *Newsweek,* Feb. 21, 1972

HATRED also see DISLIKE

Hate is a prolonged form of suicide.
DOUGLAS V. STEERE, *Dimensions of Prayer,* 1963

Hatred toward a person obliges me to exercise a certain degree of justice, which I never achieve and which exhausts me.
MAX FRISCH, *Sketchbook 1966–1971,* 1974

HEALTH also see SICKNESS

To a healthy man everything seems healthy.
RUSSIAN PROVERB

Health is the thing that makes you feel that now is the best time of the year.
FRANKLIN P. ADAMS, quoted in *Today's Health,* Feb. 1969

HELL also see **THE DEVIL**

Hell is truth seen too late.
RABBI BERNARD RASKAS, *Quote,* July 2, 1967

New York City with all the escape hatches sealed.
JAMES R. FRAKES, *New York Times,* May 19, 1974

It's wall-to-wall Wall.
STANLEY ELKIN, *The Living End,* 1979

Boredom is the one torment of hell that Dante forgot.
ALBERT SPEER, *Spandau,* 1976

HERESY also see **RELIGION**

Heresy is the lifeblood of religions. There are no heresies in a dead religion.
ANDRÉ SUARÈS

Heresy is the side that loses.
J. V. FLEMING, quoted in *Princeton Alumni Weekly,* Nov. 13, 1973

HERO/HEROISM

To go against the dominant thinking of your friends, of most of the people you see every day, is perhaps the most difficult act of heroism you can have.
THEODORE H. WHITE, *Columbia Journalism Review,* Winter 1969–1970

From hero to zero is about the average hero's fate.
EDDIE RICKENBACKER, obituary in *New York Post,* July 23, 1973

Show me a hero and I'll write you a tragedy.
F. SCOTT FITZGERALD, quoted in *New York Post,* May 17, 1969

One reason that even many heroes of the past no longer seem quite so heroic is that the art of biography has changed for the better.
GEORGE F. WILL, *Newsweek,* Aug. 6, 1979

HIGHWAYS

The horizontal line of a new Freedom extending from ocean to ocean.
FRANK LLOYD WRIGHT, *An Autobiography,* 1943

The cloverleaf is becoming our national flower.
LEE METCALF, 1966, quoted in *New York Times,* Nov. 14, 1976

Thanks to the Interstate Highway System, it is now possible to travel across the country from coast to coast without seeing anything.
CHARLES KURALT, "CBS News," CBS-TV, Sept. 7, 1971

The people in charge of road signs on, off and about the Long Island Expressway cater purely and simply to that segment of the public that already knows where it's going.
CRAIG CLAIBORNE, *New York Times,* April 15, 1971

HINDSIGHT also see THE FUTURE; THE PAST

Hindsight is much more accurate than foresight, but not as valuable.
GEN. A. J. GOODPASTER, speech at Princeton conference, Nov. 2, 1975

The average reader of the *New York Times,* equipped with hindsight, is smarter than any president.
THEODORE C. SORENSEN, *New York Times,* July 13, 1971

Get off your high and mighty hindsight!
HENRY E. PETERSEN TO SAM ERVIN, Senate Judiciary Committee hearing on Watergate, June 20, 1974

HIPPIES also see DECADE: 1960-1969

The hippie honestly believes that he is practicing Love, but if you shut your eyes while he discusses suburbanites, you would think he was a bigoted white talking about Negroes.
JUNE BINGHAM, *New York Times,* Sept. 24, 1967

The hippies who left the suburbs in protest against the worship of money and material possessions found there is more talk about money on Haight Street than on Wall Street.
EARL SHORRIS, *New York Times,* Oct. 29, 1967

A hippy wears tight pants and suffers.
FIFTH-GRADE PUPIL, quoted in *Parent-Teacher Association Magazine,* Nov. 1968

Daygloed by Tom Wolfe and dissected by Time-Life, its innovations and high spirits co-opted by Madison Avenue, the fashion industry and other points of absorption for possible revolutionary energy, the Hippie Scene spends its declining days in the purgatory reserved for social movements swallowed whole by that they sought to change.
PETER COLLIER, *New York Times,* May 18, 1969

HISTORY

History is baroque.
WILL DURANT, quoted in *Time,* Oct. 6, 1967

History does not unfold: it piles up.
ROBERT M. ADAMS, *Bad Mouth,* 1977

It is the wicked who make history.
ISAAC BASHEVIS SINGER, *A Friend of Kafka,* 1970

History has been called a story of hungry men in search of food.
Wallace's Farmer, June 13, 1970

All periods of history show a strain of madness and all are chaotic.
JACQUES BARZUN, lecture at Columbia University, Jan. 29, 1973

History is an argument without end.
PIETER GEYL, quoted in *Columbia Forum,* Fall 1972

History is full of examples of lonely thinkers who were belittled by the established figures of the time and who, it now turns out, were deservedly neglected.
LEON LIPSON, interview in *New York Times,* Apr. 1, 1969

History repeats itself in the large because human nature changes with geological leisureliness.
WILL AND ARIEL DURANT, *The Lessons of History,* 1968

Historians of literature like to regard a century as a series of ten faces, each grimacing in a different way.
RICHARD ELLMAN, *New York Times,* Feb. 5, 1967

If this instant history trend accelerates, we shall judge the next administration on the basis of the inaugural parade.
JEFF GREENFIELD, *New York Times,* Sept. 25, 1977

HOCKEY also see SPORTS

Hockey's the only place where a guy can go nowadays and watch two white guys fight.
FRANK DEFORD, *The Owner,* 1976

The Democratic National Convention on ice skates.
RON POWERS, "Special Edition," PBS, May 21, 1979

HOLLYWOOD also see ACTORS/ACTING; MOVIES; SHOW BIZ; THEATER

Hollywood is an extraordinary kind of temporary place.
JOHN SCHLESINGER, interview in *New York Times,* May 8, 1975

Daft but not boring.
J. B. PRIESTLEY, quoted in John Baxter, *The Hollywood Exiles,* 1976

Loneliness beside the swimming pool.
LIV ULLMANN, *Changing,* 1978

People wear resort clothes, but actually Hollywood is an enormous factory.
MARIE-FRANCE PISIER, quoted in *Newsweek,* May 16, 1977

Genius, geniuses everywhere I turn! If only there were some talent!
HENRI BERNSTEIN, quoted in *Coronet,* Mar. 1967

The movie business is at the moral level of the South Vietnamese Army.
JOSH GREENFIELD, quoted in *Newsweek,* Feb. 13, 1978

If you tell the press—or anyone in Hollywood—the truth, it throws them, they don't know how to deal with it.
LAUREN BACALL, *Lauren Bacall by Myself,* 1978

Harvey Korman, in honor of his former agent, is having a tree uprooted in Israel.
Daily Variety, quoted in *TV Guide*, Dec. 28, 1968

THE HOLOCAUST also see WORLD WAR II

Who still talks nowadays of the extermination of the Armenians?
ADOLF HITLER, 1939, on the Turkish genocide of 1.5 million Armenians in 1915, quoted in *New York Times*, Aug. 7, 1975

How can you understand six million of anything?
HIGH-SCHOOL STUDENT, quoted in *New York Times*, June 11, 1976

This century's blackest hole.
JOHN LEONARD, *New York Times*, Feb. 10, 1976

HOMOSEXUALITY also see BISEXUALITY

Homosexuality itself is not against the law, just practicing it is.
ANTHONY MANCINI, *New York Post*, July 21, 1975

Sexual deviations have come in for far more scrutiny than have deviations from other behavioral norms—like not wanting to own an automobile.
MARTIN DUBERMAN, *New York Times*, Dec. 10, 1972

The homosexual subculture based on brief, barren assignations is, in part, a dark mirror of the sex-obsessed majority culture.
GEORGE F. WILL, *Newsweek*, May 30, 1977

The sexual heretic has this in common with the religious heretic, that he is linked with his fellows in a community of historic suffering that somehow elevates a problem to a cause.
MAURICE EDELMAN, M.P., *New York Times*, July 5, 1970

The love that previously dared not speak its name has now grown hoarse from screaming it.
ROBERT BRUSTEIN, *New York Times*, Nov. 20, 1977

If God had wanted fags He would have created Adam and Freddy.
GRAFFITO, N.Y.C., quoted in *National Review*, Feb. 10, 1970

At the Catholic high school I attended, they spent so much time telling us how sinful heterosexual relations before marriage are, that I had 100 homosexual experiences before I knew it was sinful. A nun could talk anybody into being a homosexual.
> DICK LEITSCH, quoted in *Princeton Alumni Weekly,* May 9, 1967

"Gay" used to be one of the most agreeable words in the language. Its appropriation by a notably morose group is an act of piracy.
> ARTHUR M. SCHLESINGER, Jr., usage report for *American Heritage Dictionary,* 1976

HONESTY

"Honesty," without compassion and understanding, is not honesty, but subtle hostility.
> DR. ROSE N. FRANZBLAU, *New York Post,* Aug. 24, 1966

He who tells the truth should have one foot in the stirrup.
> ARAB PROVERB

Solitaire is the only thing in life that demands absolute honesty.
> HUGH WHEELER (book) and STEPHEN SONDHEIM (music and lyrics), *A Little Night Music* (musical), 1973

THE HORSES also see GAMBLING

I'd rathei have a bad day on the track than a goddam good day off it somewhere else.
> JOHNNY NERUD, quoted in Bill Surface, *The Track,* 1976

There's something about the turf—tomorrow is more appealing and interesting than today.
> LARRY MACPHAIL, obituary in *New York Times,* Oct. 2, 1975

At least 70 per cent of all race horses don't want to win.
> ATTRIBUTED TO EDDIE ARCARO

For the maintenance costs of one horse, approximately $250 a week, you could send two kids to Harvard.
> MIKE McGRADY, *New York Times,* Jan. 16, 1977

Horse racing is a particular interest in that the spectators, who lose money, set many fashions; while the bookmakers, who make money, set none.
QUENTIN BELL, *On Human Finery,* rev. 1976

HOSPITALS also see DOCTORS; MEDICAL CARE; SICKNESS

Blue Cross Hiltons.
DR. EDGAR BERMAN, *The Solid Gold Stethoscope,* 1976

The two places one should always go first class are in hospitals and on ships.
BARBARA A. HUFF, *New York Times,* May 26, 1974

HOUSES also see ARCHITECTURE; CITY; SKYSCRAPERS

A house is a machine for living in.
LE CORBUSIER (CHARLES ÉDOUARD JEANNERET-GRIS), quoted in *Daily Express* (London), Dec. 16, 1969

Most of them are nothing more than fancy nozzles attached to the municipal hydraulic system.
R. BUCKMINSTER FULLER, *Petroleum Today,* Fall 1968

A house should not be built so close to another that a chicken from one can lay an egg in the neighbor's yard, nor so far away that a child cannot shout to the yard of his neighbor.
PRES. JULIUS K. NYERERE OF TANZANIA, quoted in *New York Times,* Jan. 18, 1977

HOUSTON also see TEXAS

This city has been an act of real estate, rather than an act of God or man.
ADA LOUISE HUXTABLE, *New York Times,* Feb. 15, 1976

Houston is six suburbs in search for a center.
NIGEL GOSLING, *Quote,* Mar. 17, 1968

Houston is twenty of the most innovative buildings in the country and 2,000 rather ordinary gas stations.
DENNIS A. WILLIAMS, *Newsweek,* Dec. 12, 1977

It is the sassy new Pittsburgh of the Southern rim.
JAMES P. STERBA, *New York Times,* Feb. 9, 1976

Houston is rather like Los Angeles, except, that driving in Houston, one finds the thruways posted with signs saying "Drive Friendly," and for some reason Texans still do.
EDWARD HOAGLAND, *New York Times,* Dec. 23, 1973

HUMILITY also see PRIDE

Humility is a strange thing, the minute you think you've got it, you've lost it.
E. D. HULSE, *Bashford Methodist Messenger,* Feb. 1967

There is no surer sign of humility than boasting of compliments. A vain person thinks them their due.
LADY BESSBOROUGH, quoted in *Seventy Years: The Autobiography of Lady Gregory 1852–1922,* Colin Smythe, ed., 1976

HUMOR/HUMORISTS also see COMEDY/COMEDIANS; LAUGHTER; SATIRE; WIT

Humor is really laughing off a hurt, grinning at misery.
BILL MAULDIN, *Houston Post,* in *Quote,* Apr. 23, 1967

Humor is emotional chaos remembered in tranquility.
JAMES THURBER, quoted in Earl Wilson's column, Feb. 29, 1960

Humor is the most engaging cowardice. With it, I have held my enemies in play far out of gunshot.
ROBERT FROST, quoted in *Show,* May 1966

The kind of humor I like is the thing which makes me laugh for five seconds and think for ten minutes.
WILLIAM DAVIS, editor, *Punch,* quoted in Mort Crim, *Like It Is,* 1970

Humor can be dissected, as a frog can, but the thing dies in the process and the innards are discouraging to any but the pure scientific mind.
E. B. WHITE, *A Subtreasury of American Humor,* E. B. White and Katharine S. White, eds., 1941

Men will confess to treason, murder, arson, false teeth or a wig. How many will own up to a lack of humor?
FRANK MOORE COLBY, quoted in *New York Daily News,* July 4, 1976

Humorists are serious. They're the only people who are.
MARK VAN DOREN, interview in *New York Times,* June 13, 1969

A humorist, unless he is very, very good, has a life only a little longer than a moth.
FRANK SULLIVAN, obituary in *New York Post,* Feb. 19, 1976

There must be a disciplined eye and a wild mind.
DOROTHY PARKER, obituary in *New York Times,* June 8, 1967

If there's anything I hate it's that word humorist. I feel like countering with the word seriousist.
PETER DE VRIES, interview in *Time,* Nov. 15, 1968

IBM also see CORPORATIONS

IBM works so hard at succeeding that they have made it impossible for anyone else to prosper.
DAN L. McGURK, president, Computer Industry Association, quoted in *New York Times,* Apr. 28, 1974

We don't really train losers.
FRANK T. CARY, chairman, IBM, quoted in *Newsweek,* Oct. 1, 1973

IDEAS also see BELIEF; CONVICTIONS; PREJUDICES

An idea is the most exciting thing there is.
JOHN RUSSELL, *New York Times,* Jan. 7, 1979

If we watch ourselves honestly, we shall often find that we have begun to argue against a new idea even before it has been completely stated.
ARTHUR KOESTLER, *The Act of Creation,* 1964

IDENTITY also see SELF

Our wine is bitter but it is our wine.
JOSÉ MARTÍ, Cuban political martyr, quoted in *Newsweek,* Sept. 1, 1969

Identity is not found, the way Pharaoh's daughter found Moses in the bulrushes. Identity is built.
MARGARET HALSEY ON THE SEARCH-FOR-IDENTITY FAD, *Newsweek*, Apr. 17, 1978

IDEOLOGY

When you have one you suffer from the delusion that you have all the answers.
SAUL ALINSKY, quoted in *Wall Street Journal*, Apr. 4, 1969

The American ideology is not to have any ideology.
EDMUND WILSON, letter to William Faulkner, 1956, quoted in *Letters on Literature and Politics, 1912–1972*, Elena Wilson, ed., 1977

People who talk about the end of ideology in the United States must be so committed to the American ideology as not to be aware of it—like a fish who doesn't realize he's in water.
NOAM CHOMSKY, quoted in *New York Times*, Dec. 30, 1969

The function of ideologies is as much to reassure as to explain; should they cease to be absolute, we would feel abandoned to the chaos and fragility of our destiny.
ALBERT MEMMI, *New York Times*, Nov. 7, 1971

What people want in the world is not ideology; they want goods and services.
ANDREW YOUNG, interview in *Newsweek*, Mar. 28, 1977

IDLENESS

Idleness is fatal only to the mediocre.
ALBERT CAMUS, *A Happy Death*, 1972

Doing nothing—that's hard work.
JOHN FOWLES, interview in *New York Times*, Nov. 13, 1977

Life is short. Work only pleases those who will never understand it. Idleness cannot degrade anybody. It differs greatly from laziness.
BATOUALA, African chieftain, quoted in René Maran, *Batouala*, 1972

Idle people are often bored and bored people, unless they sleep a lot, are cruel.
RENATA ADLER, *Speedboat,* 1976

IMAGINATION also see ORIGINALITY

Imagination continually frustrates tradition; that is its function.
JOHN PFEIFFER, *New York Times,* Mar. 29, 1979

A man who has no imagination has no wings.
MUHAMMAD ALI, quoted in *Newsweek,* Sept. 29, 1975

Genghis Khan burned and smashed whatever he could not use because he could not imagine what else to do with it.
EVAN S. CONNELL, Jr., *New York Times,* Dec. 15, 1968

IMPERIALISM

We came here to serve God and also to get rich.
BERNAL DÍAZ DEL CASTILLO, Spanish soldier and historian, 16th century, quoted in Samuel Eliot Morison, *The European Discovery of America: The Southern Voyages,* 1974

We have destroyed the past and nothing has taken its place.
FRENCH OFFICIAL IN INDO-CHINA, 1885, quoted in *New Yorker,* Dec. 18, 1978

Thank God that we have got/The Maxim Gun, and they have not.
HILAIRE BELLOC ON THE COLONIZATION OF AFRICA, quoted in John Ellis, *The Social History of the Machine Gun,* 1976

I helped make Mexico safe for American oil interests in 1914. I helped make Haiti and Cuba a decent place for the National City Bank boys to collect revenue in. I helped purify Nicaragua for the international banking house of Brown Brothers. . . . I brought light to the Dominican Republic for American sugar interests in 1916. I helped make Honduras "right" for American fruit companies in 1903. Looking back on it, I might have given Al Capone a few hints.
MAJ. GEN. SMEDLEY D. BUTLER, U.S.M.C., interview in *New York Times,* Aug. 21, 1931

IMPOSSIBILITY

Nothing is impossible for the man who does not have to do it himself.
A. H. WIELER, *New York Times,* Mar. 17, 1968

I'll tell you in two words—im-possible.
SAM GOLDWYN, obituary in *New York Times,* Feb. 1, 1974

INDEPENDENCE: PERSONAL

Thank God I won't ever again have to be at the beck and call of every son of a bitch who's got two cents to buy a stamp.
WILLIAM FAULKNER, letter resigning as postmaster at University of Mississippi, 1924, quoted in Joseph Blotner, *Faulkner,* 1974

Don't be so inde-goddam-pendent.
BILL ROPER, Princeton football coach, to Hobey Baker, 1915, quoted in *Princeton Alumni Weekly,* May 9, 1967

God is the only one who is perfectly independent.
NOAH WEBSTER AFTER LISTING STANDARD DEFINITIONS, *American Dictionary of the English Language,* 1828

INDIA

This wounded old civilization that has at last become aware of its inadequacies and is without the intellectual means to move ahead.
V. S. NAIPAUL, *India,* 1977

A rich man invests in machines. We must invest in children.
INDIAN FARMER, quoted in Frances Moore Lappé and Joseph Collins, *Food First,* 1977

In India religion has become a booming business catering to foreigners.
Look, Mar. 19, 1979

If you say India has lost her way will you tell me one country which has not?
INDIRA GANDHI, quoted in *New York Times,* June 27, 1975

INDIANS: NORTH AMERICAN

We got off the boat and murdered a civilization.
JIM HARRISON, *New York Times,* Feb. 22, 1976

What have we done that the American people want us to stop?
SITTING BULL, quoted in Dee Brown, *Bury My Heart at Wounded Knee,* 1971

When the white man wins it is a battle. When the Indian wins it is a massacre.
INDIAN AXIOM, quoted in Evelyn Sibley Lampman, *Once Upon the Little Big Horn,* 1971

No white man uses his feet the way an Indian does. He talks to the earth.
AGNES DE MILLE, quoted in *Newsweek,* Dec. 24, 1973

As soon as you take out a pencil and paper with the Indians, you're one thing to them—an anthropologist—and what they tell to anthropologists is always distorted.
RUTH HILL, interview in *Newsweek,* Apr. 16, 1979

They seem to be waiting for us to go away.
SOL TAX, anthropologist, on the persistence of Indian culture, speaking at University of Chicago conference, April 9, 1966

INFLATION

Inflation is paying more than the products are worth.
LEE A. DUBRIDGE, news conference, Feb. 18, 1970

A dollar saved today is 75 cents earned tomorrow.
JAMES RESTON, quoted in *Stores,* Dec. 1969

Prices are going up by the elevator and wages are going up by the stairs.
ROBERT A. BEER, quoted in *Wall Street Journal,* Jan. 4, 1965

What seems to be an eternal process in which wages chase prices, prices chase wages and both chase their past history.
CLYDE H. FARNSWORTH, *New York Times,* Feb. 27, 1977

When government spends more than it gets and when labor gets more than it gives.
ROGER M. BLOUGH, speech at University of Virginia, Dec. 4, 1967

It is a hidden tax that no representative or senator needs to vote for. It is collected efficiently, automatically and silently. That is why since time immemorial it has been resorted to by every sovereign who has sought to command a larger share of his nation's output than his subjects would voluntarily spare him.
MILTON FRIEDMAN, *Newsweek*, Aug. 19, 1974

The price of admission into the coronation of Henry I was one crocard, but Henry II's went up to a pollard. At any of King John's frequent coronations it soared up to a siskin and by Henry III's time it cost a whole dodkin.
RICHARD CONDON, *New York Times*, Nov. 14, 1976

There's nothing heroic or dramatic in trying to squeeze inflation from an economy. You're trying to treat the hangover, and the fun is in the night before.
DANIEL BRILL, Assistant Treasury Secretary, quoted in *Newsweek*, Jan. 15, 1979

INFORMATION also see KNOWLEDGE; LEARNING

Information means money.
B. C. FORBES, quoted in *Forbes*, July 1, 1969

Information equals power.
IRWIN BLYE, quoted in Nicholas Pileggi, *Blye, Private Eye*, 1977

INSANITY

Insanity consists of building major structures upon foundations which do not exist.
NORMAN MAILER, speech at Theater of Ideas, N.Y.C., May 21, 1968

What shall I say? Lunacy is a confusion of the understanding.
JOHN PERCEVAL, *The Narrative of the Treatment Experienced by a Gentleman During a State of Mental Derangement*, London, 1836

The experience and behavior that gets labelled schizophrenic is a special strategy that a person invents in order to live in an unlivable situation.
R. D. LAING, *The Divided Self,* 1969

Here I sit—mad as the Hatter—with nothing to do but either become madder and madder or else recover enough of my sanity to be allowed to go back to the life which drove me mad.
LARA JEFFERSON, quoted in Otto Friedrich, *Going Crazy,* 1976

To be crazy is not necessarily to writhe in snake pits or converse with imaginary gods. It can sometimes be not knowing what to do in the morning.
CHRISTOPHER LEHMANN-HAUPT, *New York Times,* June 6, 1977

At bottom we discover nothing new in the mentally ill; rather we encounter the substratum of our own nature.
CARL G. JUNG, quoted in *New York Times,* June 27, 1977

I think most people are relieved the first time they actually know someone who goes crazy.
C. K. WILLIAMS, *With Ignorance,* 1977

INSECTS also see ANIMALS

They are . . . man's most important competitor for food and fiber.
"NOVA," PBS, Mar. 26, 1979

What a great irony it would be if, in our frantic efforts to kill insects, we eliminated man and made the world safe for bugs.
GAYLORD NELSON, asking Congress to ban DDT, *Quote,* July 31, 1966

Perhaps . . . insects are little machines in deep sleep, but looking at their rigidly armored bodies, their staring eyes, and their mute performance, one cannot help at times wondering if there is anyone inside.
V. G. DETHIER, *Science,* Mar. 13, 1964

INTELLECT/INTELLIGENCE also see STUPIDITY

Intellect distinguishes between the possible and the impossible; reason distinguishes between the sensible and the senseless. Even the possible can be senseless.
MAX BORN, *My Life and My Views,* 1968

The test of a first-rate intelligence is the ability to hold two opposed ideas in the mind at the same time, and still retain the ability to function.
    F. SCOTT FITZGERALD, quoted in *New York Times,* Mar. 4, 1979

There is no substitute for intelligence. The nearest thing to it is silence.
    KELLY FORDYCE, *Indianapolis Star,* Feb. 1967

The high IQ has become the American equivalent of the Legion of Honor, positive proof of the child's intellectual aristocracy. . . . It has become more important to be a smart kid than a good kid or even a healthy kid.
    SAM LEVENSON, *Everything but Money,* 1966

INTELLECTUALS

An intellectual is someone whose mind watches itself.
    ALBERT CAMUS, *Notebooks 1935–1942,* 1963

A person for whom thinking fulfills at once the function of work and play.
    CHRISTOPHER LASCH, *The New Radicalism in America,* 1965

A person living articulately in abstractions beyond his intellectual means—if he lives within his intellectual means he's a scholar.
    HARRY D. GIDEONSE, speech at the New School, N.Y.C., Oct. 13, 1971

The feeling of "aha, that's it," which accompanies the clothing of a situation with meaning, is emotionally very satisfying, and is the major charm of scientific research, of artistic creation, and of the solution of crossword puzzles. It is why the intellectual life is fun.
    HUDSON HOAGLAND, *Columbia Forum,* Summer 1967

Absolutized thought is the real crime of the intellectuals.
    DANIEL BELL, quoted in *Time,* May 9, 1969

Intellectuals, like fish, often move in schools following a leader.
    ISRAEL SHENKER, *New York Times,* Nov. 28, 1971

How quickly the visions of genius become the canned goods of the intellectuals.
SAUL BELLOW, *Herzog,* 1964

The job of intellectuals is to come up with ideas, and all we've been producing is footnotes.
THEODORE H. WHITE ON GOVERNMENT PROBLEMS, interview in *New York Times,* July 27, 1969

If there's anything worse than an intellectual in politics, it's an anti-intellectual in politics.
JAMES P. O'DONNELL, "Dick Cavett Show," PBS, Jan. 22, 1979

Every time the train of history goes around the corner, the thinkers fall off.
ATTRIBUTED TO KARL MARX

We started out being Communists, then we were Socialists, then Social Democrats, then Democrats, then full professors.
PROFESSOR ON THE MIDDLE-AGED INTELLECTUAL, quoted in *New York Daily News,* Sept. 7, 1975

How many intellectuals have the courage to admit they pick up a book and look first for their name in the index?
IRVING HOWE, interview in *New York Times,* Jan. 1, 1969

In some areas of New York if you have a master's degree you're automatically an intellectual.
ANONYMOUS

INVENTIONS

With all man's marvelous ability to invent things which are potentially good, he can always be counted on to make the worst possible use of what he invents; as witness the radio, printing-press, aeroplane and the internal-combustion engine.
ALBERT JAY NOCK, *Memoirs of a Superfluous Man,* 1962

Anything that won't sell, I don't want to invent.
THOMAS A. EDISON, quoted in Robert Conot, *A Streak of Luck,* 1979

Have there not been enough inventions?
SACHEVERELL SITWELL, *For Want of the Golden City,* 1973

IRELAND/THE IRISH also see DUBLIN

The last place in the world where conversation is not dead.
Lawrence Millman, *Our Like Will Not Be There Again,* 1977

The conversation hardly leaves a man time to swallow anything.
Wilfrid Sheed on the exaggeration of Irishmen's drinking, *New York Times,* Aug. 1, 1971

The only thing that all Irishmen agree about is that you're wrong.
Time, June 20, 1969

Only half the lies the Irish tell are true.
Walter O'Malley, quoted in Roger Kahn, *The Boys of Summer,* 1972

In Ireland "truth" is what people choose to believe—whatever the facts may be.
Newsweek, July 24, 1972

The Irish are all butterfly-brained, you know.
Clement A. Norton, quoted in *New York Times,* Mar. 18, 1971

The Ferocious Chastity of Ireland.
Sean O'Casey, dedication, *Figuro in the Night* (drama), 1961

I'm an Irish Catholic and I have a long iceberg of guilt.
Edna O'Brien, interview in *New York Times,* Oct. 11, 1977

There's no such thing as a merry Irish song.
Hugh L. Carey, governor of New York, speech, St. Patrick's Day celebration, Mar. 14, 1975

English authors write better than Americans—and Irish authors write better than anybody.
Dorothy Parker, quoted in *Writer's Digest,* Aug. 1967

The actual Irish weather report is really a recording made in 1922, which no one has had occasion to change. "Scattered showers, periods of sunshine."
Wilfrid Sheed, *New York Times,* Aug. 1, 1971

IRREVERENCE

Irreverence is the great weapon of the minorities; it is the engine for teasing the powerful.
QUENTIN BELL, *Bloomsbury*, 1969

There is nothing left to revere in this country, so it's pretty hard to be irreverent.
DAN ROWAN, interview in *Newsweek*, Jan. 29, 1973

ISRAEL/ISRAELIS also see MIDDLE EAST

Israel is the only country where one can say of someone that he is a Jew without being an anti-Semite.
JEAN-PAUL SARTRE, *New Outlook* (Tel Aviv), 1967

Israelis are viewed by too many as people who dance the *hora* when they are not planting trees in the desert.
AMOS ELON, *The Israelis*, 1971

As an American, I can decide on any given day whether or not I wish to think of abominations. I need not consider them. I can simply refuse to open the morning paper. In Israel, one has no such choice.
SAUL BELLOW, *To Jerusalem and Back*, 1976

Israel has no foreign policy, only domestic politics.
HENRY A. KISSINGER, quoted in Matti Golan, *The Secret Conversations of Henry Kissinger*, 1976

This country is a place where somebody always sits on top of somebody else.
EDDIE DRIBBEN, West Bank settler, quoted in *Newsweek*, Sept. 26, 1977

The twice-promised land.
CHAIM WEIZMANN ON ARAB AND JEWISH CLAIMS, quoted in *Columbia Forum*, Fall 1970

It was the historical tragedy of Zionism that it appeared on the international scene when there were no longer empty spaces on the world map.
WALTER LAQUEUR, *The History of Zionism*, 1972

I don't want to wake up in the morning and have to worry about how many Arabs were born during the night.
GOLDA MEIR ON ISRAEL'S HIGH ARAB BIRTHRATE, quoted in *Newsweek,* May 7, 1973

In the U.S., young people are rebelling against the bourgeois values of their parents. Here, they've skipped a generation and are rebelling against the socialistic idealism of their grandparents.
ISRAELI TEACHER, quoted in *Newsweek,* May 7, 1973

After three weeks, I had my first taste of unkosher food and my yarmulke went into my pocket.
DAVID STEINBERG ON HIS STUDENT DAYS, interview in *Newsweek,* Apr. 21, 1975

Israel is moving from the realm of poetry to the realm of prose.
SHIMON PERES, quoted in *Newsweek,* May 7, 1973

ITALY/ITALIANS also see ROME

Europeans may have to learn that Italy is stable in her instability.
ITALIAN NEWSPAPER EDITORIAL, 1972

Rome can't go bankrupt because it already is.
ITALIAN BANKER, quoted in *New York Times,* Jan. 25, 1976

Italy could never win a war. We are too sensitive.
BENITO MUSSOLINI, quoted in Branko Bokun, *Spy in the Vatican,* 1973

Their talk is always one octave above their actions.
CRIMINOLOGIST, quoted in *Newsweek,* Aug. 9, 1971

A "good" discussion is one which lends itself to arguments rather than answers.
NICHOLAS PILEGGI, *New York,* Aug. 12, 1968

Italians are interested in facial gestures and what the hands are saying. That's why businessmen come to Rome from Milan. When they get a letter they don't know what it means.
LUIGI BARZINI, interview in Israel Shenker, *Words and Their Masters,* 1974

Opera audiences are more concerned with a passionate performance than a beautiful vocal line.
JAMES NORMAN, interview in *New York Post,* Apr. 2, 1975

An Italian driver's reaction to any encounter with another vehicle is, first, stunned disbelief, then outrage.
JACK BURGESS, *Holiday,* Jan. 1970

Bribes? Why, they were the foundation of the Italian Republic.
ITALIAN NEWSMAN, quoted in *New York Times,* Jan. 26, 1975

It isn't that I like the boy because he's Italian. I like him because I'm Italian.
JOE PATERNO, Penn State football coach, *Quote,* Oct. 30, 1966

JAPAN/THE JAPANESE

Japan is built on the effective use of space, America on the effective use of time.
EDWIN O. REISCHAUER, quoted in *National Observer,* June 1, 1970

It's one big processing plant, competing all over the world for raw materials.
HARRISON BROWN, quoted in *Newsweek,* Nov. 19, 1973

The Japanese are a people with a genius for doing anything they set out to do as a matter of national decision.
GEORGE W. BALL, quoted in *Newsweek,* Oct. 6, 1975

The Japanese are addicted to tension as a welcome way of life, as a stimulating springboard for individual and collective advancement.
YUKIO MATSUYAMA, *New York Times,* Jan. 3, 1973

A nation of workaholics living in what Westerners regard as little better than rabbit hutches.
EUROPEAN COMMON MARKET INTERNAL REPORT, quoted in *Newsweek,* Apr. 23, 1979

They're extremely good imitators. And so polite they even copy the mistakes.
EARL SCRUGGS, interview in *Newsweek,* Mar. 25, 1968

I've never seen one Japanese-English translation that any four experts agree is accurate.
AMERICAN DIPLOMAT, quoted in *Newsweek,* Aug. 6, 1973

JAZZ see MUSIC: JAZZ

JEWS/JUDAISM also see RELIGION

We are a justice-intoxicated people.
RABBI JOACHIM PRINZ, quoted in *Look,* Apr. 20, 1971

Resurrection with us is not a miracle, but a habit.
ISAAC BASHEVIS SINGER, interview in *New York Post,* Feb. 1, 1972

Judaism . . . is not how to explain God, but how to live with him.
EMIL L. FACKENHEIM, speech at Auschwitz symposium, N.Y.C., June 8, 1974

The essence of being a Jew, in my opinion, is the idea of the Prophets—not the Torah, but the Prophets. They have two ideas: You must love one single God, and you must lead a moral life. That is all that matters.
DAVID BEN-GURION, obituary in *New York Times,* Dec. 2, 1973

Chicken soup Judaism, B'nai B'rith and Israel Bond Judaism, country-club Judaism are mere variations of an American effort to keep busy.
HERBERT GOLD, *New York Times,* Jan. 23, 1972

A Jew, reading history, must always expect to have his face pinked a little.
BEN HECHT, quoted in *New York Times,* Apr. 18, 1971

Only a Jew can ask a question and answer it in the same sentence.
APHORISM

Where two Jews, three opinions.
ANONYMOUS

The Jews have always been students, and their greatest study is themselves.
LENNY BRUCE, quoted in Albert Goldman, *Ladies and Gentleman, LENNY BRUCE!!!,* 1974

After you are born you have about five years of relaxation, but once you reach the age between 5 and 6 your parents decide you're going to be a doctor.
STUDENT, quoted in *New York Times,* Aug. 31, 1969

Remember when they used to say Jews didn't drink, that there were no gay Jews? Now we too have made it.
SOL MALOFF, *Heartland,* 1973

THE JOB also see BLUE-COLLAR BLUES; SECRETARIES; WORK

To say a man holds a job is to misstate the fact. The job holds the man.
JAMES GOULD COZZENS, *Morning, Noon and Night,* 1968

The test of a vocation is the love of the drudgery it involves.
LOGAN PEARSALL SMITH, quoted in *Forbes,* May 15, 1974

I have always been overpaid to do that which I would pay to do.
PAUL A. SAMUELSON, *Newsweek,* Dec. 30, 1974

If you have a job without aggravations, you don't have a job.
MALCOLM S. FORBES, *The Sayings of Chairman Malcolm,* 1978

Whose bread I eat, whose wine I drink, his songs I sing.
DAMON RUNYON

Yesterday's young hero who rode his bike "no hands" to impress his girl is today the executive submitting a 50-page proposal entitled "A Comprehensive Plan for Implementation of Participating Management with Particular Attention to Line-Staff Interface."
WILLIAM N. PENZER, *Public Relations Reporter,* May 6, 1974

There are no rewards for thirty years' service around here. It's what you do this year that counts.
EXECUTIVE, quoted in *Fortune,* Feb. 1973

The "organization man" is not merely a slick phrase. He is a growing menace to us all, not because of what he is—a decent and hard-working servant of his organization—but because of what he is not. He is not willing to annoy his organization by any action, and his organization is too easily annoyed.
MCGEORGE BUNDY, Ford Foundation annual report, 1966

In the office in which I work there are five people of whom I am afraid. Each of these five people is afraid of four people (excluding overlaps).
JOSEPH HELLER, *Something Happened,* 1974

On the evening bus, the tense, pinched faces of young file clerks and elderly secretaries tell us more than we care to know.
STUDS TERKEL, *New York Times,* Mar. 19, 1973

Everything can be a deadend job if you're a deadend guy.
ANTHONY CHAFFO, interview in *New York Post,* Dec. 12, 1972

No matter what the job is, it ain't final. You can always quit.
PETER DRUCKER, interview in *Psychology Today,* Mar. 1968

JOGGING see RUNNING

KNOWLEDGE also see INFORMATION; LEARNING

If I could but describe in simple words the immensity of simple knowledge.
PATRICK WHITE, *Voss,* 1965

Knowledge itself can be defined as detailed awareness of unsolved problems.
ANONYMOUS, quoted in *New York Times,* May 23, 1976

There are things that are known and things that are unknown; in between are doors.
ANONYMOUS

A man with a watch knows what time it is; a man with two watches isn't so sure.
ANONYMOUS

We know too much for one man to know much.
ATTRIBUTED TO J. ROBERT OPPENHEIMER

If a little knowledge is dangerous, where is the man who has so much as to be out of danger?
T. H. HUXLEY, "On Elementary Instruction in Physiology," 1877

We have not the reverent feeling for the rainbow that the savage has, because we know how it is made. We have lost as much as we have gained by prying into the matter.
MARK TWAIN, *Quote,* Oct. 30, 1966

KUDOS also see PUTDOWNS

Einstein was a man who could ask immensely simple questions. And what his work showed is that when the answers are simple too, then you can hear God thinking.
JACOB BRONOWSKI, "The Ascent of Man," PBS, Jan. 8, 1975

Tonight France is a widow.
GEORGES J. R. POMPIDOU ON THE DEATH OF CHARLES DE GAULLE, quoted in *New York Times,* Mar. 5, 1977

This avalanche of a man.
JACK VALENTI ON LYNDON B. JOHNSON, *A Very Human President,* 1976

He could walk into a henhouse where a fox was chasing the chickens and they'd all stop and look at him.
FRIEND ON GRIFFIN B. BELL, quoted in *Newsweek,* Feb. 28, 1977

He has swallowed the sun.
PABLO PICASSO ON HENRI MATISSE, quoted in *Newsweek,* Jan. 17, 1966

I never saw such barking colors!
OSIP MANDELSTAM ON VAN GOGH, "Journey to Armenia," 1933

Toots does more kind things accidentally than most people do on purpose.
QUENTIN REYNOLDS ON TOOTS SHOR, obituary of Shor in *New York Post,* Jan. 24, 1977

If he tells you tomorrow's Christmas, you can get your sock ready. He was that kind of person.
BEN JOHNSON ON JOHN WAYNE, obituary of Wayne in *Newsweek,* June 25, 1979

The Orson Welles of woebegone.
WILLIAM REEL ON WOODY ALLEN, *New York Daily News,* June 1, 1979

He could throw a lamb chop past a wolf.
ARTHUR "BUGS" BAER ON LEFTY GROVE, who once struck out Babe
Ruth, Lou Gehrig and Bob Meusel with nine pitches, quoted in *New
York Times*, May 26, 1975

How can you bully Niagara Falls?
BILLY ROSE AFTER TALLULAH BANKHEAD CALLED HIM "A LOATHSOME
LITTLE BULLY," obituary of Bankhead in *New York Times*, Dec. 13,
1968

The best potato masher one could wish for.
HANNAH NIXON ON HER SON, RICHARD M. NIXON, quoted in Liz
Smith, *The Mother Book*, 1978

A great social reformer.
GEORGE BERNARD SHAW ON JACK THE RIPPER, WHO SPECIALIZED IN
PROSTITUTES

LANGUAGE also see PUNCTUATION; WORDS

Perhaps of all the creations of man, language is the most astonishing.
LYTTON STRACHEY, introduction to George H. W. Rylands' *Words
and Poetry*, 1925

A people's speech is the skin of its culture.
MAX LERNER, *America as a Civilization*, 1957

There are three races—men, women and children. And none of them
speaks the same language.
Kaiser News, no. 3, 1965

If you will scoff at language study how, save in terms of language, will
you scoff?
MARIO PEI, quoted in *Newsweek*, Dec. 8, 1975

LANGUAGE: SLANG

Slang is a poor man's poetry.
JOHN MOORE, quoted in *Little Gazette*, Oct. 1969

Slang, though humanly irreverent, tends to be inhumanly loveless. It lacks tenderness and compassion; its poetry has the effulgence of a soldier's brass buttons.

> ANTHONY BURGESS, *New York Times,* July 12, 1970

Scientific jargon is superior slang.

> SANDRA RAPHAEL, Oxford English Dictionary staff, interview in Israel Shenker, *Words and Their Masters,* 1974

Do suburban ladies who use the phrases to show where they're *at* know that "funky" at first meant sex smells, or that "up tight" referred to the contraction of the testicles in times of stress?

> ARTHUR HERZOG, *The B.S. Factor,* 1973

LAST AND NEAR-TO-LAST WORDS

Have I played my part well in this comedy of life?

> AUGUSTUS CAESAR, quoted by *Suetonius*

I don't understand what I'm supposed to do.

> LEO TOLSTOY, quoted in David Hendin, *Death as a Fact of Life,* 1973

So that's how you die.

> GABRIELLE CHANEL, quoted in Edmonde Charles-Roux, *Chanel,* 1975

If this is dying, I don't think much of it.

> LYTTON STRACHEY, quoted in Michael Holroyd, *Lytton Strachey,* 1967

No, it is not.

> OLIVER GOLDSMITH WHEN ASKED IF HIS MIND WAS AT EASE, quoted in *New York Times,* Oct. 30, 1966

I did not know that we had ever quarreled.

> HENRY THOREAU WHEN ASKED IF HE HAD MADE HIS PEACE WITH GOD, quoted in Henry Seidel Canby, *Thoreau,* 1939

Why, of course, he will forgive me; that's his business.

> HEINRICH HEINE WHEN TOLD GOD WOULD FORGIVE HIS SINS, quoted in Louis Untermeyer, *Heinrich Heine,* 1937

Haven't chosen yet.

> IMOGEN CUNNINGHAM WHEN HOSPITAL ASKED HER RELIGION, *After Ninety,* introduction by Margaretta Mitchell, 1977

Lord, here I come!
IOWA FARM WOMAN, quoted in Curtis Harnack, *We Have All Gone Away,* 1973

Have the services start at 2:30 P.M.; my friends don't get up before noon.
VINCENT YOUMANS, quoted in Leonard Lyons' column, Dec. 19, 1970

Is it possible?
PAUL DOUMER, FRENCH PRESIDENT, WHEN SHOT BY ASSASSIN, 1932, according to conservative press, quoted in Janet Flanner, *Paris Was Yesterday,* 1972

Oh, lá, lá!
DOUMER'S WORDS, according to popular press, quoted in Flanner, *Paris Was Yesterday*

Remember me.
14-YEAR-OLD POLISH GIRL ABOUT TO BE HANGED, Ravensbruck concentration camp, World War II, quoted in Howard Blum, *Wanted!,* 1976

LATIN AMERICA

Americans will do anything about Latin America except read about it.
JAMES RESTON, quoted in *Columbia Journalism Review,* Winter 1969–70

In Latin America a rise of prices under 10 per cent is regarded as deflation.
GOTTFRIED HABERLER, speech at monetary conference, Claremont College, March 24, 1975

LAUGHTER also see COMEDY/COMEDIANS; HUMOR/HUMORISTS; SATIRE; WIT

Laughter is an orgasm triggered by the intercourse of reason with unreason.
JACK KROLL, *Newsweek,* May 31, 1976

Laughter is both an act of protest and an act of acceptance.
W. H. AUDEN, *Columbia Forum,* Winter 1970

We only laugh because we are surprised.
GARSON KANIN, quoted in *New York Times,* May 14, 1976

Men show their character in nothing more than what they find laughable.
Grit, Mar. 1967

I'm faintly suspicious of people who laugh out loud for a long time.
GERALD NACHMAN, *New York Daily News,* July 4, 1976

LAW also see COURTS; LAWYERS

Law is the backbone which keeps man erect.
S. C. YUTER, *Bulletin of the Atomic Scientists,* Oct. 1969

The law can never make us as secure as we are when we do not need it.
ALEXANDER M. BICKEL, *The Morality of Consent,* 1975

The life of the law has not been logic; it has been experience.
OLIVER WENDELL HOLMES, JR., *The Common Law,* 1881

The worse the society, the more law there will be. In Hell there will be nothing but law, and due process will be meticulously observed.
GRANT GILMORE, quoted in *New York Times,* Feb. 23, 1977

Colby is prepared, as we have always tried to do, to comply with the law of the land, but first it would be helpful to know what the law of the land is.
E. L. STRIDER, president, Colby College, letter to Equal Opportunity Commission, quoted in *Wall Street Journal,* Mar. 4, 1976

LAWYERS also see COURTS; LAW

About half the practice of a decent lawyer consists in telling would-be clients that they are damned fools and should stop.
ELIHU ROOT, quoted in Martin Mayer, *The Lawyers,* 1967

An odd profession that presents its greatest scholarship in student-run publications.
MORTON J. HORWITZ, quoted in *Newsweek,* Sept. 15, 1975

It's not a profession at all, but rather a business service station and repair shop.
ADLAI STEVENSON ON CORPORATE LAW, *The Papers of Adlai Stevenson, 1900–1941*, Walter Johnson and Carol Evans, eds., 1972

Lawyers are . . . operators of the toll bridge across which anyone in search of justice must pass.
JANE BRYANT QUINN, *Newsweek*, Oct. 9, 1978

A lawyer's job is to manipulate the skeletons in other people's closets.
SOL STEIN, *Other People*, 1979

We shake papers at each other the way primitive tribes shake spears.
JOHN JAY OSBORN, JR., *The Associates*, 1979

You don't approach a case with the philosophy of applying abstract justice—you go in to win.
PERCY FOREMAN, quoted in *Newsweek*, Feb. 3, 1969

You can't earn a living defending innocent people.
MAURICE NADJARI, interview in *New York Post*, May 8, 1975

Law students are trained in the case method, and, to the lawyer, everything in life looks like a case. His first thought in the morning is how to handle the case of the ringing alarm clock.
EDWARD B. PACKARD, JR., *Columbia Forum*, Spring 1967

The appearance in our courts of these learned gentlemen of the law, who can make black appear white and white appear black, is forbidden.
DECREE, GOVERNMENT OF ANDORRA, 1864; still in effect

LEADERSHIP

Leaders . . . they grasp nettles.
DAVID OGILVY, speech at American Marketing Association, Philadelphia, May 10, 1972

The only real training for leadership is leadership.
ANTONY JAY, *Management and Machiavelli*, 1968

A mean streak is a very important quality of leadership.
CHARLES E. GOODELL, *Newsweek*, Oct. 18, 1976

The great leaders have always stage-managed their effects.
CHARLES DE GAULLE, *The Edge of the Sword,* 1960

There has not been a great leader in this century who wasn't devious at certain times when it was necessary to achieve his goals.
CLINTON ROSSITER, quoted in *Newsweek,* Jan. 20, 1969

LEARNING also see INFORMATION; KNOWLEDGE

It's what you learn after you know it all that counts.
JOHN WOODEN, *They Call Me Coach,* 1973

Everybody today studies the piano but nobody learns anything.
GEORGE BALANCHINE, interview in *Newsweek,* Feb. 12, 1979

I can learn something from anything. I can learn from a pile of Nixon under the stoop.
IMAMU AMIRI BARAKA, quoted in *New York Times,* June 27, 1971

LEFTISTS see RADICALS

LEISURE

Nobody should work all the time. Everyone should have some leisure, but I believe the early morning hours are best for this—the five or six hours when you're asleep.
GEORGE ALLEN, Washington Redskins coach, quoted in *Newsweek,* Nov. 1, 1971

Of all the men of any culture in the history of the world nobody was ever worse fitted to make the adjustment to an age of leisure than the modern Americans who made it all possible.
EDWIN J. STALEY, *Quote,* Sept. 14, 1969

LETTERS also see TELEPHONES

A letter is like a present.
STEPHEN SPENDER, interview in *New York Post,* Apr. 26, 1975

Life would split asunder without letters.
VIRGINIA WOOLF, *Jacob's Room*, 1922

Letters are largely written to get things out of your system.
JOHN DOS PASSOS, *The Fourteenth Chronicle*, Townsend Ludington, ed., 1973

It is quite a mistake to suppose that one ever needs subject matter in writing a letter: I think those are most interesting which detail least of daily affairs.
JOHN ADDINGTON SYMONDS, letter to sister, *The Letters of John Addington Symonds, 1844–1868*, Herbert M. Schueller and Robert L. Peters, eds., 1969

If one is not scandalous it is difficult to write at all.
J. R. ACKERLEY, *The Ackerley Letters*, Neville Braybrooke, ed., 1975

LIBERALS/LIBERALISM also see CONSERVATIVES; RADICALS

It is one of the tendencies of liberalism to simplify, and this tendency is natural in view of the effort which liberalism makes to organize the elements of life in a rational way.
LIONEL TRILLING, *The Liberal Imagination*, 1950

The liberal . . . is better at inventing reforms than in insuring that they are well and honestly administered.
JOHN KENNETH GALBRAITH, *New York Times*, June 26, 1977

To the modern liberal mind, the word discipline has an almost pornographic sound.
DONALD BARR, *Who Pushed Humpty Dumpty?*, 1971

They've got a sense of injustice bigger than anyone else, but not so much a sense of justice—that is, they don't want to face the consequences.
ROMAIN GARY, interview in *New York Times*, Apr. 27, 1970

He's like a man with premature ejaculation. First it's, "Hey, wow!" Then, "I don't know what keeps going wrong."
ANONYMOUS

Liberalism seems to be related to the distance people are from the problem.
WHITNEY M. YOUNG, JR., *Quote*, Sept. 27, 1967

LIBERTY

The spirit of liberty is the spirit which is not too sure that it is right.
JUDGE LEARNED HAND, quoted in *New York Post*, July 16, 1976

Another man's liberty stops at the tip of my nose.
ANONYMOUS

I am prepared to give the boys more liberties, provided they do not take them.
MICHAEL McCRUM, headmaster, Eton, 1970

LIBRARIES

It is intensely frustrating to acquire insight in public places without being allowed to exclaim "Ah-ha!"
ROBERT SOMMER, interview in *New York Times*, Apr. 3, 1971

I looked into the library and everyone had his sleeves rolled up, and it looked like they were shoveling cement.
DANIEL J. BOORSTIN ON THE YALE LAW SCHOOL LIBRARY, interview in *New York Post*, May 1, 1971

With most people, libraries are like their lives. They begin with some order and go on to increasing disorder.
IRVING HOWE ON THE HOME LIBRARY, quoted in *New York Times*, Dec. 27, 1976

LIES/LIARS also see TRUTH

A lie goes around the world before the truth gets its britches on.
GEORGE HARTZOG, quoted in John McPhee, *Pieces of the Frame*, 1975

Liars share with those they deceive the desire not to *be* deceived.
SISSELA BOK, *Lying*, 1978

I suspect that people lie about their sex lives more than any other subject.
ABIGAIL VAN BUREN, "Dear Abby" column, May 31, 1977

LIFE also see DEATH

Rejoice with your family in the beautiful land of life.
ALBERT EINSTEIN, letter to Paul Ehrenfest, June 3, 1917, quoted in Martin J. Klein, *Paul Ehrenfest,* vol. 1, 1970

Life is a tragedy full of joy.
BERNARD MALAMUD, interview in *New York Times,* Jan. 29, 1979

But life is a great school. It thrashes and bangs and teaches you.
NIKITA S. KHRUSHCHEV, obituary in *New York Times,* Aug. 12, 1971

Life don't run away from nobody. Life runs at people.
JOE FRAZIER, quoted in *Newsweek,* Mar. 18, 1968

Life today is nervous, sharp and zigzag. It often stops in midair.
MARTHA GRAHAM, 1929, quoted in *New York Times,* Oct. 2, 1970

Life is what happens to us while we are making other plans.
WILLIAM GADDIS, *JR.,* 1975

In all human affairs, the odds are always 6 to 5 against.
DAMON RUNYON, quoted in *New York Times,* Dec. 20, 1964

When the risk is taken out, there isn't much left.
SIGMUND FREUD, quoted in *New York Times,* Sept. 25, 1975

We're all in this together—by ourselves.
LILY TOMLIN, quoted in *New York Times,* Sept. 12, 1976

I wanted only to try to live in accordance with the promptings that came from my true self. Why was that so very difficult?
ANONYMOUS

The saddest thing in life/Is that the best thing in it should be courage.
ROBERT FROST, *A Masque of Mercy,* 1947

I heard a bit of good news today. We shall pass this way but once.
GEORGE PRICE, cartoon, *New Yorker,* Apr. 14, 1973

And the days are not full enough/And the nights are not full enough/
And life slips by like a field mouse/Not shaking the grass.
> EZRA POUND, Prologue to "Lustra" in *Personae,* 1926

LITERATURE also see BOOKS; READING; WRITERS/WRITING

Literature is recognizable through its capacity to evoke more than it
says.
> ANTHONY BURGESS, *New York Times,* Sept. 25, 1977

Literature is the question minus the answer.
> ROLAND BARTHES, quoted in *New York Times,* Jan. 29, 1978

All modern American literature comes from one book by Mark Twain
called *Huckleberry Finn.*
> ERNEST HEMINGWAY, *The Green Hills of Africa,* 1935

LITERATURE: THE NOVEL

When we want to understand grief beyond grief, or the eternal confrontation of man and woman, man and God, man and himself, we go
to the novel.
> RICHARD CONDON, *Harper's,* Sept. 1977

A great novel is like a hunt for the answers to why we're alive and
what we're doing here.
> LEON KIRCHNER, interview in *Newsweek,* Apr. 25, 1977

A novel is a prose narrative of some length that has something wrong
with it.
> RANDALL JARRELL

There are three rules for writing a novel. Unfortunately, no one knows
what they are.
> W. SOMERSET MAUGHAM, quoted in Ralph Daigh, *Maybe You Should
> Write a Book,* 1977

Let's hope the institution of marriage survives its detractors, for without it there would be no more adultery and without adultery two-
thirds of our novelists would stand in line for unemployment checks.
> PETER S. PRESCOTT, *Newsweek,* Nov. 8, 1976

LITERATURE: POETRY

I am overwhelmed by the beautiful disorder of poetry, the eternal virginity of words.
THEODORE ROETHKE, *Straw for the Fire*, David Wagoner, ed., 1972

Information is true if it is accurate. A poem is true if it holds together.
E. M. FORSTER, quoted in Peter Gay, *Style in History*, 1974

If a poem arises from a dynamic relation with reality, it will be fresh whatever formal difficulties the poet chooses to overcome in the writing of it. If not, it will be like a group of anthropologists demonstrating a rain dance.
RICHARD WILBUR, *Responses*, 1976

Whatever poetry is, it's not self-expression.
W. H. AUDEN, quoted in *Columbia Forum*, Winter 1974

Poets have to dream, and dreaming in America is no cinch.
SAUL BELLOW, *Humboldt's Gift*, 1975

My verse represents a handle I can grasp in order not to yield to the centrifugal forces which are trying to throw me off the world.
OGDEN NASH, obituary in *New York Post*, May 20, 1971

Wherever human dignity and liberty are threatened, poets are busy in the night.
STANLEY KUNITZ, speech at Benefit for Freedom to Read Committee, N.Y.C., Oct. 8, 1975

Poetry is the only art people haven't learned yet to consume like soup.
W. H. AUDEN, quoted in *American Scholar*, Apr. 1967

The public has an unusual relation with the poet. It does not even know that he is there.
RANDALL JARRELL

Lyric poets generally come from homes run by women.
MILAN KUNDERA, *Life Is Elsewhere*, 1974

Anyone who says he likes poetry and doesn't buy poetry books is a dirty sonofabitch.
SIGN AT SWALLOW PRESS BOOTH, Modern Language Association meeting, N.Y.C., Dec. 1972

LIVING, RULES FOR

Love life for better or worse without conditions.
ARTHUR RUBINSTEIN, *My Young Years,* 1973

Don't forget to love yourself.
SØREN KIERKEGAARD, *Letters and Documents,* 1979

You're here for a short visit so be sure to stop and smell the flowers.
WALTER HAGEN, quoted in Fred Corcoran, *Unplayable Lies,* 1965

Every ten years a man should give himself a good kick in the pants.
EDWARD STEICHEN TO MUSEUM OF MODERN ART STAFFER, 1962

I'll go through life either first class or third, but never in second.
NOËL COWARD, quoted in Leonard Lyons' column, Mar. 28, 1973

Practice being excited.
BILL FOSTER, Duke University basketball coach, quoted in *Atlantic Monthly,* Feb. 1979

Never turn your back.
NIKITA S. KHRUSHCHEV, quoted on "Day at Night," PBS, Oct. 23, 1974

Never co-sign.
AL MCGUIRE, quoted in *Newsweek,* Mar. 28, 1977

Never answer the telephone if you are in the middle of something more important.
C. NORTHCOTE PARKINSON, *Mrs. Parkinson's Law,* 1968

Never dispute the referee's ability to count ten.
ANONYMOUS

Never play cards with a man named Doc. Never eat at a place called Mom's. Never sleep with a woman whose troubles are worse than your own.
ANONYMOUS, quoted in *Newsweek,* July 2, 1956

I think there is one smashing rule: *Never face the facts.*
RUTH GORDON, interview in *New York Post,* May 8, 1971

LIVING STANDARD see STANDARD OF LIVING

LONDON also see BRITAIN/THE BRITISH

The last civilized metropolis in the world.
JOHN CANADAY, *New York Times,* Sept. 24, 1972

Even the ambulance sirens can afford to be low key.
ADAM YARMOLINSKY, *Manchester Guardian,* Mar. 7, 1968

All sports news is reported subjectively—and patriotically.
FELIX KESSLER ON THE TIMES (LONDON), *Wall Street Journal,* May 13, 1970

I taste the wine and it is—how you say?—unfortunate.
COMTE DE MOUCHERON, quoted in *New York Times,* July 20, 1970

It's so cold here, yesterday I almost got married.
SHELLEY WINTERS, quoted in Leonard Lyons' column, May 11, 1971

LOS ANGELES also see CALIFORNIA

That Queen City of Plastic.
NORMAN MAILER, quoted in *Wall Street Journal,* May 2, 1969

A kind of post-urban process rather than a city.
HERBERT GOLD, "Dick Cavett Show," PBS, Jan. 31, 1978

It is present tense.
G. T. SEWALL, *New York Times,* May 31, 1977

Where people carry radios to ball games so they can be told what's happening before their eyes.
JOEL OPPENHEIMER, *New York Times,* June 17, 1979

If you ever tilted the map of the U.S.A. very sharply, Los Angeles is the spot where everything would spill out.
FRANK LLOYD WRIGHT, quoted in *New York Post,* Jan. 15, 1969

I knock him out in two rounds.
PRIMO CARNERA WHEN ASKED WHAT HE THOUGHT OF LOS ANGELES,
quoted in *New York Times,* June 30, 1967

LOSING also see FAILURE; MAKING IT; SUCCESS

Show me a good loser and I'll show you a loser.
JIMMY CARTER, *Why Not the Best?,* 1975

I'd much rather play with a poor loser than any kind of a winner.
BRIAN DONLEVY ON GIN RUMMY, quoted in Leonard Lyons' column,
Mar. 19, 1972

How can we lose when we're so sincere?
CHARLES SCHULZ, *Peanuts,* 1968

LOVE

Love is an attempt to change a piece of a dream-world into reality.
THEODOR REIK, *The Psychology of Sex Relations,* 1945

It comes in at the eyes and subdues the body. An army with banners.
My God, every poet in the world knew about it, except me.
LOUISE BOGAN, *What the Woman Lived,* Ruth Limmer, ed., 1973

Having someone wonder where you are when you don't come home at
night is a very old human need.
MARGARET MEAD, speech to National Council of Women, N.Y.C.,
Apr. 16, 1975

The mark of a true crush (whether the object is man, woman or city)
is that you fall in love first and grope for reasons afterward.
SHANA ALEXANDER, *The Feminine Eye,* 1970

Out of love you can speak with straight fury.
EUDORA WELTY, *The Eye of the Story,* 1978

Love is so misused a word. I don't even know what it means, do you?
What is it: compassion, *caritas,* pity? In any case, it has nothing to do
with lust, and the mixing up of the two is one of the reasons we're in
such trouble emotionally.
GORE VIDAL, interview in *Bookviews,* June 1978

LUCK

You can't hope to be lucky. You have to prepare to be lucky.
> TIMOTHY DOWD, N.Y.P.D. deputy inspector, "MacNeil/Lehrer Report," PBS, July 29, 1977

Smart is better than lucky.
> TITANIC THOMPSON, hustler, quoted in Jon Bradshaw, *Fast Company,* 1975

There's only one thing I believe about luck—it's unlucky to be behind at the end of the game.
> ATTRIBUTED TO BILL RUSSELL, Boston Celtics coach

This sort of thing is always happening to me.
> JAMES JONES AFTER STEPPING ON DOG DUNG IN THE WHITE HOUSE ROSE GARDEN, quoted in Willie Morris, *James Jones,* 1978

MAKING IT also see FAILURE; LOSING; SUCCESS

Be bold when you've got a hot hand.
> CHARLES H. KIRBO TO JIMMY CARTER IN 1976 CAMPAIGN, quoted in *New York Times,* July 14, 1976

When you've got it—flaunt it.
> GEORGE LOIS, *The Art of Advertising,* 1977

Always go for the top man.
> WENDELL PHILLIPS, quoted in *Newsweek,* Feb. 14, 1972

I always go where the dough is.
> GYPSY ROSE LEE, obituary in *New York Times,* Apr. 28, 1970

Win any way you can as long as you can get away with it.
> LEO DUROCHER, *Nice Guys Finish Last,* 1975

Don't get too much sleep and don't tell anybody your troubles. Appearances count; get a sun lamp . . . maintain an elegant address even if you . . . live in the attic; patronize posh watering places even if you have to nurse your drinks. Never niggle when you're short of cash. Borrow big, but always repay promptly.
> ATTRIBUTED TO ARISTOTLE ONASSIS

Cheat neat.
> RICHARD PETTY, stock-car racer, *King of the Road,* 1977

Never allow the public to cool off; never admit a fault or wrong; never concede that there may be some good in your enemy; concentrate on one enemy at a time and blame him for everything that goes wrong; people will believe a big lie sooner than a little one.

PSYCHOANALYTIC PORTRAIT OF ADOLF HITLER'S METHODS PUT TOGETHER FOR OSS, 1943, Dr. Walter C. Langer, *The Mind of Hitler,* 1972

No leisure, no pleasure, just work.

LORD THOMSON OF FLEET, obituary in *New York Times,* Aug. 5, 1976

When I was a kid in the Midwest I got straight A's in school, and I spent 13 years on the psychiatrist's couch paying for it.

WALLY COX, obituary in *Newsweek,* Feb. 26, 1973

MALE CHAUVINISM

Women when they are in power are much harsher than men. Much more cruel. Much more bloodthirsty. I'm quoting facts, not opinions.

MOHAMMED RIZA PAHLEVI, interview in Rizzoli Press Service—Europo, Dec. 1973

The traits that compose the core of the female personality are feminine narcissism, masochism and passivity.

DR. J. ROBERT WILLSON, *Obstetrics and Gynecology,* 1971

I have come across some women in analytic practice who lacked the faculty of being catty. They were either emotionally perverted, masochistic, homosexual, or neurotic.

THEODOR REIK, obituary in *New York Times,* Jan. 1, 1970

I like girls, but they're different from us. They're always trying to get something in exchange.

ROBERTO GOMEZ, student, quoted in Osvaldo A. Quijada Cerda, *Sexual Behavior in Mexico,* 1977

I fired my female employees because they weren't beautiful any more.

TAIJI KAWATE, Japanese broadcasting executive, quoted in *Newsweek,* Nov. 27, 1972

I want a healthy woman handy to steady my nerves & leave my mind free for real things.

H. G. WELLS, letter to wife, quoted in Gordon N. Ray, *H. G. Wells and Rebecca West,* 1974

Lovemaking grows tedious to me—the emotion has evaporated from it. This is your fault.

> GEORGE BERNARD SHAW, letter to Alice Lockett, Parke-Bernet auction, N.Y.C., May 1972

All animals are sad after making love except the rooster and the human female.

> PAGE SMITH AND CHARLES DANIEL, *The Chicken Book,* 1975

When anyone mentions a cultivated woman to me I imagine her with parsley in her ears.

> SACHA GUITRY, quoted in *New York Times,* Sept. 17, 1972

No Girls Aloud.

> SIGN ON BEDROOM DOOR OF JONATHAN LEVINSON, 8, quoted in *New York Times,* Dec. 20, 1974

MANKIND also see PEOPLE

Man is a puny, slow, awkward, unarmed animal.

> JACOB BRONOWSKI, *The Ascent of Man,* 1974

A dirty animal.

> ROBERT A. McCORMICK, interview in *New York Times,* May 20, 1970

An unfinished animal.

> THEODORE ROSZAK, *The Unfinished Animal,* 1975

The most dangerous animal in the world.

> SIGNS BELOW FULL-LENGTH MIRRORS IN SEVERAL U.S. ZOOS

Human beings are animals with a zest for going beyond the immediate.

> LIONEL TIGER AND ROBIN FOX, *The Imperial Animal,* 1971

In the eye of nature we are just another species in trouble.

> TIGER AND FOX, *The Imperial Animal*

We are an impossibility in an impossible universe.

> RAY BRADBURY, "World Hunger," PBS, Jan. 27, 1975

We are as gods and might as well get good at it.

> STEWART BRAND, *Whole Earth Catalog,* 1969

Man transforms everything he encounters into a tool; and in doing so he himself becomes a tool. But if he asks, a tool for what, there is no answer.
PAUL TILLICH, *Saturday Evening Post,* June 14, 1958

With his laziness, his selfishness, his cowardice, he has also a power to endure and at times a willingness to die for distant and abstract ideas.
WALTER LIPPMANN, obituary in *Newsweek,* Dec. 13, 1974

We know more about the atom than about ourselves, and the consequences are everywhere to be seen.
CARL KAYSEN, quoted in *Time,* Mar. 19, 1973

If man goes through the present stage of the universe, it will be because he has discovered himself.
R. BUCKMINSTER FULLER, interview in *New York Post,* Apr. 26, 1971

MARKETING also see MERCHANDISING; SALESMEN/SELLING; SUPERMARKETS

I once made a design for Zenith, and they turned it down because it was a design that would not go out of fashion. They asked, "What will we do next year?"
ISAMU NOGUCHI, interview in *Newsweek,* Apr. 29, 1968

In a consumer society, the best product you can manufacture is one that must be replaced immediately. Like munitions. . . . You make a bomb and sell it to the government. They . . . *blow it up.* . . . They have to come right back to you and buy another one.
GENE LEES, *True,* Feb. 1969

The armpit had its moment of glory, and the toes, with their athlete's foot. . . . We went through wrinkles, we went through diets. . . . We conquered hemorrhoids. So the businessmen sat back and said, "What's left?" And some smart guy said, "The vagina." . . . Today the vagina, tomorrow the world.
JERRY DELLA FEMINA, *From Those Wonderful Folks Who Gave You Pearl Harbor,* 1970

One billion toothbrushes and two billion armpits.
MARKETING MAN ON THE CHINA POTENTIAL, quoted in *Newsweek,* Feb. 5, 1979

MARRIAGE also see ADULTERY; DIVORCE

There are no successful marriages. There are only those that are succeeding—or failing.
DR. WELLS GOODRICH, *Redbook*, Dec. 1968

Marriage isn't a 50–50 proposition very often. It's more like 100–0 one moment and 0–100 the next.
BILLIE JEAN KING, *Billie Jean*, 1974

The perfect mate, despite what "Cosmopolitan" says, does not exist, no matter how many of those tests you take.
SUZANNE BRITT JORDAN, *Newsweek*, June 11, 1979

Marriage is the hell of false expectations, where both partners, expecting to be loved, defined and supported, abdicate responsibility for themselves and accuse the other of taking away freedom.
KATHRIN PERUTZ, *Marriage Is Hell*, 1972

We would have broken up except for the children. Who were the children? Well, she and I were.
MORT SAHL, *Heartland*, 1976

Thinking your married friends have it made is the same as thinking your single friends have it made.
MARCIA SELIGSON, MORT GERBERG AND AVERY CORMAN, *The Everything in the World That's the Same as Something Else Book*, 1970

There's nothing worse than solitude, growing old without a shoulder to lean on. Marry, marry—even if he's fat and boring.
GABRIELLE CHANEL

MARRIAGE, SECOND also see DIVORCE

The first time you buy a house you see how pretty the paint is and buy it. The second time you look to see if the basement has termites. It's the same with men.
LUPE VELEZ, quoted in *Women, Women, Women*, Leta W. Clark, ed., 1977

People enter second marriages as lemmings head for the sea.
LESLIE ALDRIDGE WESTOFF, *New York Times*, Aug. 10, 1975

MASS TRANSIT see SUBWAYS; TRANSPORTATION

MATHEMATICS

Mathematics is the language of size.
> LANCELOT HOGBEN, *Mathematics for the Million*, 1936

Mathematics is what the world is when we subtract our own perceptions.
> DON DELILLO, *Rainer's Star*, 1976

Mathematics goes along behind physics, making respectable what the physicists find sensible.
> G. S. WATSON, quoted in *Princeton Alumni Weekly*, Nov. 13, 1973

Spurious moral grandeur is generally attached to any formulation computed to a large number of decimal places.
> DAVID BERLINSKI, *On Systems Analysis*, 1976

I never could make out what those damned dots meant.
> LORD RANDOLPH CHURCHILL, Chancellor of the Exchequer, on decimals, 1866, quoted in Winston Churchill, *Lord Randolph Churchill*, 1906

When you are dissatisfied and would like to go back to youth, think of algebra.
> GENE YASENAK, *Successful Farming*, from *Quote*, Oct. 2, 1966

"X" is almost always eleven, and "y" is almost always nine.
> CHARLES SCHULZ, *Peanuts*, Feb. 8, 1971

Since the mathematicians have attacked the relativity theory, I myself no longer understand it.
> ALBERT EINSTEIN, quoted in Ronald W. Clark, *Einstein*, 1972

MEDICAL CARE also see DOCTORS; HEALTH; HOSPITALS; SICKNESS

It should be the function of medicine to help people die young as late in life as possible.
> DR. ERNST WYNDER, speech at American Health Foundation symposium, N.Y.C., Sept. 29, 1975

The truth is that medical care today goes where the money is.
Dr. Michael DeBakey, *Quote,* July 26, 1970

Most people think that medical care is good for you. The fact is that some medical care is good for you, a great deal is irrelevant and, unfortunately, some of it is harmful.
Dr. Lester Breslow, quoted in *Newsweek,* Dec. 23, 1974

THE MEDITATION KICK also see ZEN

America's neo-Oriental county fair.
Harvey Cox, *Turning East,* 1977

Many of these imported practices are as un-Oriental as a carry-out bucket of chop suey in a Minneapolis diner.
Francine du Plessix Gray, *New York Times,* Dec. 25, 1977

TM is the . . . McDonald's of the meditation business . . . a relatively low fixed price, a standard item, and increasing numbers of franchises, or outlets.
"Adam Smith" (George Goodman), *Powers of Mind,* 1975

Change-your-life-in-a-weekend sessions that feature a little applied fascism and sound like Grossinger's ads written by Hermann Hesse.
Richard R. Lingeman on est, *New York Times,* Nov. 8, 1976

THE MELTING POT

The bleaching of America.
Irving Howe, quoted in *Newsweek,* July 4, 1977

It takes two or three generations to get over the scars, the mutations and the damage to personality from immigration.
James T. Farrell, speech at City College, N.Y., conference, Apr. 12, 1972

The third generation remembers what the second generation would like to forget—his ethnic identity.
Paul Mundy, quoted in *New York Times,* Nov. 27, 1970

MEMORY also see HINDSIGHT; NOSTALGIA; THE PAST

Of all liars, the smoothest and most convincing is memory.
ANONYMOUS

When I was younger I could remember anything whether it happened or not.
MARK TWAIN, Twain Papers, Vassar College

Much of what the mind stores up is the rubbish of experience.
PETER QUENNELL, *The Marble Foot,* 1977

My mind is like a tape recorder with one button—Erase.
ANDY WARHOL, *The Philosophy of Andy Warhol (from A to B and Back Again),* 1975

MEN also see WOMEN

A man must be potent and orgasmic to ensure the future of the race. A woman need only be available.
WILLIAM H. MASTERS AND VIRGINIA E. JOHNSON, *McCall's,* May 1970

An erection at will is the moral equivalent of a valid credit card.
ALEX COMFORT, *New York Times,* Mar. 12, 1978

Men think they know a woman if they've seen her naked.
ALAIN TANNER AND JOHN BERGER, *The Middle of the World* (film), 1978

What have Hemingway and Hefner and Bogart and (even) John Kennedy and Charles Atlas and the sins of our fathers before them done to our males that they continue to labor under their own ghostly machismo?—which must be the loneliest, most fragile state in the world, this worship of form without content.
CYNTHIA BUCHANAN, *New York Times,* Feb. 9, 1972

Males have made asses of themselves writing about the female sexual experience.
WILLIAM H. MASTERS, quoted in *Newsweek,* May 5, 1975

Watch out for men who have mothers.
LAURA SHAPIRO, *Ms.,* Apr. 1978

MERCHANDISING also see MARKETING; SALESMEN/SELLING; SUPERMARKETS

It is our job to make women unhappy with what they have.
> B. EARL PUCKETT, president, Allied Stores, obituary in *Newsweek*, Feb. 23, 1976

The public doesn't know what it wants. We offer beautiful things that we like. Anyone who disagrees with our taste is free to go elsewhere.
> WALTER HOVING, chairman, Tiffany & Co., quoted in *Wall Street Journal*, Dec. 24, 1968

Next to the American corpse, the American bride is the hottest thing in today's merchandising market.
> KITTY HANSON, *For Richer, For Poorer*, 1968

Closed Until We Open.
> SIGN ON BICYCLE SHOP, Szcecin, Poland, 1970

Customers Giving Orders Will Be Swiftly Executed.
> SIGN ON TAILOR SHOP, Kowloon, Hong Kong, quoted in Leo Rosten, *The 3:10 to Anywhere*, 1976

MIDDLE AGE also see AGING; OLD AGE

It begins at that precise moment when you realize that all you had thought of as preparation was, in fact, fulfillment, while all you had anticipated as fulfillment is likely to turn out as merely more of the same.
> *Unitarian Universalist Register-Leader*, Mar. 1967

You have to pass 40 to know what not to hope for.
> WEBSTER SCHOTT, *New York Times*, Sept. 12, 1976

The only people who can't enjoy middle age are those who wear themselves out aping the young.
> HAL BOYLE'S COLUMN, Aug. 26, 1969

You no longer spend your life hurrying around the corner for something which is never there.
> REX HARRISON, *Quote*, Sept. 25, 1966

You all of a sudden realize that you are being ruled by people you went to high school with. You all of a sudden catch on that life is nothing *but* high school . . . class officers, cheer-leaders, and all.
KURT VONNEGUT, *Our Time Is Now,* John Birmingham, ed., 1970

A Midlife Crisis is a lot like the Army, only the food is better.
GERALD NACHMAN, *Playing House,* 1978

MIDDLE EAST also see ISRAEL/ISRAELIS

If God is dead, he died trying to solve the dilemma of the Middle East.
I. F. STONE, *Polemics and Prophecies,* 1971

Jews and Muslims can live, and have lived, harmoniously together—particularly if there are barbarous and bloodthirsty Christians somewhere near.
C. P. SNOW, speech at New York School of Hebrew Union College–Jewish Institute of Religion, Mar. 31, 1969

The Egyptians are unstable and we're neurotic. It won't be an easy co-existence.
ZEEV SCHIFF, Israeli newsman, quoted in *Newsweek,* Feb. 6, 1978

MINING see CONSERVATION: MINING

MODERN TIMES also see CENTURY: TWENTIETH; CIVILIZATION; DECADES; TECHNOLOGY

We are living and seeing one of those great turning points in history when a whole era dissolves and disappears.
JACQUES BARZUN, lecture at Columbia University, Jan. 29, 1973

Modern man . . . strides about the globe in scientific splendor, matter in one hand, energy in the other, proclaiming his conquest of the elements. But once back from the campaign, he hasn't the faintest idea of what to do with all this technological plunder.
VAN CLEVE MORRIS, *Existentialism in Education,* 1966

It is like the story of Jack who marveled at his unexpected beanstalk only to glimpse, as he neared the top, the ominous form of a disturbed giant.
RICHARD N. GOODWIN, *The American Condition,* 1974

The modern urban-industrial society is based on a series of radical disconnections between body and soul, husband and wife, marriage and community, community and earth. At each of these points of disconnection the collaboration of corporation, government, and experts sets up a profit-making enterprise that results in the further dismemberment and impoverishment of the Creation.
WENDELL BERRY, *The Unsettling of America,* 1977

We may go down in history as an elegant technological society which underwent biological disintegration through lack of economic understanding.
DAVID M. GATES, quoted in *This Week in Public Health,* Sept. 19, 1968

We have not had time to learn inside ourselves the things that have happened to us.
JOHN STEINBECK, *America and Americans,* 1966

At the age of 40 these days, an average man's alarm mechanism is shot.
RUSSELL BAKER, quoted in *Business Week,* Oct. 24, 1964

No one will live all his life in the world into which he was born and no one will die in the world in which he worked in his maturity.
MARGARET MEAD, quoted in *Vital Speeches,* Dec. 15, 1969

We're living in a Babylonian society perhaps more Babylonian than Babylon itself. It's what's called a late sensate period.
MAX LERNER, quoted in *Newsweek,* Nov. 13, 1967

The turbulence of the machine is soothed by the consoling hum of a unified society.
JACQUES ELLUL, *The Technological Society,* 1964

Who can really feel comfortable in this culture now except maybe a few guys who are good at mathematics?
THOMAS HART BENTON, interview in *New York Times,* June 9, 1968

Has anyone noticed that we no longer produce a literature of utopia?
DOUGLAS DAVIS, *Newsweek,* June 14, 1976

MONEY also see POVERTY; RICHES

Money is applause.
JACQUELINE SUSANN

To have money is to have time.
ALBERT CAMUS, *A Happy Death,* 1972

Money is a sixth sense which makes it possible for us to enjoy the other five.
RICHARD NEY, "Day at Night," PBS, June 4, 1974

The fuel that keeps the new people moving faster than the speed of worry is money.
WILFRID SHEED, *The Morning After,* 1971

There is something about making money. You can bitch at it and talk about your ego, but make money and it all becomes easy. It even improves your personality.
JOHN M. KING, quoted in *Forbes,* Aug. 15, 1969

That most versatile of all abstractions. . . . Only the poor appreciate the physicality of cash.
KENNETH BAKER, *New York Times,* Feb. 3, 1974

Nobody is a gentleman when big money is involved.
JOHN LEONARD, *New York Times,* July 6, 1976

I figure if somebody's got a dollar, 40 cents of it is mine.
GUY DRAKE, songwriter and hustler, quoted in *Newsweek,* Apr. 13, 1970

I've got all the money I'll ever need if I die by 4 o'clock.
HENNY YOUNGMAN, quoted on "Tomorrow," NBC-TV, Feb. 22, 1977

Because that's where the money is.
ATTRIBUTED TO WILLIE SUTTON ON WHY HE ROBBED BANKS, THOUGH HE DISCLAIMS IT, *Where the Money Was,* 1976

If you want to make money, go where the money is.
> JOSEPH P. KENNEDY, quoted in *New York Herald-Tribune,* Oct. 11, 1964

Money brings some happiness. But, after a certain point, it just brings more money.
> NEIL SIMON, interview in *Newsweek,* Feb. 2, 1970

I have the feeling that in a balanced life one should die penniless. The trick is dismantling.
> ART GARFUNKEL, interview in *Newsweek,* Apr. 3, 1978

MOON also see SUN

Tell me what you feel in your room when the full moon is shining in upon you and your lamp is dying out, and I will tell you how old you are, and I shall know if you are happy.
> HENRI-FRÉDÉRIC AMIEL, *Amiel's Journal,* 1885

It is perhaps of passing interest that man has named two major areas on the moon, "The Sea of Tranquility" and "The Sea of Serenity." He has few such names for places on earth.
> *Kaiser News,* no. 5, 1966

MOONLANDING also see ASTRONAUTS; DECADE: 1960–1969

One small step for a man, one giant leap for mankind.
> NEIL A. ARMSTRONG ON FIRST MOONWALK, July 20, 1969

America audaciously pointed to the center-field bleachers and then hit the ball to the spot.
> GEORGE F. WILL, *Newsweek,* July 23, 1979

Pointless and high spirited.
> JACOB BRONOWSKI ON "The Ascent of Man," PBS, Nov. 16, 1975

Public amusement.
> EDWARD TELLER on "Day at Night," PBS, Dec. 27, 1974

MORNING

To have reason to get up in the morning, it is necessary to possess a guiding principle. A belief of some kind. A bumper sticker, if you will.
JUDITH GUEST, *Ordinary People,* 1976

I arise in the morning torn between a desire to improve, or save, the world and a desire to enjoy, or savor, the world. This makes it hard to plan the day.
E. B. WHITE, interview in *New York Times,* July 11, 1969

Getting out of bed in the morning is an act of false confidence.
JULES FEIFFER, *Hold Me!* (drama), 1963

MOTHERS also see CHILDREN; FAMILY; FATHERS; PARENTS

The commonest fallacy among women is that simply having children makes one a mother—which is as absurd as believing that having a piano makes one a musician.
SYDNEY J. HARRIS, *The Progressive,* May 1967

It is impossible for any woman to love her children 24 hours a day.
DR. MILTON R. SAPIRSTEIN, *Paradoxes of Everyday Life,* 1953

You can't change your mind—you know, and say, this isn't working out, let's sell.
FRAN LEBOWITZ, interview in *Philadelphia Magazine,* Nov. 1978

No mother wants to let go.
ANTHONY BURGESS, lecture at City College, N.Y.C., Sept. 15, 1972

My darling Katya, my heart's blood, straight as a rowan tree, sweet as a cherry, what have I done to you?
SVETLANA ALLILUYEVA, letter, after defecting, to daughter in Soviet Union, *Atlantic Monthly,* June 1967

Which one?
MOTHER OF DWIGHT D. EISENHOWER, 1945, when asked if she was proud of her son, quoted in Doris Faber, *The Presidents' Mothers,* 1978

Dear Mother: I'm all right. Stop worrying about me.
PAPYRUS LETTER OF 17-YEAR-OLD EGYPTIAN GIRL, ca. 2000 B.C., Metropolitan Museum of Art

MOVIES also see ACTORS/ACTING; HOLLYWOOD; SHOW BIZ; THEATER; TV: MOVIES/DRAMA

Movies are just another form of merchandising. We have our factory, which is called a stage. We make a product, we color it, we title it and we ship it out in cans.
CARY GRANT, interview in *Newsweek*, June 3, 1968

They're the most expensive art form ever invented. Leonardo didn't need a studio chief for the money to draw a lower jaw. All he needed was a nickel for a pencil.
MEL BROOKS, interview in *Newsweek*, Feb. 17, 1975

The camera likes some people and the people it likes can't do any wrong.
HOWARD HAWKS, quoted in *Newsweek*, Mar. 6, 1978

Aside from the anonymous obscene phone call, modern technology provides no potentially sneakier way of getting across a punchy message than film-editing.
RICHARD EDER, *New York Times*, Aug. 17, 1975

If my fanny squirms, it's bad. If my fanny doesn't squirm, it's good.
HARRY COHN, Columbia Pictures president, quoted in *New York Times*, Oct. 31, 1971

Imagine, the whole world wired into Harry Cohn's ass.
HERMAN J. MANKIEWICZ, who was fired for this comment, quoted in *New York Times*, Oct. 31, 1971

I think moviegoers should be forewarned that any theater that is peddling oatmeal cookies instead of Jujyfruits is a good bet to be showing a movie with subtitles and a lot of rain in it.
PETE AXTHELM, *Newsweek*, Apr. 10, 1978

I can't ever remember staying for the end of a movie in which the actors wore togas.
JIMMY CANNON, *Nobody Asked Me, But . . .*, Jack and Tom Cannon, eds., 1978

MS. also see WORDS

A syllable which sounds like a bumblebee breaking wind.
> HORTENSE CALISHER, *New York Times,* Sept. 22, 1974

Is the sibilant in Ms. any more disagreeable to the ear than the hiss in Miss?
> CASEY MILLER AND KATE SWIFT, *Words and Women,* 1976

MUSEUMS

Essentially a museum is a collection of objects taken out of context.
> RUSSELL LYNES, *New York Times,* Jan. 1, 1967

It's a place for the people to battle against the blows of technology and the misery of life.
> THOMAS HOVING, interview in *Newsweek,* Apr. 1, 1968

I get tired immediately upon entering a museum.
> LOUIS KAHN, who, among other things, designed them, quoted in *Newsweek,* Apr. 1, 1968

MUSIC

Music is "Ordered Sound."
> HAROLD SAMUEL, *The Mystery of Music,* Walter E. Koons, ed., 1977

Music is the most expensive of all noises.
> JOSEF HOFMANN, *The Mystery of Music,* Walter E. Koons, ed., 1977

Every kind of music is good, except the boring kind.
> GIOACCHINO ROSSINI, quoted in *Image,* July 1973

If I had to choose between music and sex, I would pause a long time.
> DONALD BARTHELME, interview in *New York Post,* Dec. 13, 1975

Actually I love it more than myself—but it is vastly more lovable.
> GEORGE SZELL, obituary in *Newsweek,* Aug. 10, 1970

To see itself through, music must have either idea or magic. The best has both. Music with neither dies young, though sometimes rich.
> NED ROREM, *New York Times,* Aug. 29, 1971

Everyone wants to ride around in the newest automobile and listen to the oldest music. They want their heads in the seventeenth century and their behinds in the twentieth.
EDGARD VARÈSE, quoted in *Newsweek,* Dec. 24, 1973

We must remember, Mozart and Beethoven didn't hear all of the sounds we hear. They never heard the sound of a motor car starting, running, grinding, stopping. They never heard a telephone ring, or an airplane roar.
GREGOR PIATIGORSKY ON MODERN MUSIC, interview at City University of New York Oral History Project, Apr. 1975

MUSIC: BLUES

How many things can you do with a knife? You can cut fish, you can cut your toenails. I seen men shave with it, you can eat beans with it, you can kill a man. There. You name five things you can do with a knife, you got five verses. You got yourself a blues.
BIG BILL BROONZY, quoted in Studs Terkel, *Talking to Myself,* 1977

White and black are completely different things. To really sing the blues, you have to pay your dues.
OLIVER KILLENS, quoted in *Newsweek,* June 16, 1970

Yes. I, too, have said that I would exchange all the blues to save one starving child. I was wrong, not only because the exchange is not in my power, but also because this singing of the Lord's song in so strange a land has saved more children than anyone will ever know.
JAMES BALDWIN, *New York Times,* Oct. 16, 1977

MUSIC: COMPOSERS

Essentially, we are a breed of men and women concerned with the arrangement of the same seven notes.
RICHARD RODGERS, foreword, Robert Kimball and Alfred Simon, *The Gershwins,* 1973

We all know how to get a hand at the end of a piece by making a loud noise with a big drum.
AARON COPLAND, interview in *Newsweek,* Nov. 23, 1972

I write music with an exclamation point!
RICHARD WAGNER, quoted in *Music Educators' Journal,* Oct. 1969

MUSIC: CONDUCTING

Tall or short, conductors must give unmistakable signals to the orchestra, not choreography to the audience.
GEORGE SZELL, obituary in *Newsweek,* Aug. 10, 1970

If you want to please only the critics, don't play too loud, too soft, too fast, too slow.
ARTURO TOSCANINI, quoted in *Newsweek,* Jan. 23, 1978

Never, under any circumstances, *never* look at the brass.
RICHARD STRAUSS, quoted in *New York Times*, June 9, 1968

The members of major orchestras never think highly of conductors, unless they are long dead.
HAROLD C. SCHONBERG, *New York Times,* May 15, 1977

MUSIC: DISCO

Disco is like a musical iron lung for a culture in respiratory distress.
JACK KROLL, *Newsweek,* Dec. 25, 1978

It's a '70s sedative: music to look in the mirror by.
BILLY JOEL, interview in *Newsweek,* Dec. 11, 1978

We're in a period of the McDonald's of music.
MELBA MOORE, quoted in *Newsweek,* Apr. 2, 1979

MUSIC: FOLK

In this country, at any rate, real folk music long ago went to Nashville and left no known survivors.
DONAL HENAHAN, *New York Times,* May 8, 1977

All music is folk music. I ain't never heard no horse sing.
LOUIS ARMSTRONG, obituary in *New York Times,* Aug. 7, 1971

MUSIC: JAZZ

It's an art of the city.
STEWART DAVIS, quoted in Brian O'Doherty, *American Masters,* 1973

If you don't know what it is, don't mess with it.
ATTRIBUTED TO FATS WALLER

What do you think we were doing up there—kidding?
DIZZY GILLESPIE WHEN ASKED IF HE ALSO PLAYED SERIOUS MUSIC, interview in *New York Post*, July 1, 1975

We all go *do, re, me,* but you got to find the other notes for yourself.
LOUIS ARMSTRONG, interview in *Reader's Digest,* Dec. 1971

I would like to play for audiences who are not using my music to stimulate their sex organs.
ORNETTE COLEMAN, interview in *Newsweek,* Dec. 12, 1966

Historians in the future, in my opinion, will congratulate us on very little other than our clowning and our jazz.
KURT VONNEGUT, introduction to Bob Elliott and Ray Goulding, *Write If You Get Work,* 1975

MUSIC: OPERA

No good opera plot can be sensible, for people do not sing when they are feeling sensible.
W. H. AUDEN, quoted in Mona McCormick, *Who-What-When-Where,* 1971

Singers never look at each other until the curtain call.
PETER HALL, *Glyndebourne Festival Program,* 1972

Their gestures are planned for a stage with a 58-foot opening.
VIRGIL THOMSON, quoted in *New York Times,* Nov. 10, 1968

No opera manager is known for saving money. He's known for great performances. Bankers are known for saving money.
RUDOLF BING, interview in *Newsweek,* May 1, 1972

When the Latin mass and grand opera were reduced to English, both our sins and our passions seemed smaller. . . . If the romantic soul is to operate, a dash of voodoo is needed.
JOE FLAHERTY, *New York Times,* June 27, 1976

MUSIC: RAGTIME

Basically it is a formation, an organization of folk melodies and musical techniques into a brief and fairly simple quadrille-like structure.
WILLIAM J. SCHAFER AND JOHANNES RIEDEL, *The Art of Ragtime,* 1973

Syncopated melody over a regularly accented rhythmic accompaniment.
GUNTHER SCHULLER, quoted in *New York Times,* Mar. 3, 1974

Notice: Do not play this piece fast. Ragtime is never to be played fast.
SURPRINT ON ORIGINAL SHEET MUSIC FOR SCOTT JOPLIN'S PIANO RAGS

It is artistically and morally depressing and should be suppressed by press and pulpit.
Musical Courier, 1899

MUSIC: ROCK

Rock 'n' roll is about sex.
ELVIS COSTELLO, interview in *Newsweek,* May 8, 1978

Clean soap-bubble simplicity.
NED ROREM, *New York Times,* Aug. 29, 1971

They seem to want to suppress all competitive life.
DAVID COURT ON THE NOISE, *New York Times,* Nov. 29, 1970

There's one advantage to the music the younger generation goes for today; nobody can whistle it.
GLORIA PITZER, *Quote,* Jan. 1, 1978

MUSIC: SINGERS

Every time the curtain rises their lives are at stake.
RUDOLF BING, interview in *Newsweek,* May 1, 1972

Am I afraid of high notes? Of course I am afraid! What sane man is not?
LUCIANO PAVAROTTI, interview in *Thirteen,* PBS, Feb. 1978

They have a disease of the throat.
RUDOLF BING ON SINGERS, interview in *Newsweek*, May 1, 1972

The vibrations of high notes beating frequently on a singer's brain make him stupid.
ARTURO TOSCANINI ON TENORS, quoted in *Newsweek*, Mar. 15, 1976

It's a very athletic profession. You need tremendously strong back and stomach muscles.
MARILYN HORNE, interview in *New York Post*, Apr. 17, 1976

Madame, she doesn't sing with her ankles.
ATTRIBUTED TO COL. CREIGHTON WEBB, WHEN WOMAN SAID OF GERAL-DINE FARRAR, "MY AREN'T HER ANKLES BIG."

MUSICIANS

I'm in a profession, like law.
ALEXIS WEISSENBERG, interview in *Newsweek*, Nov. 7, 1977

Learning to perform on stage is really learning to live comfortably with fear.
ISAAC STERN, "Dick Cavett Show," PBS, Jan. 11, 1979

Musicians are ordinarily the least sophisticated of political animals, perhaps because for so many of their formative years they are shut up in practice rooms communicating with the dead.
DONAL HENAHAN, *New York Times*, June 14, 1970

String players often take on the vocal level of their instruments—violinists have high-pitched voices, cellists low-pitched voices, and violists somewhere in between.
HENRI TEMIANKA, *Facing the Music*, 1973

Politicians are among our worst musicians. And when they become President, they are at their very worst. . . . Doctors are better jazz musicians than lawyers. Lawyers' minds are more like CPA's. They're bookish. Doctors are more romantic.
LEN LIEBER ON AMATEUR MUSICIANS, interview in *New York Times*, May 25, 1975

MYTHS

A myth is a religion in which no one any longer believes.
James K. Feibleman, *Understanding Philosophy*, 1973

Myths are public dreams. Dreams are private myths.
Joseph Campbell, quoted in *Time*, Jan. 17, 1972

Gossip grown old.
R. P. Blackmur, *Language as Gesture*, 1952

NAKEDNESS

The body of someone we love is not altogether naked, but clothed and framed in our feelings.
Anatole Broyard, *New York Times*, July 4, 1979

A mass of naked figures does not move us to empathy, but to disillusion and dismay.
Lord Kenneth Clark, *The Nude*, 1972

NAMES

Your name begins with a caress and ends with the crack of a whip.
Jean Cocteau to Marlene Dietrich, quoted in Charles Higham, *Marlene*, 1977

I can't remember the last time anybody called me Francis. I'll have to think about that.
Frankie De Paula, rough-and-tumble light heavyweight contender, christened Francis, quoted in *New York Times*, Jan. 19, 1969

No one ever sat on her beulah.
Fanny Hurst wishing her mother had named her that, obituary in *New York Times*, Feb. 24, 1968

Till I was 13, I thought my name was "Shut Up."
Joe Namath, *I Can't Wait Until Tomorrow*, 1969

One 1950's college classmate of mine who made the mistake of naming his son James III has lived to see that child change his entire name to "Yossarian"—or, more informally, "Yo-yo."
JAMES C. THOMSON, *New York Times*, Sept. 12, 1976

NATURE also see **CONSERVATION/CONSERVATIONISTS; EARTH**

In nature there are neither rewards nor punishments—there are consequences.
ROBERT C. INGERSOLL, *Quote*, July 19, 1970

Nature is what she is—amoral and persistent.
STEPHEN JAY GOULD, *New York Times*, May 6, 1979

We seldom see the bones of pain that hang beyond the green summer day. The woods and fields and gardens are places of endless stabbing, impaling, squashing and mangling. We see only what floats to the surface: the colour, the song, the nesting, and the feeding. I do not think we could bear a clear vision of the animal world.
J. A. BAKER, *The Hill of Summer*, 1969

I do not know of a flowering plant that tastes good and is poisonous. Nature is not out to get you.
EUELL GIBBONS, obituary in *Newsweek*, Jan. 12, 1976

NEUROSIS/NEUROTICS

The necessary equipment man has for dealing with his civilized surroundings.
SIGMUND FREUD, quoted in *Wall Street Journal*, Nov. 6, 1974

We're all controlled neurotics.
HARRY REASONER, interview in *TV Guide*, Mar. 20, 1971

What's the point of being "adjusted"? You'll just gurgle along like Elsie the Cow.
MAURICE SAMUEL, in Mark Van Doren and Maurice Samuel, *The Book of Praise*, 1975

I have all the women's ills. All I lack is the uterus.
GIOACCHINO ROSSINI, quoted in *New York Times*, Mar. 17, 1968

I'd like everyone to spend a little time each day thinking about my problems.
STANLEY SIEGEL, quoted in *Newsweek,* Aug. 8, 1977

In my day we called that hysterics, and naughtiness, and we knew exactly how to deal with it.
DOROTHY L. SAYERS, *Clouds of Witness,* 1931

I prefer neurotic people. I like to hear rumblings beneath the surface.
STEPHEN SONDHEIM, interview in *Newsweek,* Apr. 23, 1973

NEW also see OLD

Every new idea is obscure at first. It is or it wouldn't be new.
ROBERT IRWIN, interview in *Newsweek,* Dec. 29, 1976

The pursuit of novelty is one of the least original and most meretricious of aesthetic strategies.
STANLEY KUNITZ, *A Kind of Order, A Kind of Folly,* 1975

The new and bold can also be crappy.
WHITE HOUSE STAFFER, quoted in *Newsweek,* Aug. 11, 1975

NEWS/NEWSPAPERS also see COLUMNISTS; TV: NEWS

News is what someone somewhere wants, everything else is advertising.
LORD NORTHCLIFFE, quoted in *Columbia Journalism Review,* Jan.–Feb. 1972

A first draft of history.
ELIZABETH DREW, *Washington Journal,* 1975

The truth, just as approximate as we can make it.
ERIC SEVAREID, dedicating Edward R. Murrow Park, Washington, Apr. 27, 1979

The front page is a paper's most precious commodity. It helps set the nation's agenda.
JONATHAN POWER, *International Herald Tribune* (Paris), Oct. 1975

When a reporter sits down at the typewriter, he's nobody's friend.
THEODORE H. WHITE, interview in *Newsweek,* Oct. 23, 1972

An old editor once told me to walk down the middle of the street and shoot windows out on both sides.
PETER LISAGOR

I don't like to hurt people. I really don't like it at all. But in order to get a red light at the intersection, you sometimes have to have an accident.
JACK ANDERSON, interview in *Newsweek,* Mar. 3, 1972

I am reading it more and enjoying it less.
JOHN F. KENNEDY ON THE PRESS, quoted in *Columbia Journalism Review,* Winter 1969–1970

The newspaper business is the only enterprise in the world where a man is supposed to become an expert on any conceivable subject between 1 o'clock in the afternoon and a 6 P.M. deadline.
ROBERT S. BIRD, obituary in *New York Times,* Feb. 19, 1970

I think the press has a lot of problems. One of them being that the first 20 stories written about a public figure set the tone for the next 2,000 and it is almost impossible to reverse it.
CHARLES W. COLSON, interview in *New York Times,* July 7, 1974

Hastiness and superficiality are the psychic diseases of the twentieth century, and more than anywhere else this disease is reflected in the press.
ALEKSANDR SOLZHENITSYN, speech at Harvard University commencement, June 7, 1978

One Englishman is a story. Ten Frenchmen is a story. One hundred Germans is a story. One thousand Indians is a story. Nothing ever happens in Chile.
NOTICE IN LONDON NEWSROOM, quoted in *International Herald Tribune* (Paris), Oct. 1975

While other corporations economize on pencils and paper clips, the *Times* saves money on chairs.
WILL WENG, *New York Times* puzzle editor, who in 47 years "never had a decent place to sit," *New York Times,* Feb. 27, 1977

A lot of girls go to journalism school because of Robert Redford, but I tell them newsrooms are much fuller of Dustin Hoffmans.
BARBARA BRUNDAGE COLEGRAVE, speech at Columbia Journalism School, Nov. 1977

NEW YORK

Skyscraper National Park.
KURT VONNEGUT, *Slapstick,* 1976

The nation's thyroid gland.
CHRISTOPHER MORLEY, quoted in *New York Times,* Mar. 2, 1970

The insecurity center of America.
JOHN WEITZ AND EVERETT MAHLIN, *Man in Charge,* 1974

The city of right angles and tough, damaged people.
PETE HAMILL, *New York Daily News,* Nov. 15, 1978

Listen to it roar.
DAMON RUNYON, quoted in *Reader's Digest,* Aug. 1968

New York is a city where everyone mutinies but no one deserts.
HARRY HERSHFIELD, obituary in *New York Post,* Dec. 16, 1974

There's no room for amateurs, even in crossing the streets.
GEORGE SEGAL, interview in *Newsweek,* Dec. 14, 1972

Robinson Crusoe, the self-sufficient man, could not have lived in New York City.
WALTER LIPPMANN, *Newsweek,* Feb. 26, 1968

The thing I can't tell is whether cab drivers yield to each other out of fear or respect.
NEW YORK POLICEMAN, quoted in *New York Times,* Mar. 10, 1968

A car is useless in New York, essential everywhere else. The same with good manners.
MIGNON McLAUGHLIN, *The Second Neurotic's Notebook,* 1966

If you are confused ask somebody. New Yorkers are very helpful. However, the first person you ask will give you the wrong answer. So ask loudly enough that others will overhear and make corrections. New Yorkers love to correct each other.
GEORGE WELLER, note on subway map he designed and published, 1977

This city is the size of a country but it has been operated like a candy store.
JOEL HARNETT, speech to City Club of N.Y., May 7, 1976

Prostitution is the only business that isn't leaving the city.
ROY GOODMAN, New York state senator, speech to N.Y. Press Club,
Oct. 24, 1976

Africa, for New Yorkers, begins at East Orange.
RAYMOND A. SOKOLOV, *New York Times,* Feb. 14, 1971

I have withdrawal symptoms at picnics on Long Island.
JOE FLAHERTY, *New York Times,* July 25, 1971

New York is where I *have* to be. I wish I knew why.
SECRETARY, quoted in Jack Olsen, *The Girls in the Office,* 1972

This is good-bye, God—we're moving to New York.
CHILD'S PRAYER

NOBEL PRIZE see AWARDS

NOSTALGIA also see MEMORY; THE PAST

Nostalgia is a seductive liar.
GEORGE W. BALL, *Newsweek,* Mar. 22, 1971

What nostalgia does, exactly, is to "select out."
JOHN ROMANO, *New York Times,* June 3, 1979

After a man makes a visit to his boyhood town he finds that it wasn't
the old home he wanted, but his boyhood.
Arkansas Baptist Newsmagazine, Mar. 5, 1970

Whatever we do in the present instantly becomes the past; we manufacture our nostalgia from moment to moment.
JOSEPH MORGENSTERN, *Newsweek,* Mar. 10, 1969

We are not so much in love with the past as afraid of the present, and
in positive horror of the future.
DONAL HENAHAN, *New York Times,* Aug. 15, 1971

Enjoy yourself. These are the good old days you're going to miss in
1990.
Ohio Grange, June 1969

NOTORIETY also see FAME; GLORY

Men often mistake notoriety for fame, and would rather be remarked for their vices and follies than not to be noticed at all.
HARRY S. TRUMAN, quoted in *New York Times,* Oct. 31, 1965

No one knows who built the temple at Ephesus, but Erostratus is remembered for having burned it down.
JEAN-PAUL SARTRE, quoted in *Newsweek,* Apr. 30, 1973

NUMBERS see MATHEMATICS

OBJECTIVITY

Show me a man who claims he is objective and I'll show you a man with illusions.
HENRY R. LUCE, quoted in *New York Times,* Mar. 1, 1967

If I were objective or if you were objective or if anyone was, he would have to be put away somewhere in an institution because he'd be some sort of vegetable.
DAVID BRINKLEY, "Public Broadcasting Laboratory," PBS, Dec. 2, 1968

OCCULT AND PSYCHIC PHENOMENA

[Psychic experience gives] the sense of bumping into one's self around the corner of time.
Time, Mar. 4, 1974

I've gone into hundreds of [fortune-tellers' parlors], and have been told thousands of things, but nobody ever told me I was a police woman getting ready to arrest her.
NEW YORK CITY DETECTIVE, quoted in Jess Stearn, *The Door to the Future,* 1963

Most chemists are tolerant—even proud—about alchemy, but astronomers take a hard line toward astrology. Possibly chemists would be less broadminded if they were surrounded by rich alchemists and saw columns of alchemical advice in all the daily newspapers.
RICHARD FURNALD SMITH, *Prelude to Science,* 1975

When the Mandans undertake to make it rain, *they never fail to succeed,* for their ceremonies never stop until rain begins to fall.
GEORGE CATLIN, *Letters and Notes on the North American Indians,* 1841

Today we know four types of forces—electromagnetic, gravitational and the strong and weak nuclear forces. But the existence of the latter two was not even suspected before this century. I don't believe that we have found all the forces in nature yet. There is probably at least one more type of energy operating at the physical level which serves to support psychic phenomena.
WILLIAM TILLER, quoted in *Newsweek,* Mar. 4, 1974

This is the kind of thing I wouldn't believe even if it were true.
ANONYMOUS, *Journal of Electrical and Electronic Engineers,* Dec. 1976

OCEAN

Its fumbling, deep-structured roar.
JAMES DICKEY, poem for President Carter's inauguration, "The Strength of Fields," Jan. 21, 1977

The thing itself is dirty, wobbly and wet.
WALLACE STEVENS, quoted in Helen Bevington, *Along Came the Witch,* 1976

If I were a capitalist, I would not hesitate to put my last shirt on the ocean.
ALEKSANDR P. LISITZIN, Soviet geologist, on undersea mineral potential, quoted in *New York Times,* Aug. 10, 1969

OLD also see NEW

If a thing is old, it is a sign that it was fit to live. . . . The guarantee of continuity is quality.
EDDIE RICKENBACKER, quoted in *Kiwanis,* Jan. 1970

One can hope that our habit of equating "old" with obsolete and "new" with best will in time disappear.
VICE ADM. HYMAN RICKOVER ACCEPTING FRANKLIN MEDAL FOR DISTINGUISHED SERVICE, Jan. 16, 1967

OLD AGE also see AGING; MIDDLE AGE; RETIREMENT

It's a damned nuisance, getting older, but it's not exactly depressing.
ELSA LANCHESTER, interview in *New York Daily News*, June 4, 1976

The worst thing about old age is the rapidity with which your periphery sinks.
DOROTHY REED MENDENHALL, quoted in Edmund Wilson, *Upstate*, 1971

It strikes suddenly, like a Kansas cyclone!
ALDEN PALMER, *Fraternal Monitor*, Apr. 1970

You can't even take salt for granted.
GROUCHO MARX, quoted in Charlotte Chandler, *Hello, I Must Be Going*, 1978

The real curse of being old is the ejection from a citizenship traditionally based on work.
ALEX COMFORT, *A Good Age*, 1976

I would willingly stand at street corners, hat in hand, begging passersby to drop their unused minutes into it.
BERNARD BERENSON, quoted on "A Renaissance Life," PBS, Apr. 12, 1971

The denunciation of the young is a necessary part of the mental hygiene of elderly people, and greatly assists the circulation of their blood.
LOGAN PEARSALL SMITH, *Quote*, June 18, 1967

Strangely enough, the aged have a lot in common with youth; they are largely unemployed, introspective and often depressed; their bodies and psyches are in the process of change, and they are heavy users of drugs. If they want to marry, their families tend to disapprove. Both groups are obsessed with time. Youth, however, figures its passage from birth; the aged calculate backward from their death day.
Time, Aug. 3, 1970

There are many virtues in growing old. I am just trying to think of what they are.
> W. SOMERSET MAUGHAM, quoted in Garson Kanin, *Remembering Mr. Maugham,* 1966

As you grow old, your tastes broaden. Your enthusiasm may diminish, but your tolerance expands.
> ROBERT C. ALBERTS, *New York Times,* Nov. 17, 1974

Old persons have nothing to lose by telling the truth.
> MALCOLM COWLEY, *Life,* Dec. 1978

One of the delights known to age, and beyond the grasp of youth, is that of Not Going.
> J. B. PRIESTLEY, *Delight,* 1973

Old age is a special problem for me because I've never been able to shed the mental image I have of myself—a lad of about 19.
> E. B. WHITE, interview in *New York Times,* July 11, 1969

I'm growing old! I'm falling apart! And it's VERY INTERESTING!
> WILLIAM SAROYAN, interview in *New York Times,* May 20, 1979

My doctors have forbidden me to chase women unless they are going downhill.
> OCTOGENARIAN, quoted in *Harvard University Class of 1919 Bulletin,* May 1978

How can I die? I'm *booked.*
> GEORGE BURNS, quoted in Garson Kanin, *It Takes a Long Time to Become Old,* 1978

OPEC also see ENERGY CRISIS

Our neck is stretched over the fence and OPEC has the knife.
> CITIZEN TO JIMMY CARTER, quoted in Carter speech, July 15, 1979

Those fellows are not considerate and they're not malicious. They're just trying to do the best for themselves, squeezing the goose without killing it.
> MORRIS A. ADELMAN, petroleum economist, quoted in *Newsweek,* Jan. 1, 1979

It certainly has demonstrated that economic forces are primary, diplomatic maneuvers are secondary.
GEORGE F. WILL, *Newsweek,* July 9, 1979

Why is it that all oil wells are found in the ass ends of the world?
GARY GOERLICH, tool pusher, quoted in *Newsweek,* Oct. 28, 1974

OPERA see MUSIC: OPERA

ORDER also see DISORDER; PLAN/PLANNERS

Order and harmony arise as an accidental byproduct of individuals pursuing their own self-interests.
STEPHEN JAY GOULD, *New York Times,* May 6, 1979

Perfect order is the forerunner of perfect horror.
CARLOS FUENTES, *Terra Nostra,* 1976

The graveyard is completely ordered because absolutely nothing happens there.
C. J. FRIEDRICH, *An Introduction to Political Theory,* 1967

ORGAN

If you press the right notes at the right time the organ will play itself.
JOHANN SEBASTIAN BACH, quoted in *New York Times,* Jan. 14, 1975

You have to wear narrow shoes or your feet get stuck.
ERROLL GARNER, quoted in Leonard Lyons' column, Oct. 24, 1972

With the introduction of the electronic organ . . . the wonderful old paaah and chaaah became just plain aaah.
E. POWER BIGGS, obituary in *Newsweek,* Mar. 21, 1977

ORGANIZATIONS also see BUREAUCRACY; CORPORATIONS; THE JOB

Today the large organization is lord and master, and most of its employees have been desensitized much as were the medieval peasants who never knew they were serfs.
RALPH NADER, quoted in *Newsweek,* Apr. 17, 1972

All organizations are at least 50 per cent waste—waste people, waste effort, waste space, and waste time.
ROBERT TOWNSEND, *Up the Organization,* 1970

The only things that evolve by themselves in an organization are disorder, friction and malperformance.
PETER DRUCKER, quoted in John J. Tarrant, *Drucker,* 1976

Reorganization is the permanent condition of a vigorous organization.
ROY L. ASH, Executive Reorganization Advisory Council report, Feb. 7, 1971

The last gasp of an expiring organization is to publish a new set of old rules.
Kaiser News, no. 2, 1967

ORGASM also see SEX

Like a slight attack of apoplexy.
DEMOCRITUS, 5th cent. B.C., quoted in James K. Feibleman, *Understanding Philosophy,* 1973

Like the tickling feeling you get inside your nose before you sneeze.
CHILDREN'S SEX EDUCATION MANUAL, quoted in *Newsweek,* Aug. 21, 1972

ORIGINALITY also see IMAGINATION

That romantic disease.
WILLIAM GADDIS, *Recognitions,* 1955

It is better to be good than to be original.
LUDWIG MIES VAN DER ROHE, obituary in *National Observer,* Aug. 25, 1969

PAINTING also see ART: CREATIVE PRODUCT

When we look at a great painting (i.e., a painting uniformly held to be "great") we are seeing the world through a creator's eyes, and we are seeing it as no pair of eyes before in history had regarded the world.
HAROLD C. SCHONBERG, *New York Times,* Feb. 1, 1976

If you could say it in words there'd be no reason to paint.
EDWARD HOPPER

Those trying to explain pictures are as a rule completely mistaken.
PABLO PICASSO, *Picasso on Art,* Dore Ashton, ed., 1972

You know, when you were a little boy, you drew like a man. Now you're a man, you draw like a little boy.
ZERO MOSTEL'S MOTHER ON HIS FIRST ART EXHIBIT, quoted in *National Observer,* May 19, 1969

If it sells, it's art.
FRANK LLOYD, art gallery director, quoted in Lee Seldes, *The Legacy of Mark Rothko,* 1978

PARENTAL GUIDANCE

Son, get up! Every boy in town has a two-hour start on you.
LYNDON B. JOHNSON'S FATHER, quoted in *New York Times,* Jan. 23, 1973

Never get sick, Hubert; there isn't time.
HUBERT H. HUMPHREY'S FATHER, quoted in *New York Times,* July 11, 1969

Always go with people who are smarter than you are—and in your case it won't be difficult.
FRANCIS CARDINAL SPELLMAN'S FATHER, quoted in Stephen Birmingham, *Real Lace,* 1973

Never have partners.
HOWARD HUGHES' FATHER, quoted in Donald L. Bartlett and James B. Steele, *Empire,* 1979

Do not take liberties with a woman whose husband is listening.
ONCHSHESHONQY TO SON, ancient Egypt, Archives, Oriental Institute, University of Chicago

You will do foolish things, but do them with enthusiasm.
COLETTE TO DAUGHTER, quoted in *Women, Women, Women,* Leta W. Clark, ed., 1977

If a man starts a sentence with the word "frankly," you know he's going to lie to you.
STEWART ALSOP'S FATHER, quoted in *Newsweek,* Oct. 15, 1973

You can always be perfectly natural with people of high rank, but with everybody else please behave like an Englishman.
MOZART'S FATHER, quoted in *New York Times,* Aug. 6, 1967

PARENTS also see CHILDREN; FAMILY; FATHERS; MOTHERS

Those two giants.
DR. CLARICE KESTENBAUM, quoted in *New York Times,* July 1, 1977

Parenthood remains the greatest single preserve of the amateur.
ALVIN TOFFLER, *Future Shock,* 1970

Accepting a child's dictation is the equivalent of robbing the child of a parent.
MILDREW NEWMAN AND BERNARD BERKOWITZ, *How to Be Your Own Best Friend,* 1973

The permissive fallacy is that children learn good things from bad experience.
DONALD BARR, *Who Killed Humpty Dumpty?,* 1971

To provide some degree of child training at home requires that both parents and children be there together at the same time.
DR. J. HAROLD SMITH, *Quote,* Jan. 1, 1978

Raising kids is part joy and part guerilla warfare.
EDWARD ASNER, "Raised in Anger," PBS, Jan. 14, 1979

What I pray for this year is not the remission of my sins, but the wit to remember them when they come back to me as my offspring's.
WILLIAM GIBSON, quoted in Thomas J. Cottle, *Time's Children,* 1971

PARIS also see FRANCE/THE FRENCH

I like Paris. They don't talk so much of money, but more of sex.
VERA STRAVINSKY, interview in *New York Times,* May 11, 1969

Any talk about Paris in this moonwalking age is, first and foremost, talk about the motor-car.
FRANÇOIS NOURISSIER, *Cartier-Bresson's France,* 1971

THE PAST also see HINDSIGHT; THE FUTURE; NOSTALGIA; MEMORY

The past is a foreign country; they do things differently there.
L. P. HARTLEY, quoted in *Newsweek,* Apr. 11, 1977

Nothing is as far away as one minute ago.
JIM BISHOP, *Coronet,* June 1968

The past is really the only source of information we have about the future.
FINNISH AMBASSADOR TO U.N. MAX JAKOBSON, quoted in *Foundation News,* Oct. 1971

It is a fallacy now widely current that the dead were less intelligent than we are.
JOHN RUSSELL, *New York Times,* July 18, 1976

PATIENCE

Patience means holding back your inclination to the seven emotions: hate, adoration, joy, anxiety, anger, grief, fear.
JAMES CLAVELL, *Shōgun,* 1975

Patience has its limits. Take it too far and it's cowardice.
GEORGE JACKSON, *Soledad Brother,* 1970

Laziness is often mistaken for patience.
FRENCH PROVERB

PATRONAGE

Patronage is for people who are looking for jobs but not for work.
POLITICAL AXIOM

An occupational hazard of democracy.
MARTIN AND SUSAN TOLCHIN, *To the Victor,* 1971

PEACE also see WAR

The pursuit of peace is complicated because it has to do with people, and nothing in this universe baffles man as much as man himself.
ATTRIBUTED TO ADLAI STEVENSON

There is no way to peace, peace is the way.
A. J. MUSTE, quoted in *Newsweek,* Dec. 25, 1967

If there is ever to be peace in the world, governments will have to agree either to inculcate no dogmas, or all to inculcate the same.
BERTRAND RUSSELL, *The Basic Writings of Bertrand Russell, 1903– 1959,* Lester E. Dennon and Robert E. Egner, eds., 1961

PENTAGON

Puzzle Palace.
NEWSMEN'S TERM, quoted in James W. Canan, *The Superwarriors,* 1975

A log going down the river with 25,000 ants on it, each thinking he's steering.
ASSISTANT SECRETARY OF DEFENSE, quoted in Hank Searls, *Pentagon,* 1971

All War Departments are now Defense Departments. That is part of the double talk of our time.
GEORGE WALD, speech at M.I.T. anti-Vietnam rally, Mar. 4, 1969

The Budget Bureau trembles before the Defense Department, . . . all other agencies tremble before the Budget Bureau.
REP. WILLIAM MOOREHEAD, quoted in William Proxmire, *Report from the Wasteland,* 1970

The welfare program of the rich.
STAUGHTON LYND ON DEFENSE CONTRACTS, *Newsweek,* July 6, 1970

Costs . . . are almost always rounded to the *nearest tenth of a billion dollars.*
C. MERTON TYRRELL, *Pentagon Partners,* 1970

PEOPLE also see MANKIND

Most people are hidden most of the time, their appearances are brief and controlled, their movements secret, the outlines of their lives obscured.
JONATHAN RABAN, *Soft City,* 1974

One thing that has always haunted me about people is that strange absent look of solitude they have when they're walking down the street or just standing around. It's like the ferocious loneliness of the desert.
RAPHAEL SOYER, interview in *Newsweek,* Nov. 13, 1967

People, like Russia, are more attractive from the distance.
EDWARD KUZNETSOV, *Prison Diaries,* 1975

There are two groups of people, those who divide people into two groups and those who don't.
ROBERT BENCHLEY, quoted on "Dick Cavett Show," PBS, Mar. 9, 1978

Whatever you may be sure of, be sure of this, you are dreadfully like other people.
JAMES RUSSELL LOWELL, quoted in *Forbes,* May 1, 1974

PERSECUTION

We have the term "paranoia" for someone who feels he's persecuted when he isn't. But there's no term for someone who doesn't feel persecuted when he really is. And that's much more the normal state of affairs these days.
R. D. LAING, lecture at Tulane University, 1972

Persecution makes people unpleasant. You can't expect people to be charming about it; being hated is apt to make you return the hate.
CHRISTOPHER ISHERWOOD, interview in *New York Post,* Dec. 11, 1976

PHILOSOPHY/ PHILOSOPHERS

All *definite . . .* knowledge belongs to science; all *dogma* as to what surpasses definite knowledge belongs to theology. But between theology and science there is a No Man's Land, exposed to attack from both sides, this No Man's Land is philosophy.
BERTRAND RUSSELL, *A History of Western Philosophy,* 1945

The big task of philosophy amid the new technology is to stand aside and say "however."
ABRAHAM KAPLAN, quoted in *New York Times,* Jan. 12, 1969

It is one of the failures of American philosophy that we confuse education and intelligence as much as we confuse plumbing and civilization.
LOUIS BROMFIELD, quoted in *Good Reading,* Mar. 1969

When critical philosophers point their finger at reality, orthodox "philosophers" study the finger.
BLACKBOARD GRAFFITO, American Philosophical Association meeting, N.Y.C., Dec. 29, 1969

I wanted to be a philosopher, but cheerfulness kept breaking in.
ANONYMOUS

PHOTOGRAPH/PHOTOGRAPHERS

Today everything exists to end in a photograph.
SUSAN SONTAG, *On Photography,* 1977

You can go into all sorts of situations with a camera and people will think they should serve it.
SUSAN SONTAG, interview in *New York Times,* Dec. 18, 1977

Photography is a tool for dealing with things everybody knows about but isn't attending to.
EMMET GOWIN, quoted in *Newsweek,* Oct. 21, 1974

A photographer is able to capture a moment that people can't always see.
HARRY CALLAHAN, interview in *Newsweek,* Dec. 13, 1976

A single photograph found in the ruins of Troy, or in the loot of a Hun, home from sacking Rome, might provoke a rewriting of the fiction of history.
WRIGHT MORRIS, *New York Times,* Nov. 28, 1976

A still photographer is a mechanic, you know. He's not an artist, despite all you read.
EARL OF SNOWDON, interview in *New York Times,* Mar. 16, 1968

I like the word "craftsman." I don't know anything about art.
LEE FRIEDLANDER, interview in *Newsweek,* July 24, 1978

The more gadgets you use, the worse the picture.
FELIX MAN, speech at George Eastman House, Rochester, N.Y., May 13, 1971

I try to be as dumb as the camera. It's an immense discipline.
GARRY WINOGRAND, quoted in *Newsweek,* Nov. 7, 1977

Snapshots show nothing but joy. Year after year of it.
WILLIAM MAXWELL, *Over the River,* 1977

PLAN/PLANNERS also see DISORDER; ORDER

To preplan too thoroughly is to kill life.
PAUL GOODMAN, *Drawing the Line,* Taylor Stoehr, ed., 1977

Merely making proposals takes only a typewriter; making workable proposals takes time.
RICHARD M. NIXON, Legislative Message to Congress, Apr. 1969

A planner can neither improve things nor make them much worse.
GEORGE KONRAD ON URBAN PLANNING, *The City Builder,* 1977

The only military plan that goes according to schedule is a parade.
U.S. GENERAL, Vietnam, quoted in *Newsweek,* Apr. 5, 1971

You've got to be very careful if you don't know where you are going, because you might not get there.
YOGI BERRA, quoted in *Business Week,* Oct. 12, 1974

Who plans the planners?
MARCUS PORCIUS CATO THE ELDER, quoted in *Saturday Review,* July 26, 1975

POKER also see GAMBLERS, GAMBLING

Poker is a game of discipline and management, and the second is really a factor of the first. Beyond that, it is a game of subtle questions and shouted answers that can only be heard by a deaf man. The opening bet is the question. What your opponents do is the answer. If it's loud enough—a big bet—you had better be deaf to the pounding of your heart or you will be misled by it.
CRANDALL ADDINGTON, gambler, interview in *New York Times,* May 19, 1973

The game exemplifies the worst aspects of capitalism that have made our country so great.
> WALTER MATTHAU, quoted in *New York Times,* Mar. 31, 1977

POLICE

The policeman is the little boy who grew up to be what he said he was going to be.
> RAYMOND BURR, quoted in *American Opinion,* Mar. 1968

You can't measure what a patrolman standing on a corner has prevented. There is no product at the end of a policeman's day.
> CHARLES E. MCCARTHY, New York deputy chief inspector, interview in *New York Times,* July 21, 1968

If you aren't in complete control of a situation, anything you do can make it worse.
> HOWARD LEARY, New York police commissioner, quoted in Barry Gottehrer, *The Mayor's Man,* 1975

I'm so used to pressure I'm afraid if it stopped I'd get the bends.
> WALTER E. HEADLEY, Miami police chief, obituary in *New York Times,* Nov. 17, 1968

I'd love to be a policeman here, but I'm not brave enough.
> CHRIS KAY, British constable, training in U.S.A., interview in *New York Times,* May 28, 1972

There's only one Dick Tracy and he's in the funny papers.
> CHICAGO POLICE LIEUTENANT, quoted in *Newsweek,* June 27, 1967

The police can't use clubs or gas or dogs. I suppose they will have to use poison ivy.
> WILLIAM F. BUCKLEY, JR., campaigning for mayor, New York City, 1965

POLITICS: THE CAMPAIGN

From July to November a national candidate is not a living person who wakes up queasy in the morning and gets cramps in the stomach; he is an abstract plaything for the nation, and his hometown is inside a television set.
> LEONARD C. LEWIN, *New York Times,* May 20, 1973

Charge and warn, never offer a concrete solution.
> FRANZ JOSEF STRAUSS, leader, German Christian Social Union, speech at party meeting, Sonthofen, Bavaria, Nov. 1974

Never let the public know all your opinions, but make sure it knows about selected portions of your opponent's views.
> MURRAY CHOTINER TO RICHARD M. NIXON IN HIS FIRST CONGRESSIONAL CAMPAIGN, 1946, quoted in Henry D. Spalding, *The Nixon Nobody Knows,* 1972

If you can't dazzle 'em with brilliance, baffle 'em with bull.
> SLOGAN ON WALL OF STUART SPENCER, campaign manager, 1976

Sometimes at the end of the day when I'm smiling and shaking hands, I want to kick them.
> RICHARD M. NIXON, quoted in Theodore H. White, *The Making of the President, 1968,* 1969

It's shattering to be told your father stinks.
> JULIE NIXON, interview in *New York Times,* Mar. 10, 1969

The best time to listen to a politician is when he's on a stump on a street corner in the rain at night when he's exhausted. Then he doesn't lie.
> THEODORE H. WHITE, interview in *New York Times,* Jan. 2, 1969

I don't want to spend the next two years in Holiday Inns.
> WALTER F. MONDALE, withdrawing from Democratic race for presidential nomination, Nov. 21, 1975

With the money I'm spending I could elect my chauffeur.
> ATTRIBUTED TO JOSEPH P. KENNEDY ON J.F.K.'S ELECTION, Fred Sparks, *National Star,* Sept. 28, 1974

POLITICS: THE ELECTION also see VOTING

Democracy's ceremonial, its feast, its great function, is the election.
> H. G. WELLS, *Democracy Under Revision,* 1927

A circus wrestling match.
> NIKITA S. KHRUSHCHEV, *Khrushchev Remembers,* 1971

Governments lose elections, oppositions don't win them.
> DAVID MARQUAND, quoted in *Newsweek,* Apr. 9, 1979

The men who study groups of white rats in cages might do better to study what happens when groups of bright, egocentric and ambitious—oh, ambitious—people come together to grab for public power in a short scramble to the tape marked Election Day.
RICHARD REEVES, *New York Times*, July 19, 1970

Haldeman and Ehrlichman are gone, but the beast that bore them is always in heat in an election year.
GODFREY HODGSON, *New York Times*, Aug. 14, 1977

You have to get the election certificate before you can be a statesman.
LYNDON B. JOHNSON, quoted in *Newsweek*, Oct. 25, 1971

POLITICS: THE JOB

Politics is the science of who gets what, when and why.
ATTRIBUTED TO SIDNEY HILLMAN

Politics in America is the binding secular religion.
THEODORE H. WHITE, *Breach of Faith*, 1975

Presidential politics is a contest between the 35-yard lines.
BEN WATTENBERG, quoted in *Newsweek*, Nov. 13, 1972

The first law of politics is arithmetic.
MARTIN RYAN HALEY, *Public Relations Journal*, Dec. 1968

Money is the mother's milk of politics.
JESSE UNRUH, quoted in George Thayer, *Who Shakes the Money Tree?*, 1974

The tool of politics (which frequently becomes its objective) is to extract resources from the general taxpayer with minimum offense and to distribute the proceeds among innumerable claimants in such a way as to maximize support at the polls.
JAMES R. SCHLESINGER, *Journal of Law and Economics*, Oct. 1968

Politics is a flexible art; the minute you take a fixed position, you're in trouble.
NORMAN MAILER, interview in *New York Post*, Mar. 15, 1969

If you can't deliver the pie in the sky that you promised, you'd better redefine the pie.
PAUL A. SAMUELSON, *Newsweek*, Jan. 31, 1972

A little vagueness goes a long way in this business.
EDMUND G. BROWN, JR., quoted in *New York Times,* June 6, 1976

There is a thin line between politics and theatricals.
JULIAN BOND, quoted in *Newsweek,* Aug. 16, 1976

Politics is far more complicated than physics.
ALBERT EINSTEIN, quoted in Sir Robert Watson-Watt, *Man's Means to His End,* 1961

Disgusted with politicians, some people from time to time yearn for government without politics. Sometimes, to their dismay, they get it, as in Soviet Russia, Poland and North Korea, where the political process has been abolished.
S. I. HAYAKAWA, quoted in *Newsweek,* Apr. 24, 1978

POLITICS: THE POL also see WASHINGTON, D.C.

They're among the few people in America who still work, live by their wits, have no job security, endure brutal hours, and show great ingenuity even when they're thieves.
RUSSELL BAKER, interview in *New York Times,* Jan. 30, 1972

The typical political leader of the contemporary managerial society is a man of strong will, a high capacity to get himself elected, but no very great conception of what he is going to do when he gets into office.
HENRY A. KISSINGER, quoted in *Newsweek,* July 28, 1969

I know that if one waits for the politician to find a solution, it is almost always the wrong one because politicians, by definition, react to headlines. And that's always treating the symptoms and leaving the basic conditions untouched.
PETER DRUCKER, speech at National Association of Manufacturers marketing conference, Apr. 10, 1969

The impact of immediacy created by TV has placed a premium not on reflection and reason but on the glib answer and the bland statement. The politician is concerned with public relations, not with public principles.
RICHARD B. MORRIS, quoted in *New York Times,* May 5, 1973

The demon of political activity moves public men to speak wistfully about "quiet hours," but one suspects that this wistfulness about the contemplative life is part of a secret formula or incantation to avoid the terrors of sitting still.

> SAUL BELLOW, *New York Times,* Apr. 2, 1978

Good politicians don't make wrong moves. Doing nothing is sometimes better.

> SENATE AIDE, quoted in Penn Kimball, *Bobby Kennedy and the New Politics,* 1968

When attacked, politicians are expected to strike back and to seek friends among the enemies of their enemies.

> *Fortune* EDITORIAL, June 1970

A real politician has to know the right moment to hit an opponent just a bit below the belt.

> KONRAD ADENAUER, quoted in *Newsweek,* Dec. 19, 1966

Every time a school site is bought, a politician goes into the real-estate business.

> FIORELLO LA GUARDIA, quoted in *New York Times,* Jan. 2, 1966

My deepest feeling about politicians is that they are dangerous lunatics to be avoided when possible, and carefully humored: people, above all, to whom one must never tell the truth.

> W. H. AUDEN, *The English Auden,* Edward Mendelson, ed., 1978

Heavens, I'd always be polite to a politician. They are our public servants.

> PHILADELPHIA MATRON, quoted in Stephen Birmingham, *The Right People,* 1968

POLLS also see PUBLIC OPINION; STATISTICS

Polls give some politicians, weaker ones, more information than is good for them, particularly if they can't resist the temptation to follow the 51 per cent of their district who seemed to be against the Bill of Rights between Tuesday and Thursday of last week.

> RICHARD REEVES, *Newsweek,* July 2, 1973

How far would Moses have gone if he had taken a poll in Egypt?

> HARRY S. TRUMAN, quoted in *Show,* Nov. 1964

The only thing I have ever been asked was the age at which I first indulged in oral sex (which, since it was a *Yale Daily News* poll, meant kissing).

PAUL RUDNICK, student, *New York Times,* Sept. 7, 1976

POLLUTION also see CONSERVATION/CONSERVATIONISTS

The air and water grow heavier with the debris of our spectacular civilization.

LYNDON B. JOHNSON, Message to Congress, Jan. 30, 1967

We have broken out of the circle of life, converting its endless cycles into man-made, linear events.

BARRY COMMONER, *The Closing Circle,* 1971

We are presently in the predicament of the Australian who went crazy trying to throw away his old boomerang.

WILLIAM L. SPRINGER, quoted in *Wall Street Journal,* June 29, 1970

Ecological devastation is the excrement, so to speak, of man's power worship.

ERNEST BECKER, *Escape from Evil,* 1975

All of us have opted for environmental damage, albeit unwittingly, by voting for convenience with our dollars.

RUSSELL W. PETERSON, speech to American Association for Advancement of Science, N.Y.C., Jan. 30, 1975

Humans may be in the same plight as a frog placed in a pan of cold water which is very slowly heated. If the rise in temperature is gradual enough he will be boiled without ever knowing what happened to him.

JEROME FRANK, quoted in *University* (Princeton), Winter 1969–1970

A new generation is being raised—with DDT in their fat, carbon monoxide in their systems and lead in their bones. That is technological man.

BARRY COMMONER, quoted in *New York Times,* Aug. 3, 1969

The irony of the matter is that future generations do not have a vote. In effect, we hold their proxies.

CHARLES J. HITCH, *Annual Report,* Resources for the Future, 1976

Once you prime the pump of free enterprise, it doesn't stop where you want it.
> STANLEY K. HATHAWAY, former governor of Wyoming, speech at Green River Chamber of Commerce, Mar. 1975

"Environment" and "safety" are fine objectives, but they have become sacred cows about which it is almost heresy to ask whether the return justifies the cost.
> MILTON FRIEDMAN, Newsweek, Aug. 19, 1974

Environment is one-tenth science and nine-tenths politics.
> BRITISH DELEGATE TO U.N. CONFERENCE ON HUMAN ENVIRONMENT, Stockholm, June 1972

POP CULTURE

Pop is ultimately the point of convergence, where art and entertainment, literature and journalism, sincerity and fraud, engagement and alienation, even art and life, meet and mingle in profound ambiguity.
> ALBERT GOODMAN, Freakshow, 1971

The elite culture is always judged by the best it produces, the pop culture is judged by the worst it produces. Ninety per cent of novels are junk, 90 per cent of films are junk, 90 per cent of Ph.D. theses are junk.
> MAURICE C. HORN, speech to American Studies Association conference, Washington, Sept. 29, 1976

Pop has the capacity to spread like oil from a wrecked tanker. It often befouls, but there the simile must end, since an injection of pop can also invigorate. It has tremendous adaptability.
> JOHN CANADAY, New York Times, Dec. 28, 1969

The lyrics of pop songs are so banal that if you show a spark of intelligence they call you a poet.
> PAUL SIMON, interview in New York Times, Oct. 13, 1968

There are many ways to evade issues, and for the educated classes (the uneducated ones have other devices) pop sociology, pop anthropology and pop history are among the best.
> CLIFFORD GEERTZ, New York Times, Apr. 28, 1968

POPULATION EXPLOSION also see BIRTH CONTROL

The goal of nature is zero population growth, and only man violates that goal.
> JOHN F. EISENBERG, interview in *New York Times*, Mar. 22, 1970

The problem is no longer that with every pair of hands that comes into the world there comes a hungry stomach. Rather it is that, attached to those hands are sharp elbows.
> PAUL A. SAMUELSON, *Newsweek*, June 12, 1967

People are everywhere. Some people say there are too many of us, but no one wants to leave.
> CHARLES SCHULZ, *Peanuts*, Jan. 23, 1971

If the world's population were to maintain its present growth rate for 6,000 years (about the period of recorded history), it would end in a mass of human flesh the periphery of which would be expanding at the speed of light.
> PHILIP M. HAUSER, speech at Albert Einstein College of Medicine commencement, June 1963

It is my observation that the disadvantages of a larger population are seen most vividly by those who were born in an earlier era. Often the current inhabitants see nothing wrong with many of the changes that the older citizens decry.
> ANSLEY J. COALE, speech to Population Society of America, June 1968

Zero Population Growth and Zero Economic Growth occasionally sound like the latter-day equivalent of Lent.
> *Newsweek*, June 12, 1972

Quite without outside interference, time and human nature will probably take care of the population problem. It has taken us barely a century to come down from the twelve-child family to the three-child family.
> HENRY C. WALLICH, *Newsweek*, June 29, 1970

They shout and scream about "standing room only." But we believe in reincarnation, my friend, so don't worry. We'll be back.
> KARAN SINGH, Indian delegate to U.N. Conference on Population, Aug. 1974

PORNOGRAPHY

Pornography is in the groin of the beholder.
CHARLES REMBAR, *The End of Obscenity,* 1968

Words that give me an erection.
BRITISH JUDGE, quoted in William Gass, *On Being Blue,* 1976

Pornography is not in the hands of the child who discovers his sexuality by masturbating, but in the hands of the adult who slaps him.
BERNARDO BERTOLUCCI, interview in *Newsweek,* Feb. 12, 1973

Murder is a crime. Writing about it isn't. Sex is not a crime, but writing about it is. Why?
LARRY FLYNT, quoted in *New York Daily News,* Feb. 9, 1977

I think it quite likely that there is no such thing as good pornography. If it's good, then it's not pornography.
VINCENT CANBY, *New York Times,* June 23, 1974

Pornography . . . is presumably intended to arouse sexual desire and procure solitary orgasms, against which—so far as I know—there has never been any law except that of the scoutmasters.
ANTHONY BURGESS, *New York Times,* Aug. 1, 1973

If the purpose of pornography is to excite sexual desire, it is unnecessary for the young, inconvenient for the middle aged and unseemly for the old.
MALCOLM MUGGERIDGE, quoted in *American Libraries,* Jan. 1970

I would like to suggest that at least on the face of it a stroke by stroke story of copulation is exactly as absurd as a chew by chew account of the consumption of a chicken's wing.
WILLIAM GASS, *On Being Blue,* 1976

Porno film . . . encounters are presented with all the charm of open-heart surgery.
WALTER GOODMAN, *New York Times,* Nov. 23, 1977

It is something that future generations will look back on as we do on things like the death of Little Nell.
GEORGE ORWELL ON MANDATORY SEX IN MODERN FICTION, *The Collected Essays, Journalism and Letters of George Orwell,* Sonia Orwell and Ian Angus, eds., 1968

If porno is your bag, you don't have much of an imagination of your own.
SOL GORDON, *Ten Heavy Facts about Sex* (educational comic book)

POVERTY also see MONEY; RICHES

Student radicals accuse me of organizing the poor for decadent, degenerate, bourgeois, bankrupt, immoral values. But do you know what the poor want? They want a bigger slice of those decadent, degenerate, bourgeois, bankrupt, immoral values.
SAUL ALINSKY

Poor people have more fun than rich people, they say; and I notice it's the rich people who keep saying it.
JACK PAAR, *Three on a Toothbrush,* 1965

Poverty is no disgrace, but there are few disgraces that cause such keen humiliations.
LEONARD MERRICK, *Cynthia,* 1896

It kills love, it debases men and women, it stunts life, it withers the marrow.
CHRISTY BROWN, interview in *Newsweek,* June 8, 1970

POWER

Power is what it's perceived to be.
MARILYN BERGER, "Washington Week in Review," PBS, Dec. 19, 1975

Power means not needing to raise your voice.
GEORGE F. WILL, *Newsweek,* May 16, 1977

It is . . . the ability not to have to please.
ELIZABETH JANEWAY, quoted in *Cosmopolitan,* June 1978

Power is the ultimate aphrodisiac.
HENRY A. KISSINGER, quoted in *New York Times,* Oct. 28, 1973

Power is not a statement over the news media; it has to do with organizing people.
REV. HERBERT DAUGHTRY, sermon, Dec. 26, 1976

Being powerful is like being a lady. If you have to tell people you are, you ain't.
JESSE CARR, quoted in *Newsweek,* Sept. 27, 1976

When you've got them by the balls, their hearts and minds will follow.
CARR, quoted in *Newsweek,* Sept. 27, 1976

If a man can accept a situation in a place of power with the thought that it's only temporary, he comes out all right. But when he thinks that he is the *cause* of the power, that can be his ruination.
HARRY S. TRUMAN, quoted in Merle Miller, *Plain Speaking,* 1974

If it's going to be responsible, it has to be insecure. It has to have something to lose.
RALPH NADER, interview in *New York Times,* Jan. 24, 1971

The lust for power is not rooted in strength but weakness.
ERICH FROMM, quoted in *New York Times,* Oct. 30, 1972

Power! What do we know about it? We don't know anything about it. We have sex education. Why don't we have power education?
REV. JOHN J. MCLAUGHLIN, interview in *New York Times,* June 2, 1974

Never forget the kindness of the honorable men in power.
FROM 400-YEAR CODE OF THE MITSUI FAMILY OF JAPAN, quoted in John G. Roberts, *Mitsui,* 1973

Never forget that as Parks Commissioner you have a weapon possessed by very few people—something which Bobby Kennedy doesn't have, which Cardinal Spellman doesn't have—you have 800 trucks.
THOMAS HOVING, retiring N.Y.C. Parks Commissioner, to his successor, August Heckscher, quoted in August Heckscher, *Alive in the City,* 1974

PREJUDICES also see BELIEF; CONVICTIONS; IDEAS; STEREOTYPES

Most people do not think, they merely rearrange their prejudices.
ANONYMOUS

But I hang onto my prejudices. They are the testicles of my mind.
ERIC HOFFER, *Before the Sabbath,* 1979

PRESIDENTS also see VICE PRESIDENTS

Presidents in general are not lovable, they've had to do too much to get where they are.
WALTER LIPPMANN, quoted in *New York Times,* Sept. 24, 1974

A new President proceeds on the assumption "Before me, the deluge."
W. AVERELL HARRIMAN, quoted in Leonard Lyons' column, Nov. 12, 1968

Presidents deal with power. Power is real. Power is not pretty.
LYNDON B. JOHNSON

One of the essential attributes of the Presidency is the power to make people fear you.
SUB-CABINET OFFICER, quoted in *Newsweek,* Aug. 7, 1978

Who knows what Napoleonic postures our Presidents take in front of White House mirrors.
ROBERT SHERRILL, *New York Times,* Jan. 18, 1976

You know, this is a damned good job.
JOHN F. KENNEDY, quoted by George F. McGovern, ABC-TV, Aug. 19, 1976

Presidents quickly realize that while a single act might destroy the world they live in, no one single decision can make life suddenly better or can turn history around for the good.
LYNDON B. JOHNSON, obituary in *Time,* Feb. 5, 1973

Presidents since Franklin D. Roosevelt have seen their task as deciding between painful choices or, to put the matter another way, as one of distributing pain.
MARCUS G. RASKIN, *Notes on the Old System,* 1974

By definition, a President's economic projections are more optimistic than others'.
WHITE HOUSE AIDE, quoted in *New Yorker,* Jan. 15, 1979

The man who bats most often has the opportunity to hit the most foul balls—the President has a chance to bat every day.
LYNDON B. JOHNSON, quoted in *Newsweek,* Feb. 26, 1968

I have found in my short term of office that it's very easy to get advice and very hard to get consent.
RICHARD M. NIXON ON SENATE-PRESIDENTIAL RELATIONS, news conference, June 19, 1969

In a romantic nation such as this, where soap opera, Mother's Day and June Allyson were invented, the power to inspire, not the power to command, is the most potent tool of Presidential leadership.
MEL ELFIN, *Newsweek,* Jan. 20, 1969

Corruption appears to visit the White House in 50-year cycles. This suggests that exposure and retribution inoculate the Presidency against its latent criminal impulses for about half a century. Around the year 2023 the American people would be well advised to go on the alert and start nailing down everything in sight.
ARTHUR M. SCHLESINGER, JR., *The Imperial Presidency,* 1973

The president we're going to elect in 2000 is 20 years old; he's out there somewhere.
JOHN W. GARDNER, quoted in *New York Times,* July 31, 1970

PRIDE also see HUMILITY

Pride was invented by the ruling class.
RICHARD COURANT, obituary in *New York Times,* Jan. 29, 1972

Pride, like humility, is destroyed by one's insistence that he possesses it.
KENNETH B. CLARK, *The Pathos of Power,* 1974

The question we do not see when we are young is whether we own pride or are owned by it.
JOSEPHINE JOHNSON, quoted in *Forbes,* Feb. 15, 1968

Step on my face and Ill make you swollow it.
GRAFFITO, N.Y.C., 1974

PRISONS also see CRIME

This metallic world that is society's outrageous attempt to imitate a wrathful god.
JACK KROLL, *Newsweek,* Jan. 19, 1976

Prisons don't rehabilitate, they don't punish, they don't protect, so what the hell do they do?
> EDMUND G. BROWN, JR., *Thoughts,* 1976

It is basically a place that warehouses human beings. I'm one of the stock items, so to speak.
> ANTHONY TANNAS, San Quentin Prison, quoted in *Newsweek,* July 4, 1976

America has the longest prison sentences in the West, yet the only condition long sentences demonstrably cure is heterosexuality.
> BRUCE JACKSON, *New York Times,* Sept. 12, 1968

Prisons contain not one but two groups of terrible people—criminals and the guards—each hating and fearing the other.
> LAWYER, quoted in *Newsweek,* July 8, 1974

I would rather be caught with a knife by a guard than be caught without one by another inmate.
> PRISONER, quoted in *Newsweek,* Jan. 26, 1976

Our system nurtures criminals with the same care the Air Force Academy uses to turn out second lieutenants.
> JO WALLACH, quoted in *Newsweek,* Sept. 14, 1970

The animal factory.
> EDWARD BUNKER, ex-con, San Quentin, *The Animal Factory,* 1977

PRIVACY also see RIGHTS

The right to be alone is the most comprehensive of rights, and the right most valued by civilized men.
> LOUIS D. BRANDEIS, 1928, quoted in *Newsweek,* Mar. 9, 1964

Guessing about other people's private habits is more interesting than knowing for sure.
> CHARLES MICHENER, *Newsweek,* Apr. 5, 1976

Don't tell the bastards anything.
> WILLIAM FAULKNER, 1930, letter to agent when magazine asked for biographical sketch, quoted in Joseph Blotner, *Faulkner,* 1974

By the year 2000, man's technical inventiveness may, in terms of privacy, have turned the whole nation into the equivalent of an army barracks.
HARRY KALVEN, JR., *Nation's Business,* from *Quote,* Dec. 3, 1967

PRIZEFIGHTING

There ain't nothing like being in the corner, and the trainer is whispering in your ear and another guy is putting in your mouthpiece. Five seconds to go, then boom! The bell. It's more exciting than looking down a cliff.
GEORGE FOREMAN, quoted in *Newsweek,* Jan. 26, 1976

The raucous art.
JOE FLAHERTY, *New York Times,* Nov. 6, 1977

Hurting people is my business.
SUGAR RAY ROBINSON TO N.Y.S. BOXING COMMISSION, May 23, 1962

Fighting is the only racket where you're almost guaranteed to end up as a bum.
ROCKY GRAZIANO, quoted in Earl Wilson's column, Nov. 19, 1976

THE PRO

A man who can do his best at a time when he doesn't particularly feel like it.
ALISTAIR COOKE, "The Way It Was," PBS, Mar. 4, 1976

One of the differences between an amateur and a pro is that an amateur will settle for allowances and a pro won't.
LARRY BLYDEN, letter to *New York Times,* Aug. 25, 1974

It is good for a professional to be reminded that his professionalism is only a husk, that the real person must remain an amateur, a lover of the work.
MAY SARTON, *Plant Dreaming Deep,* 1968

Professions, like nations, are civilized to the degree to which they can satirize themselves.
PETER DE VRIES, *The Glory of the Hummingbird,* 1974

PROBLEMS

I have yet to see any problem, however complicated, which, when you look at it the right way, did not become still more complicated.
POUL ANDERSON, quoted in *Kaiser News,* no. 1, 1970

For every problem there is one solution which is simple, neat, and wrong.
H. L. MENCKEN, quoted on "MacNeil/Lehrer Report," PBS, Dec. 17, 1975

Some problems never get solved. They just get older.
CHAIM WEIZMANN, quoted on PBS, Apr. 10, 1972

You can't pick up a jellyfish by the corners.
MCGEORGE BUNDY ON ELUSIVE PROBLEMS, quoted in *Newsweek,* Dec. 26, 1967

Obviously, for wolves, be they in sheep's clothing or in mufti, it is always best to refer to the lamb problem in the interest of public relations, as well as for the good of the lupine conscience.
LINDA NOCHLIN, *Woman in Sexist Society,* Vivian Gornick and Barbara K. Moran, eds., 1971

Did you ever consider hitting it closer to the hole?
BEN HOGAN TO GOLFER WITH PUTTING PROBLEM, quoted in *Newsweek,* Feb. 3, 1975

Swing at the strikes.
ATTRIBUTED TO YOGI BERRA ADVISING BATTER IN A SLUMP

A solved problem creates two new problems, and the best prescription for happy living is not to solve any more problems than you have to.
RUSSELL BAKER, interview in *Time,* Jan. 19, 1967

PROFESSORS see TEACHERS/TEACHING

PROFIT also see CAPITALISM

Profits are part of the mechanism by which society decides what it wants to see produced.
HENRY C. WALLICH, *Newsweek,* Jan. 16, 1967

If one has not made a reasonable profit, one has made a mistake.
> LI XIANNIAN, finance minister, People's Republic of China, 1968, quoted in *Newsweek,* Oct. 25, 1976

The worst crime against the working people is a company which fails to make a profit.
> ATTRIBUTED TO SAMUEL GOMPERS

Volume times zero isn't too healthy.
> LEE IACOCCA, president, Ford Motor Company, quoted in *Newsweek,* Aug. 30, 1971

The next guy who talks to me about tonnage is going to get his salary in tons, and we'll see how he converts that into dollars.
> JOHN C. LOBB, president, Crucible Steel Company, quoted in *New York Times,* May 29, 1967

PROGRESS also see CHANGE

The art of progress is to preserve order amid change and to preserve change amid order.
> ANONYMOUS, quoted in *Grit,* Sept. 28, 1969

Progress is man's ability to complicate simplicity.
> THOR HEYERDAHL, *Fatu-Hiva,* 1974

It is said that modern societies alternate between exhilaration about the achieving of progress and disappointment about the fruits of it.
> GEORGE F. WILL, *Newsweek,* June 26, 1978

How do you measure progress? Greater personal security? Shorter work week? Better education? Improved medical protection? Higher culture? More happiness? In none of these ways does there seem to be progress commensurate with the enormous effort Americans have been putting out.
> ARTHUR HERZOG, *The B.S. Factor,* 1973

A society might be better off in the long run if we did not always equate progress with doing something faster.
> WILLIAM T. COLEMAN, JR., Secretary of Transportation, quoted in *Newsweek,* Feb. 16, 1976

PROPHECY also see HINDSIGHT

If you keep saying things are going to be bad you have a good chance of being a prophet.
ISAAC BASHEVIS SINGER, "Dick Cavett Show," PBS, July 17, 1978

What is prophecy but a denial of possibility, of adventure, of the dream of becoming?
ANATOLE BROYARD, *New York Times,* Oct. 16, 1977

Prophecy is the wit of the fool.
VLADIMIR NABOKOV, quoted in *New York Times,* July 31, 1977

PROSTITUTION

Prostitution is an exacting talent, though not an art, since it requires falsification rather than the disciplined expression of feeling.
EDGAR Z. FRIEDENBERG, *The Disposal of Liberty,* 1975

It's a gentleman's trip. A man propositions you, a man busts you, a man judges you, a man jails you, and a man bails you out.
LUCIA, prostitute, speech to COYOTE convention, June 1974

The oldest profession in the world is also the solidest.
PROSPECTUS FOR THE PURCHASE OF LIMITED PARTNERSHIPS IN KOHLS LIE-GENSCHAFTEN KG, operators of a brothel chain, West Germany, quoted in *Wall Street Journal,* Dec. 31, 1971

PROTEST also see FREE SPEECH

Most people do not go to the dentist until they have a toothache; most societies do not reform abuses until the victims begin to make life uncomfortable for others.
CHARLES ISSAWI, *Columbia Forum,* Summer 1970

Group violence has no necessary relationship to group protest, although there continue to be those who decry the one as though it were the other.
REPORT, National Commission on Causes and Prevention of Crime, Sept. 8, 1970

PROTESTANTISM see CHRISTIANITY; THE CHURCHES; RE-
LIGION

PSYCHIC PHENOMENA see OCCULT AND PSYCHIC PHE-
NOMENA

PSYCHOANALYSIS/PSYCHOTHERAPIES

An oasis in the desert of reticence.
    PHILIP REIFF, quoted in John Murray Cuddihy, *The Ordeal of Civil-
    ity*, 1974

Psychotherapy can free us, it cannot show us how to use freedom.
Here ethics and religion must take over.
    ABRAHAM KAPLAN, *Saturday Evening Post*, Sept. 23, 1961

Psychoanalysts love their insights. They are like gifts they give to
themselves.
    DR. DAVID S. VISCOTT, *The Making of a Psychiatrist*, 1972

Do psychiatrists drive their kids crazy?
    ROSS WETZSTEON, *Village Voice* (New York), Feb. 14, 1977

Why should I tolerate a perfect stranger at the bedside of my mind?
    VLADIMIR NABOKOV, *Strong Opinions*, 1973

The point of therapy is to get unhooked, not to thrash around on how
you got hooked.
    MARIANNE WALTERS, family therapist, quoted in Mel Roman and
    Sara Blackburn, *Family Secrets*, 1979

Patients . . . identify with a psychiatrist on a one-to-one basis but the
rest of the week they are home and that is where the problem is.
    ALAN KING, interview in *New York Times*, Aug. 1, 1972

When I look at some of my friends who have "outgrown," or been psy-
choanalyzed away from, the peculiarities that originally drew me to
them, I wish there were something like an Institute of Regression
where they could go and have their psyches turned back like a clock or
speedometer.
    ANATOLE BROYARD, *New York Times*, Oct. 29, 1975

Narcissists who go to Freudian analysts are like alcoholics who buy
saloons.
    RICHARD BOETH, *Newsweek*, Sept. 26, 1977

[Freud's] emphasis on the role of sexual repression in neurosis has been distorted to fit the current idealization of the momentary kick.
HERBERT HENDIN, *New York Times,* Aug. 26, 1976

It is one of the charms of the Freudian method that one does not need to refute the evidence of an opponent; simply question his methods.
JOHN H. DAVIS, *Princeton Alumni Weekly,* Mar. 7, 1967

Did Freud ever write the word happiness?
ANDRÉ MALRAUX, quoted in *New York Times,* Nov. 24, 1976

We are bringing them the plague.
SIGMUND FREUD ON VOYAGE TO U.S.A., 1909, quoted in O. Mannoni, *Freud,* 1970

I finally had an orgasm and my doctor told me it was the wrong kind.
WOODY ALLEN AND MARSHALL BRICKMAN, *Manhattan* (film), 1979

PSYCHOLOGY

Psychology is justified by its problems, not by its answers.
DONALD CAMPBELL, quoted in *New York Times,* Nov. 9, 1975

Unfortunately for psychology, everybody thinks of himself as a psychologist.
JEAN PIAGET, *Columbia Forum,* Fall 1969

Sometimes a cigar is just a cigar.
SIGMUND FREUD, quoted in *New York Times,* Feb. 29, 1976

PUBLIC OPINION also see POLLS

That great compound of folly, weakness, prejudice, wrong feeling, right feeling, obstinacy, and newspaper paragraphs, which is called public opinion.
SIR ROBERT PEEL, 1820

Public opinion in this country runs like a shower bath. We have no temperature between hot and cold.
HEYWOOD BROUN, *The Algonquin Wits,* Robert E. Drennan, ed., 1968

We must abandon the prevalent belief in the superior wisdom of the ignorant.
DANIEL J. BOORSTIN, *Democracy and Its Discontents*, 1974

PUBLIC RELATIONS

The public-relations man ... works on the periphery of organized power, serving it as a necessary but not quite trusted instrument.
KENNETH HENRY, *Defenders and Shapers of the Corporate Image*, 1972

Until Image Words came along, "communication" meant "sharing"— but the communication division doesn't want any backtalk. It wants to dish it out, not take it, so it "municates" instead.
ARTHUR HERZOG, *The B.S. Factor*, 1973

Regardless of my industry and ingenuity, more than once I've been haunted by the suspicion that I'm yodeling in an echo chamber.
RICHARD MANEY, obituary in *New York Times*, July 2, 1968

I am not a lobbyist. I am a traditional flak.
HOWARD J. RUBENSTEIN, interview in *New York Times*, Mar. 16, 1977

PUNCTUATION also see LANGUAGE; WORDS

A period is a stop sign. A semicolon is a rolling stop sign; a comma is merely an amber light.
ANDREW J. OFFUTT, *Writer's Digest*, July 1978

The comma is ... the most ingenious device ever invented to mimic the human voice rhythms, improve the writing of writers, or help readers to read, while often dividing the teaching of teachers into squabbling groups of comma here advocates, comma there nay-sayers, and some with a cool *comme ci, comme ça* attitude about the whole bloody business.
DELBERT JONES, *New York Times*, Dec. 26, 1976

When we are very young, we tend to regard the ability to use a colon much as a budding pianist regards the ability to play with crossed hands.
ERIC PARTRIDGE, *You Have a Point There*, 1953

If you take hyphens seriously you will surely go mad.
> JOHN BENBOW, *Manuscript and Proof*, 1943

PUTDOWNS also see KUDOS

Jimmy would cut the cards if he was playing poker with his mother.
> NEWSMAN ON JIMMY CARTER, quoted in *New York Times*, Aug. 1, 1976

He looks and talks like he just fell off Edgar Bergen's lap.
> DAVID STEINBERG ON GERALD R. FORD, quoted in *Newsweek*, Apr. 21, 1975

His phones are never out of order and no one ever beats him to a cab.
> BILL MOYERS ON RICHARD M. NIXON, *Newsweek*, Apr. 8, 1973

Would you buy a second-hand bank from this man?
> ANONYMOUS ON BERT LANCE, quoted on "Weekend," NBC-TV, Aug. 6, 1977

Hamilton Jordan has always seemed like a son to me: slovenly, tardy, disrespectful—and generally broke.
> JIMMY CARTER, telegram to Jordan testimonial dinner, Albany, Ga., Nov. 5, 1977

Peel away the plastic, and you find more plastic. But that's the secret; he's sincere.
> POLITICIAN ON RONALD F. REAGAN, quoted in *Newsweek*, May 22, 1967

He's not an intellectual, he's a humorist.
> WILLIAM E. SIMON ON JOHN KENNETH GALBRAITH, interview in *New York Times*, Nov. 19, 1978

Dr. Graham has with great self-discipline turned himself into the thinking man's Easter Bunny.
> GARRY WILLS ON BILLY GRAHAM, *New York Times*, May 20, 1979

He looks like a man who has just swallowed an entire human being.
> TRUMAN CAPOTE ON WILLIAM PALEY, quoted in David Halberstam, *The Powers That Be*, 1979

If the Italians knew about his taste in wines, they never would have agreed to have him as Pope.
> FRIEND ON POPE JOHN PAUL II, quoted in *Time*, Oct. 30, 1978

No Rockefeller in the record is ever known to have had a good time.
> LUCIUS BEEBE, quoted in *Wall Street Journal*, July 9, 1968

She is a woman who acts her age, which is 50. She has, in fact, acted that age since she was little more than 20.
> FERN MARJA ECKMAN ON QUEEN ELIZABETH II, *New York Post*, July 3, 1976

The Billy Carter of the British monarchy.
> ROBERT LACEY ON PRINCESS MARGARET, quoted in *Newsweek*, May 22, 1978

A Cardinal Richelieu with a plumber's face.
> VIRGIL DAY ON GEORGE MEANY, interview in *New York Post*, Nov. 24, 1976

The Jacqueline Onassis of the sweat set.
> JOHN LEONARD ON MUHAMMAD ALI, *New York Times*, Oct. 30, 1975

The burlesque emcee with the tie that lights up.
> WILFRID SHEED ON HOWARD COSELL, *New York Times*, Jan. 18, 1976

The designated gerbil.
> BOSTON RED SOX PITCHER BILL LEE ON MANAGER DON ZIMMER, who favors designated batters, quoted in *Newsweek*, July 3, 1978

His face had that look people get when they ride in an elevator.
> ANATOLE BROYARD ON STEVE McQUEEN, *New York Times*, June 9, 1976

He has turned almost alarmingly blond—he's gone past platinum, he must be in plutonium; his hair is coordinated with his teeth.
> PAULINE KAEL ON ROBERT REDFORD, *Reeling*, 1976

She was good at playing abstract confusion in the same way that a midget is good at being short.
> CLIVE JAMES ON MARILYN MONROE, "Dick Cavett Show," PBS, Jan. 18, 1979

He looks like an extra in a crowd scene by Hieronymous Bosch.
> KENNETH TYNAN ON DON RICKLES, *New Yorker*, Feb. 20, 1978

He looks like a stork that dropped a baby and broke it and is coming to explain to the parents.
MEL BROOKS ON MEL TOLKIN, quoted in *New Yorker,* Oct. 30, 1978

Nothing but a pack of lies but very interesting in spots.
DAMON RUNYON ON *Alice in Wonderland,* quoted in *New York Times,* Jan. 24, 1976

RACISM see BLACKS; GHETTOS; INDIANS: NORTH AMERICAN

RADICALS also see CONSERVATIVES; LIBERALS/LIBERALISM

It is love of candor that makes men radical thinkers.
ERIC BENTLEY, *Thirty Years of Treason,* 1971

They appear to love an idea rather than the increase of happiness which that idea is supposed to bring.
GERALD BRENAN, *Personal Record, 1920–1972,* 1975

It is not better when all is in vain, as some members of the Cyrano Left believe.
BERNARD GERT, speech to American Philosophical Association, Dec. 30, 1969

We veteran critics of this life-adjustment education recognize under the mod sideburns and whiskers of the romantic radicals the same old face of anti-intellectualism.
MORTIMER SMITH, quoted in *Newsweek,* July 19, 1972

You have never suffered—how can you be a leftist?
MAO ZEDONG TO NEPHEW, obituary in *New York Times,* Sept. 10, 1976

The right no longer exists, and today everybody is on the left, which means the left no longer exists.
ANDRÉ MALRAUX, quoted in *New York Times,* Nov. 24, 1976

RADIO also see TV

Radio is a creative theater of the mind.
"WOLFMAN JACK" SMITH, interview in *Newsweek,* Dec. 24, 1973

TV just feeds you. Radio involves you.
HIMAN BROWN, interview in *Newsweek,* Jan. 14, 1974

You don't have to keep that straight line between your head and the set.
MICHAEL O'DONOGHUE, interview in *Newsweek,* Jan. 14, 1974

Always sound plausible, because no one is really listening anyway.
BOB ELLIOTT AND RAY GOULDING, *Write If You Get Work,* 1975

RAGTIME see MUSIC: RAGTIME

RAILROADS also see TRANSPORTATION

I like trains because their landing gear is always down.
EX-BOMBER PILOT, 1957

You can see the ground all the way.
MARY Z. GRAY, train passenger, *New York Times,* July 18, 1976

There's one nice thing about driving a train. No one's gonna put a gun at your head and say, "Havana."
E. B. SELOVER, motorman, interview in *New York Times,* Jan. 16, 1969

When you go by on a train, everything looks beautiful. But if you stop, it becomes drab.
EDWARD HOPPER

There is no sound so evocative as a distant train whistle. If you contrast it with the screech of a jet, you get a tragically clear sense of the difference between the two ages.
ANATOLE BROYARD, *New York Times,* Aug. 20, 1975

Railroad terminals, in the American mind, were what cathedrals are to Europeans.
LUCIUS BEEBE, *Petroleum Today,* Fall 1962

RANDOMNESS also see DISORDER; ORDER

17 is *the* one arbitrary random number. It's also called a "Feller" number. Feller, who was a Princeton man but is now dead, always used to say, "Pick any random number, say 17." The point is, if you're going to pick an arbitrary number, you don't want it to be even, and you want it to be less than 20. 19 is pushing it a little. Also, it better not be divisible by 5 if it's going to be random. 1 is obviously out. 3 is the Trinity; that's no good. 5 is divisible by 5, so we don't want that. 7 is lucky; 9 is a perfect square. 11 is also lucky, as in "7 come 11." 13 is *un*lucky, and 15 is divisible by 5. We've already thrown out all the evens, so 17 is the only number that's left.
　　P. BENACERRAF, quoted in *University* (Princeton), Winter 1970–1971

Only God can make a random selection.
　　MARION L. LEVY, JR., quoted in *University* (Princeton), Winter 1970–1971

RAPE

Rape is a dull, blunt, ugly act committed by punk kids, their cousins and older brothers, not by charming, witty, unscrupulous, heroic, sensual rakes, or by timid souls deprived of a "normal" sexual outlet, or by *supermenschen* possessed of uncontrollable lust.
　　SUSAN BROWNMILLER, *Against Our Will*, 1975

Rape is a function of power. The sex is incidental.
　　SOL STEIN, *Other People*, 1979

Short of homicide, it is the "ultimate violation of self."
　　SUPREME COURT JUSTICE BYRON W. WHITE, quoted in *Newsweek,* July 11, 1977

READING also see BOOKS; LITERATURE; WRITERS/WRITING

It is not a spectator sport but a performing art.
　　PETER S. PRESCOTT, *Newsweek,* Dec. 24, 1973

People are used to reading in blocks, and the idea that one sentence has any meaning, as opposed to a paragraph, escapes them.
　　GORE VIDAL, interview in *Bookviews,* June 1978

I'm not a speed reader. I'm a speed understander.
ISAAC ASIMOV, interview in *New York Times,* Jan. 28, 1979

Most reading is no more cultural or intellectual or imaginative than shooting pool or watching "What's My Line."
DONALD HALL, *New York Times,* Jan. 26, 1969

The struggle [is] to keep up with what is most often not worth reading in the first place.
JOHN RUSSELL, *New York Times,* Apr. 30, 1978

I also like to read a little bit of history to help me understand the damnation of time.
STANLEY NABI, interview in *Dun's Review,* May 1969

REAL ESTATE

The world is a fairly untidy place and the most valuable thing one can give to one's children is land. That's the only security.
BERNARD BENSON, interview in *Newsweek,* Feb. 14, 1972

Real estate is the closest thing to the proverbial pot of gold.
ADA LOUISE HUXTABLE, *Will They Ever Finish Bruckner Boulevard?,* 1970

The last remaining frontier of tycoon capitalism, where a fortune can still be made by pyramiding borrowed money and taking tax deductions as you grow.
BOB KUTTNER, *New York Times,* Apr. 28, 1974

Whoever sells land sells his mother.
MEXICAN PROVERB

Look at every Main Street of every town in America and ask yourself "who cares?" Nobody cares about community, divinity and humanity, and you can prove it by asking people what they do care about. In terms of shelter they care about downpayment and location. Give me downpayment and location and I'll outsell community, divinity and humanity on any street corner.
VICTOR H. PALMIERI, land developer, quoted in *Kaiser News,* no. 2, 1966

The creativity of real-estate brokers when it comes time to take to the typewriter and compose advertising has always been a source of amazement.
PAUL GOLDBERGER, *New York Times,* May 29, 1977

REALISTS see DREAMERS/REALISTS

REALITY also see DREAMERS/REALISTS

What we call reality is an agreement that people have arrived at to make life more livable.
LOUISE NEVELSON, interview in *Newsweek,* Feb. 4, 1974

What men perceive as real is real in its consequences.
SOCIOLOGICAL AXIOM

We should tackle reality in a slightly joky way, otherwise we miss its point.
LAWRENCE DURRELL, *Tunc,* 1968

Human kind/Cannot bear very much reality.
T. S. ELIOT, "Burnt Norton," *Four Quartets,* 1943

REASONS

On this earth, there is one thing which is terrible, and that is that everyone has his own good reasons.
JEAN RENOIR, *The Rules of the Game* (film), 1939

Reasons are whores.
LEONARD MICHAELS, *New York Times,* Nov. 21, 1971

RELIGION also see CATHOLICISM; THE CHURCHES; GOD; JEWS/JUDAISM

Religion is behavior and not mere belief.
S. RADHAKRISHNAN, *Theosophical Movement* (Bombay), Mar. 1968

It is ... that cluster of memories and myths, hopes and images, rites and customs that pulls together the life of a person or group into a meaningful whole.
HARVEY COX, *The Seduction of the Spirit,* 1973

There is only one religious problem—being religious.
SOLON B. COUSINS, *Quote,* Oct. 2, 1966

Being religious means asking passionately the question of the meaning of our existence and being willing to receive answers, even if the answers hurt. Such an idea of religion makes religion universally human, but it certainly differs from what is usually called religion.
PAUL TILLICH, *Saturday Evening Post,* June 14, 1958

Organized religion is most efficient when it serves the status quo.
WILLIAM CUTTER, speech at Central Conference of American Rabbis, June 1969

We must respect the other fellow's religion ... to the extent that we respect his theory that his wife is beautiful.
H. L. MENCKEN, *Minority Report,* 1956

Faith is, at one and the same time, absolutely necessary and altogether impossible.
STANISLAW LEM, *The Star Diaries,* 1976

The enormous fatigue of trying to live without religion.
DONALD BARR, *Who Pushed Humpty Dumpty?,* 1971

REPUBLICANS/REPUBLICAN PARTY also see DEMO-CRATS/DEMOCRATIC PARTY

An endangered species.
SIDNEY VERBA, quoted in *Newsweek,* Aug. 23, 1976

If Jerry Brown says we have to cut down on big government, that's regarded as a liberal coup. If a Republican says that, he's considered as a first-class sonofabitch.
WILLIAM STEIGER, congressman, quoted in *Newsweek,* Aug. 23, 1976

Republicans never have mastered the knack, as Democrats seem to have, of winking while knifing an opponent's jugular.
JAMES M. NAUGHTON ON INTRA-PARTY CONFLICTS, *New York Times,* May 9, 1976

It seems to be a law of nature that Republicans are more boring than Democrats.
STEWART ALSOP, *Newsweek,* Dec. 30, 1968

For some goddam reason Republicans can't write.
HENRY R. LUCE ON WHY SO MANY LIBERALS WERE ON HIS STAFF, quoted in W. A. Swanberg, *Luce and His Empire,* 1972

Brains, you know, are suspect in the Republican Party.
WALTER LIPPMANN, obituary in *New York Times,* Dec. 15, 1974

Now you can't make the Republican Party pure by more contributions because contributions are what got it where it is today.
WILL ROGERS, four decades before Watergate, quoted in Richard Ketchum, *Will Rogers,* 1973

True Republicanism requires . . . that every American shall be free to become as unequal as he can.
How to Behave, 1850 etiquette book

RESEARCH

Research is the process of going up alleys to see if they're blind.
MARSTON BATES, *Quote,* Nov. 5, 1967

The chance of the bread falling butter-side-down is directly proportional to the cost of the project.
ANONYMOUS

You can't make a baby in a month by getting nine women pregnant.
RESEARCHER ON CRASH PROJECTS, quoted in *Forbes,* Oct. 15, 1974

Since one must publish to get grants, and promotion in many institutions hinges on the size of the grants, publication and grants rather than discovery become the goals in the laboratory.
ERNEST BOREK, *New York Times,* Jan. 22, 1975

Among advocates of any group—black, white or Oriental—social research is welcome only to the degree that it can be used to advance a desired cause.
WALTER GOODMAN, *New York Times,* June 17, 1979

Ninety percent of the historical researcher's time is spent at the intellectual level of collecting postage stamps.
LAWRENCE STONE, quoted in *Princeton Alumni Weekly,* Oct. 18, 1971

If you copy from one author, it's plagiarism. If you copy from two, it's research.
WILSON MIZNER, quoted in Alva Johnston, *The Legendary Mizners,* 1953

RESPONSIBILITY

Responsibility is to keep the ability to respond.
ROBERT DUNCAN, *New York Times,* Feb. 18, 1968

There are plenty of recommendations on how to get out of trouble cheaply and fast. Most of them come down to this: Deny your responsibility.
LYNDON B. JOHNSON, speech at Democratic fund-raising ball, Sept. 1967

If you can't stand the heat, get out of the kitchen.
HARRY S. TRUMAN

RESTAURANTS also see EATING

No elegant restaurant can be better than the sense of excitement it conveys to women. Many women come to a fashionable place and act as if they were on stage.
CHARLES RITZ, quoted in *New York Times,* Feb. 27, 1972

The murals in restaurants are on a par with the food in museums.
PETER DE VRIES, *Madder Music,* 1977

If you can't pronounce it, you can't afford it.
Dublin Opinion, quoted in Earl Wilson's column, May 21, 1976

I've run more risk eating my way across the country than in all my driving.
DUNCAN HINES, quoted in *New York Times,* Nov. 26, 1967

RETIREMENT also see AGING; OLD AGE

The role of a retired person is no longer to possess one.
SIMONE DE BEAUVOIR, *The Coming of Age,* 1972

Retirement is getting up, going to bed, eating and television in between.
JOHN DECK, *Rancho Paradise,* 1972

Statutory senility.
GEN. EMMETT O'DONNELL, obituary in *Newsweek,* Jan. 10, 1972

The big difference is that it isn't mandatory for anyone to listen to you any more.
WALTER WRIGHT, ex-president, General Telephone Co. of Illinois, interview in *Wall Street Journal,* Sept. 22, 1972

Now I will be able to stop dealing with the urgent and start thinking about the important.
PAUL G. HOFFMAN, quoted in *Newsweek,* Jan. 17, 1972

Twice as much husband on half as much money.
WIFE

Retirement is great, but it ruins my weekends.
ANONYMOUS, quoted in Sam Shulsky's column, Jan. 5, 1976

I miss the Xerox.
ANONYMOUS

The one thing you can say in favor of retirement is that you can brush your teeth after every meal.
DAVID GORDEN, *Harvest Years,* Mar. 1968

I am convinced that the best service a retired general can perform is turn in his tongue along with his suit.
GEN. OMAR BRADLEY, speech at New Canaan, Conn., May 16, 1959

A good retirement is about two weeks.
ALEX COMFORT, *A Good Age,* 1976

REVOLUTIONS

It is not poverty but rising expectations that impel people to revolt.
RICHARD B. MORRIS, *The American Revolution Reconsidered,* 1967

Whatever promotes the triumph of the revolution is moral, whatever hinders it is immoral.
SERGEI NECHAYEV, nineteenth-century Russian terrorist, quoted in *Newsweek,* Feb. 25, 1974

Anyone who makes plans for after the revolution is a reactionary.
MIKHAIL BAKUNIN, founder of anarchism, quoted in Isaiah Berlin, *Russian Thinkers,* 1978

Revolutions, all revolutions, mean: Let's go kill the others, and then everything will be all right.
ALEKSANDR SOLZHENITSYN, Paris TV interview, Apr. 11, 1975

The bloodier the revolution is, the longer it goes on, the more the country pays for it and the closer this revolution comes to the title "great."
ALEKSANDR SOLZHENITSYN, *August 1914,* 1972

I never realized that revolutions involve so much talk.
AMITAI ETZIONI ON 1968 STUDENT UPRISING, COLUMBIA UNIVERSITY, *New York Times,* Sept. 15, 1968

Revolutions are always verbose.
LEON TROTSKY, quoted in *Newsweek,* Oct. 23, 1967

Revolution, like a hard-working housemaid, sounds as if she were smashing the fine crystalware when she is simply polishing and arranging it.
JACQUES ELLUL, *Autopsy of Revolution,* 1971

The fact is, we now see that a revolution cannot change a nation, its tendencies and qualities and traits. Revolution only changes the form of power and property but not the nation itself.
MILOVAN DJILAS, interview in *New York Times,* Nov. 27, 1968

Revolutions always start with singing, and they end by devouring their own children.
LUDECK PACHMAN, *Checkmate in Prague,* 1975

The Robespierres always win out over the Dantons.
E. J. HOBSBAWM ON THE "PURITANICAL TENDENCIES" OF REVOLUTIONARY MOVEMENTS, quoted in *New York Times,* Feb. 5, 1976

Every revolution evaporates and leaves behind only the slime of a new bureaucracy.
FRANZ KAFKA, quoted in *Newsweek,* Oct. 14, 1968

Every decent man who has taken part in a revolution knows very well—no matter who is in power—searches take place from 2:30 A.M. to 6:15 A.M. in winter and from midnight to 4 P.M. in summer.
MIKHAIL BULGAKOV, *The White Guard,* 1971

Mao Tse-tung didn't have to deal with people who were watching seven hours of television every day.
ELAINE BROWN, Black Panthers leader, quoted in *Newsweek,* Nov. 22, 1976

RICHES also see MONEY; POVERTY

I've been rich and I've been poor and, believe me, rich is better.
JOE E. LEWIS

The rich aren't like us, they pay less taxes.
PETER DE VRIES, *I Hear America Swinging,* 1976

The rich only give to the rich.
HELEN LAWRENSON, *Stranger at the Party,* 1975

Keep company with the very rich and you'll end up picking up the check.
STANLEY WALKER, *Quote,* July 17, 1968

Since I am known as a "rich" person, I feel I have to tip at least $5 each time I check my coat. On top of that, I would have to wear a very expensive coat, and it would have to be insured. Added up, without a topcoat I save over $20,000 a year.
ARISTOTLE ONASSIS, quoted in Frank Brady, *Onassis,* 1977

For David Rockefeller, the Presidency of the United States would be a demotion.
WILLIAM HOFFMAN, *David,* 1971

Behavior that would be branded as bad taste or bad manners or simply bad by us ordinary mortals becomes a charming idiosyncrasy or eccentricity if one is a genius or has $ jillions.
MALCOLM S. FORBES, *Forbes,* Oct. 1, 1968

Wealth does not corrupt nor does it ennoble. But wealth does govern the minds of privileged children, gives them a particular kind of identity they never lose, whether they grow up to be stockbrokers or communards, and whether they lead healthy or unstable lives.
ROBERT COLES, *Privileged Ones,* 1978

I'd like to be rich enough so I could throw soap away after the letters are worn off.
ANDY ROONEY, "60 Minutes," CBS-TV, July 15, 1979

Because you're so goddam rich.
GEORGE LUKS TO GERTRUDE VANDERBILT WHITNEY WHEN SHE ASKED WHY HE KEPT TRAILING HER, quoted in *Newsweek,* Oct. 3, 1966

RIGHT: ETHICAL

✓ Doing what is right isn't the problem; it's knowing what is right.
LYNDON B. JOHNSON, quoted in *New York Times,* Feb. 22, 1975

People will always do what is right, so long as someone insists on it.
ANONYMOUS

Frequently when you do what is right, it turns out to be also very clever.
ALEX ROSE, interview in *New York Times,* Oct. 3, 1976

Must the "right" always be considered wholly "right" and the "wrong" definitely cast into outer darkness? Is the modern world, in sum, no more than a poor imitation of the Old Testament?
JEAN LACOUTURE, *New York Times,* July 10, 1977

RIGHTS also see PRIVACY

A right is not what someone gives you; it's what no one can take from you.
RAMSEY CLARK, quoted in *New York Times,* Oct. 2, 1977

Human rights as a rallying cry is a little like "environment"—a catchall so loose and ill-defined that campaigns organized around it are peculiarly susceptible to posturing, pointlessness and blather.
MEG GREENFIELD, *Newsweek,* July 18, 1977

It is time, in the West, to defend not so much human rights as human obligations.
ALEKSANDR SOLZHENITSYN, speech at Harvard University commencement, June 7, 1978

In much of the world the chief human right that people recognize is 800 calories a day.
JESSICA TUCHMAN, quoted in *Newsweek,* June 20, 1977

RISKS also see FEAR; SECURITY

Take calculated risks. That is quite different from being rash.
LT. GEN. GEORGE S. PATTON, JR., letter to son, June 6, 1944

There's no such thing as "zero risk."
WILLIAM DRIVER, quoted in *New York Times*, June 20, 1976

ROCK see MUSIC: ROCK

ROME also see ITALY/ITALIANS

I have never known a city where people speak about their relatives so much.
FEDERICO FELLINI, *New York Times*, June 3, 1973

The intellectuals, the artists, who always live in a state of friction between two different dimensions—reality and fantasy—find in Rome the right liberating thrust for their mental activity.
FELLINI, *New York Times*, June 3, 1973

In Rome . . . at first, you are full of regrets that Michelangelo died, but by and by you only regret that you did not see him do it.
MARK TWAIN, quoted in *New York Times*, Apr. 17, 1977

Remove the Roman Forum and you are left with Roman inflation.
HERBERT MITGANG, *New York Times*, Oct. 10, 1975

ROYALTY

Most of the trappings of royalty are not the fripperies of self-indulgence. They were deliberately evolved to evoke awe, fear, or respect. Unless a monarch evokes one or more such emotions, he or she is just another person sitting on an oversized chair.
WILLIAM V. SHANNON, quoted in *New York Times*, June 5, 1977

Like clowns, they amuse the people, even with their funerals, and keep them contented,
MARIE, QUEEN OF ROMANIA, quoted in Hamilton Fish Armstrong, *Peace and Counter-Peace*, 1971

Duty without responsibility, pomp without power.
EDWARD, DUKE OF WINDSOR, *A King's Story,* 1951

Only two rules really count. Never miss an opportunity to relieve yourself; never miss a chance to sit down and rest your feet.
EDWARD, DUKE OF WINDSOR, *A King's Story*

You do not become the friend of a king by saying you are his friend. He has to say you are his friend.
ARISTOTLE ONASSIS, quoted in *New York Post,* Oct. 22, 1968

Never fall in love with royalty, they'll break your heart.
DAME NELLIE MELBA, quoted in *New York Times,* Dec. 12, 1976

One advantage in marrying a princess or someone from a royal family is that they know what happens.
CHARLES, PRINCE OF WALES, quoted in *Newsweek,* Apr. 11, 1977

My grandmother used to say that she loved snobs because they were the only people who took her seriously.
PRINCE ALEXANDER OF YUGOSLAVIA, quoted in *Newsweek,* June 26, 1978

I may be uninspiring, but I'll be damned if I'm alien.
KING GEORGE V WHEN H. G. WELLS ATTACKED BRITAIN'S "UNINSPIRING ALIEN COURT "

Kings are no trouble. It's the queens.
LUIGI DONZELLI, Claridge's manager, quoted in *Newsweek,* June 5, 1978

I don't want the job. I want to be a taxi driver.
SWEDEN'S KING CARL XVI GUSTAV, when, at 7, he learned he would be king, quoted in Leonard Lyons' column, Sept. 18, 1973

RULES FOR LIVING see LIVING, RULES FOR

RUMOR

The rumor mop swishes through every life.
PAUL COWAN, *New York Times,* Dec. 26, 1971

Rumors begin to feed on one another and they become cumulative, self-fulfilling prophecies.
> U.S. DIPLOMAT, quoted in *Newsweek,* June 18, 1973

Now rumor travels faster but it don't stay put as long as truth.
> WILL ROGERS, quoted in Richard Ketchum, *Will Rogers,* 1973

If you were to believe all the rumors you hear and were to build a hotel to house all those rumors, you would have the largest hotel in the world.
> VIDA BLUE, interview, "Evening News," CBS-TV, Oct. 18, 1973

RUNNING

Those who run year in and year out make it clear they run for the same reasons as the dog, for the psychological satisfaction, the feeling of feeling good.
> DONALD PORTER, *Inner Running,* 1978

My body likes to run.
> SABINA CHEBICHI, Kenyan middle-distance runner, interview in *Newsweek,* June 25, 1973

Some sedentary types say they have never seen a runner who looked happy.
> HARRY REASONER, "Evening News," ABC-TV, Apr. 18, 1977

I remember once during a sweltering marathon in Australia passing a store window, and greatly envying a goldfish in a bowl.
> PETER D. WOOD, *New York Times,* Apr. 21, 1975

This modish mortification of the flesh.
> PETER S. PRESCOTT ON JOGGING, *Newsweek,* Feb. 12, 1979

SALESMEN/SELLING also see MARKETING; MERCHANDISING; SUPERMARKETS

Inequality of knowledge is the key to a sale.
> DEIL O. GUSTAFSON, real-estate tycoon, quoted in *Newsweek,* May 20, 1974

When my client gives me an absolute no, I blow a whistle and announce, "The second half is just beginning."
LARRY LEVITT, insurance salesman, quoted in *Newsweek*, May 27, 1968

No one has endurance/Like the man who sells insurance.
INSURANCE BROKERS' AXIOM

You can see the way he walks; he always has the bags with him, even when he doesn't.
TOM CONGDON, quoted in *New York Times*, Apr. 21, 1974

Friendliness stops as soon as the sale is made.
JONATHAN LARKIN on retail selling, quoted in *Business Week*, Sept. 1, 1973

SAN FRANCISCO also see CALIFORNIA

San Francisco is the only city I can think of that could survive all the things people are doing to it and still look beautiful.
FRANK LLOYD WRIGHT, quoted in *Newsweek*, Dec. 28, 1970

Nobody thinks of building a sober house. Of all the efflorescent, floriated bulbousness and flamboyant craziness that ever decorated a city, I think San Francisco may carry off the prize.
San Francisco Real Estate Circular, 1883

The coldest winter I ever spent was a summer in San Francisco.
MARK TWAIN, quoted in *New York Times*, Sept. 26, 1975

We get baseball weather in football season and football weather in July and August.
HERB CAEN, *New York Times*, Sept. 26, 1975

You can relax and listen in San Francisco. You can't in New York.
RALPH J. GLEASON, publisher, *Rolling Stone*, obituary in *New York Times*, June 4, 1975

SATIRE also see COMEDY/COMEDIANS; HUMOR/HUMORISTS; LAUGHTER; WIT

Satire is moral outrage transformed into comic art.
PHILIP ROTH, *Reading Myself and Others*, 1975

The purpose of satire is to strip off the veneer of comforting illusion and cozy half-truth.
MICHAEL FLANDERS, obituary in *Newsweek,* Apr. 28, 1975

Satire concerns itself with logically extending a premise to its totally insane conclusion, thus forcing onto an audience certain unwelcome awarenesses.
JULES FEIFFER, interview in *Playboy,* 1971

The satirist's congenital vice . . . is heartlessness.
GEORGE STADE, *New York Times,* Nov. 9, 1975

Satire is what closes on Saturday night.
GEORGE S. KAUFMAN, quoted in Howard Teichmann, *George S. Kaufman,* 1972

SCHOOLS also see COLLEGES/UNIVERSITIES; EDUCATION; TEACHERS/TEACHING

I've come to see that the real job of the school is to entice the student into the web of knowledge and then, if he's not enticed, to drag him in.
MARA WOLYNSKI, *Newsweek,* Aug. 30, 1976

The students are used to being entertained. They are used to the idea that if they are just the slightest bit bored, they can flip the switch and turn the channel.
IRENE KRAMSKY, quoted in *New York Times,* May 29, 1977

An American public school must have winners and losers.
JAMES HERNDON, *How to Survive in Your Native Land,* 1971

Our nursery for endless striving.
MURRAY MILNER, JR., *The Illusion of Equality,* 1972

The play *Waiting for Godot* is a very difficult one to write about because there are no real incidents in the sense that the Board of Regents means.
HIGH-SCHOOL STUDENT'S COMPOSITION, quoted in Israel Shenker, *Words and Their Masters,* 1974

High school regulations are chillingly similar to the Army's.
IRA GLASSER, interview in *New York Post,* Feb. 21, 1969

Most schools have more assistant football coaches than assistant principals.
DAVID BYRNE, quoted in *Newsweek,* Mar. 13, 1978

SCIENCE

The natural history of science is the study of the unknown. If you fear it, then you're not going to study it, and you're not going to make any progress.
DR. MICHAEL E. DEBAKEY, interview in *New York Times,* Sept. 7, 1976

A new scientific truth does not triumph by convincing its opponents and making them see the light, but rather because its opponents eventually die, and a new generation grows up that is familiar with it.
MAX PLANCK, *Scientific Autobiography,* 1949

There is a tendency in the 20th century to forget that there will be a 21st century science, and indeed a 30th century science, from which vantage points our knowledge of the universe will appear quite different. We suffer, perhaps, from temporal provincialism, a form of arrogance that has always irritated posterity.
J. ALLEN HYNEK, quoted in *Time,* Aug. 4, 1967

A declaration that "science has discovered" has been for Americans a final judgment to which there is no court of appeal.
DAVID F. MUSTO, *New York Times,* May 15, 1975

One of the most pernicious falsehoods ever to be almost universally accepted is that the scientific method is the only reliable way to truth.
RICHARD H. BUBE, quoted in *Time,* Apr. 23, 1973

The same system that produced a bewildering succession of new-model, style-obsolescent autos and refrigerators can also produce an endless outpouring of new-model, style-obsolescent science.
HARVEY WHEELER, *New York Times,* Aug. 11, 1975

I can't help thinking that science would be more appealing if it had no practical use. In what we call progress, 90 per cent of our efforts go into finding a cure for the harms linked to the advantage brought by the remaining 10 per cent.
CLAUDE LÉVI-STRAUSS, interview in *Diacritics,* Winter 1971–1972

Science is wonderfully equipped to answer the question "How?" But it gets terribly confused when you ask the question "Why?"
ERWIN CHARGAFF, *Columbia Forum,* Summer 1969

We manipulate nature as if we were stuffing an Alsatian goose. We create new forms of energy; we make new elements; we kill crops; we wash brains. I can hear them in the dark sharpening their lasers.
CHARGAFF, *Columbia Forum,* Summer 1969

We are in danger of killing ourselves with our scientific knowledge at a time when we are stripped of the comfort of our religious beliefs. That's quite a situation.
WILL DURANT, interview in *New York Times,* Nov. 6, 1975

The stone age may return on the gleaming wings of science.
ATTRIBUTED TO WINSTON CHURCHILL

SCIENTISTS

Scientists have reduced the number of calamities we can blame on God.
JOHN LEONARD, *New York Times,* Apr. 9, 1978

Peeping Toms at the keyhole of eternity.
ARTHUR KOESTLER, *The Roots of Coincidence,* 1972

In assessing the claims, prophecies and lamentations of the inhabitants of the scientific community, it is often useful to apply a generous discount. Their profession, having made a rapid ascent from deep poverty to great affluence, from academe's cloisters to Washington's high councils, still tends to be a bit excitable—not unlike a *nouveau riche* in a fluctuating market.
DANIEL S. GREENBERG, *The Politics of Pure Science,* 1968

Most scientists play to a very narrow constituency of their own peers. It assures the quality of their work, but it does tend to keep them less sensitive to the needs of society as a whole.
BRUCE MURRAY, NASA director, quoted in *Newsweek,* Aug. 15, 1977

Sometimes it is suggested that since scientists and engineers have made the bombs, insecticides, and autos, they ought to be responsible for deciding how to deal with the resultant hazards. . . . This approach would . . . force us to rely on the moral and political wisdom of scientists and engineers, and there is no evidence that I know of that suggests they are better endowed in this respect than other people.
BARRY COMMONER, *Columbia Forum*, Spring 1968

The most remarkable discovery made by scientists is science itself.
JACOB BRONOWSKI, *A Sense of the Future*, 1977

I have learned to have more faith in the scientist than he does in himself.
DAVID SARNOFF, obituary in *Newsweek*, Dec. 27, 1971

SECOND MARRIAGE see MARRIAGE, SECOND

SECOND THOUGHTS

If I had my life to live over, I would have liked to have ended up as a sportswriter.
RICHARD M. NIXON, quoted in *Newsweek*, Dec. 22, 1969

I've had a lifelong ambition to be a professional baseball player, but nobody would sign me.
GERALD R. FORD, quoted by United Press International, Dec. 4, 1976

If I were to begin life again, I should want it as it were. I would only open my eyes a little more.
JULES RENARD, *The Journal of Jules Renard*, Louise Bogan, ed., 1964

If I could just do it over, I would do it better, maybe even right.
WILLIAM FAULKNER, quoted in *New York Daily News*, Mar. 9, 1977

If I had this side of life to live over again, I'd again be just such a fool as I was.
JAMES MONTGOMERY FLAGG ON HIS LOVE AFFAIRS, quoted in Susan E. Meyer, *America's Great Illustrators*, 1978

Reading this letter years afterwards—I unthink all these unthought thinks.
JAMES STEPHENS, 1929 note on earlier criticism of James Joyce, *The Letters of James Stephens*, Richard F. Finneran, ed., 1974

SECRETARIES also see THE JOB; WORK

A good secretary can save her boss more time in a year than a business jet plane can.
MALCOLM BALDRIGE, president, Scoville Manufacturing Co., *Quote*, Mar. 17, 1968

The boss' secretary can wield great power, like the king's mistress, without any authority at all.
ANTONY JAY, *Management and Machiavelli*, 1968

If I had learned to type, I never would have made brigadier general.
WAC BRIG. GEN. ELIZABETH P. HOISINGTON, interview in *New York Times*, June 20, 1970

SECURITY also see FEAR; RISKS

Security depends not so much upon how much you have, as upon how much you can do without. And that is true for society as well as for the individual.
JOSEPH WOOD KRUTCH, quoted in *American Scholar*, June 1967

We spend our time searching for security, and hate it when we get it.
JOHN STEINBECK, "News Special," NBC-TV, Dec. 3, 1967

Security is an invitation to indolence.
ROD MCKUEN, Vietnam peace speeches, 1968

Only foolish people are completely secure.
JOHN KENNETH GALBRAITH, *New York Times*, Mar. 19, 1972

SELF also see IDENTITY

In infinite space, in infinite time, in infinite matter, an organism like a bubble was formed; it lasts a short while and then bursts; and that bubble is myself.
THORNTON WILDER, *The Eighth Day*, 1967

Each one of us is a statistical impossibility around which hover a million other lives that were never destined to be born.
LOREN EISELEY, *The Unexpected Universe*, 1969

We are all special cases.
ALBERT CAMUS, quoted in *New York Times,* May 1, 1977

Poor brother donkey.
ST. FRANCIS ON HIS BODY, quoted on "Civilisation," PBS, Nov. 8, 1976

Though estimates vary statistically, about one in every three people is troubled. I'd like each of you to think of your two closest friends. If they both seem all right to you—well, then you're the one.
EDWARD CONOLLEY, quoted in *Wall Street Journal,* Apr. 17, 1974

Every man is crucified upon the cross of himself.
WHITTAKER CHAMBERS, *Witness,* 1952

SELF-APPRAISAL

I am the king. I am the king.
LYNDON B. JOHNSON, striding down the aisle of *Air Force One,* quoted in Helen Thomas, *Dateline: White House,* 1975

I'm an introvert in an extravert's profession.
RICHARD M. NIXON, quoted in H. R. Haldeman, *The Ends of Power,* 1978

I'm not the Carter who'll never tell a lie.
BILLY CARTER, interview in *Newsweek,* Nov. 4, 1977

We are all worms, but I do believe I am a glow worm.
WINSTON CHURCHILL WHEN A YOUNG MAN, *Churchill: A Profile,* Peter Stansky, ed., 1973

I seem to be a verb.
R. BUCKMINSTER FULLER, quoted in Hugh Kenner, *Bucky,* 1973

I am not a great man. I have made a great discovery.
SIGMUND FREUD, quoted in Paul Roazen, *Freud and His Followers,* 1975

My power to follow a long and purely abstract train of thought is very limited.
CHARLES DARWIN, *The Life and Letters of Charles Darwin,* Francis Darwin, ed., 1887

I am the primitive of the method I have invented.
PAUL CÉZANNE, quoted in *Newsweek,* Oct. 17, 1977

Who, me? A genius? What rot!
PIERRE AUGUSTE RENOIR, quoted in *Newsweek,* Oct. 21, 1968

When I go, I'll take New Year's Eve with me.
GUY LOMBARDO, obituary in *Newsweek,* Nov. 14, 1977

I look like somebody's bartender.
ATTRIBUTED TO DEAN RUSK

I am 54 years old, weigh 220 pounds, and look like the chief dispatcher of a long-distance hauling concern.
JAMES M. CAIN, 1946, quoted in *New York Times,* Mar. 2, 1969

A fat little man like me appearing there in an evening dress looks like an undertaker.
ARTHUR RUBINSTEIN, interview on PBS, Jan. 26, 1977

Having practiced for hours in front of the mirror, I can work up a fairly ferocious expression, but I have not got, and never will have a natural-born fighting face.
LT. GEN. GEORGE S. PATTON, JR., quoted in Martin Blumenson, *The Patton Papers: 1940–1945,* 1972

If I only had a little humility I would be perfect.
TED TURNER, owner of Atlanta Braves and winner of 1977 America's Cup, quoted in *New York Times,* Sept. 19, 1977

SELF-DECEPTION

We all invent ourselves as we go along, and a great man's myths about himself merely tend to stick better than most.
ATTRIBUTED TO SIR DENIS BROGAN

If horses could paint they would draw gods like horses.
XENOPHANES, sixth century B.C., quoted in James K. Feibleman, *Understanding Philosophy,* 1973

Not one in a million men thinks of himself as Hamlet, but every man sees himself as Lear.
ANONYMOUS

He who despises himself esteems himself as a self-despiser.
SUSAN SONTAG, *Death Kit,* 1967

SELF-EXAMINATION

Seriously to contemplate one's abject personal triteness is probably the most painful act a man can perform.
ROBERT M. ADAMS, *Bad Mouth,* 1977

You can't go around examining yourself subjectively. It's like pulling up potatoes in the field to see if they're growing.
ROY HARRIS, interview in *Newsweek,* Feb. 19, 1968

SELF-INTEREST

No matter who you are the basic truth is that your interests are nobody's else's concern, your gain is inevitably someone else's loss, your failure somebody else's victory.
MICHAEL KORDA, *Power!,* 1975

Men are not against you; they are merely for themselves.
GENE FOWLER, quoted in *Forbes,* May 15, 1967

SELF-KNOWLEDGE

In the main it is not by introspection but by reflecting on our living in common with others that we come to know ourselves.
ATTRIBUTED TO REV. BERNARD J. F. LONERGAN

To seek to know oneself is good advice if you are, say, Montaigne or Thoreau. But for most men, it might be a good idea merely to control, use, express, nurture the self.
HERBERT GOLD, *New York Times,* May 16, 1976

At nineteen I was a stranger to myself. At forty I asked: Who am I? At fifty I concluded I would never know.
EDWARD DAHLBERG, *The Confessions of Edward Dahlberg,* 1971

How do I know what I think till I see what I say?
E. M. FORSTER, quoted in *New York Times,* Nov. 14, 1976

SELF-PRESERVATION

The Ten Commandments must be silent when self-preservation is at stake.
WILL AND ARIEL DURANT ON WAR FOR SURVIVAL, *The Lessons of History*, 1968

If self-preservation is the first law of nature, what's the second?
PHONE QUESTION TO N.Y. PUBLIC LIBRARY, quoted in *New York Times*, May 26, 1972

SENATE see CONGRESS

SENSE, COMMON see COMMON SENSE

SERVANTS also see CLASS: SOCIAL; THE JOB

The wealthy matron and her cleaning woman now compete for the same taxi.
IRVING KRISTOL, *New York Times*, Jan. 22, 1967

The answering-service operator has become the surrogate servant of the servantless society.
Newsweek, June 12, 1967

SEX also see ORGASM

Sex created the family.
CARL E. FEHRLE, *Education Leadership*, Mar. 1970

Our biological drives are several million years older than our intelligence.
ARTHUR E. MORGAN, interview in *New York Times*, June 21, 1968

To my mind, the two most fascinating subjects in the universe are sex and the eighteenth century.
BRIGID BROPHY, reviewing *Fanny Hill*

Though a man be a dignified judge, a captain of industry, a national golf champion, or a distinguished physicist, he feels worthless and debased if he cannot perform an act which he shares in common with dogs, rabbits, cattle and rats.

> HOWARD R. LEWIS AND MARTHA E. LEWIS, *Psychosomatics,* 1972

Sex *is* work.

> ANDY WARHOL, *The Philosophy of Andy Warhol (From A to B and Back Again),* 1975

If we do not accept the fact that a great deal of sex is intrinsically funny, we fall into the new heresy in which all sexual diversions are profoundly serious.

> SIR DENIS BROGAN, interview in *Saturday Evening Post,* June 8, 1963

Sex: The Breakfast of Champions.

> SLOGAN ON RACING CAR OF JAMES HUNT, where his competitors have commercial slogans, 1974

When you're young you always assume that sex was invented the day you hit puberty.

> JOHN P. ROCHE, quoted in *Newsweek,* Feb. 20, 1967

If whoever invented it, you know, didn't want us to have intercourse, why did he make us fit together so perfectly?

> 15-YEAR-OLD GIRL, quoted in Robert C. Sorensen, *Adolescent Sexuality in Contemporary America,* 1973

You can, after all, produce an orgasm yourself if that's what you want, so we must go to bed for something more.

> MERLE SHAIN, *Some Men Are More Perfect Than Others,* 1973

It is nothing less than astonishing to discover how many modern, well-informed couples still believe the Victorian idea that there is something called the "sex act" and that a man does it to a woman.

> WILLIAM H. MASTERS AND VIRGINIA E. JOHNSON, *McCall's,* May 1970

Of all the animals on the earth, none is so brutish as man when he seeks the delirium of coition.

> EDWARD DAHLBERG, *The Edward Dahlberg Reader,* Paul Carroll, ed., 1967

If the sex laws were applied drastically, I wonder who the jailers would be.

> WILLIAM H. MASTERS, quoted in *New York Times,* Apr. 27, 1970

We may eventually come to realize that chastity is no more a virtue than malnutrition.
ALEX COMFORT, *New York Times,* Feb. 18, 1968

How has it happened, what have we come to, that the scarlet letter these days isn't A but V?
JOYCE MAYNARD ON VIRGINITY, *Looking Back,* 1973

If I had as many love affairs as you have given me credit for, I would now be speaking to you from a jar in the Harvard Medical School.
FRANK SINATRA, press conference, Hollywood, Apr. 1965

SEX, GROUP

Folks whose only other hobby is The Tube.
MARCIA SELIGSON, *New York Times,* July 25, 1971

They have gone from Puritanism into promiscuity without passing through sensuality.
MOLLY HASKELL, quoted in *Newsweek,* June 21, 1971

SEX MANUALS

These books are deadening because some want to be reassured that sex is as shallow and dull as everything else in their lives—that they're not really missing that much. And smart authors know this.
PSYCHOLOGIST, quoted in *New York Times,* Feb. 11, 1974

The fact is there hasn't been a thrilling new erogenous zone discovered since de Sade.
GEORGE GILDER, *Sexual Suicide,* 1973

I read a book called *The Art of Loving.* A lot of things seemed clear while I was reading it but afterwards I went back to being more or less the same.
ALICE MUNRO, *Something I've Been Meaning to Tell You,* 1974

You should be able to discover all this by yourself.
JOSÉ DE VINCK AND FATHER JOHN CATOIR ON THE 16 BASIC POSITIONS, *The Challenge of Love,* 1969

SEXES, WAR OF THE: HERS also see MARRIAGE; WIVES

Men and women, women and men. It will never work.
ERICA JONG, *Fear of Flying*, 1973

Women are the only oppressed group in our society that lives in intimate association with our oppressors.
EVELYN CUNNINGHAM, speech at women's symposium, New York, May 16, 1969

Had I been crested, not cloven, my Lords, you had not treated me thus.
QUEEN ELIZABETH I TO COURTIERS, quoted in Nigel Nicolson, *Portrait of a Marriage*, 1973

There is perhaps only one human being in a thousand who is passionately interested in his job for the job's sake. The difference is that if that one person in a thousand is a man, we say, simply, that he is passionately keen on his job; if she is a woman, we say she is a freak.
DOROTHY L. SAYERS, 1938 speech, "Are Women Human?" *Unpopular Opinions*, 1947

No one should have to dance backward all their lives.
JILL RUCKELSHAUS, quoted in *New York Times*, Aug. 3, 1973

Men are too emotional to vote. Their conduct at baseball games and political conventions shows this, while their innate tendency to appeal to force renders them particularly unfit for the task of government. . . . Man's place is the armory.
ALICE DUER MILLER, *Are Women People?*, 1915

Man seems not so much wicked as frail, unable to face pain, trouble and growing old. A good woman knows that nature is her enemy. Look at what it does to her.
FAY WELDON, *Down Among the Women*, 1972

Where did your Christ come from? From God and a woman! Man had nothing to do with him.
SOJOURNER TRUTH, speech at first women's rights convention, 1851

Beware of the man who/denounces women writers;/his penis is tiny & cannot spell.
ERICA JONG, "Seventeen Warnings in Search of a Feminist Poem," *Half-Lives*, 1973

Men have been trained and conditioned by women, not unlike the way Pavlov conditioned his dogs, into becoming their slaves. As compensation for their labors men are given periodic use of women's vaginas.
ESTHER VILAR, *The Manipulated Man,* 1972

Delivering a baby is the ultimate male ego trip.
BARBARA SEAMAN, quoted in *New York Post,* Sept. 28, 1973

A woman can do anything a man can do—except be a grandfather, maybe.
FIFTH-GRADE GIRL, quoted in *New York Times,* June 12, 1975

SEXES, WAR OF THE: HIS

The American girl makes a servant of her husband and then finds him contemptible for being a servant.
JOHN STEINBECK, *Steinbeck: A Life in Letters,* Elaine Steinbeck and Robert Wallston, eds., 1975

Women will go to you because of your intensity. They will leave you for the same reason.
JAMES T. FARRELL, quoted in Sloan Wilson, *What Shall We Wear to This Party?,* 1976

A man no more believes a woman when she says she has an aversion for him than when she says she'll cry out.
WILLIAM WYCHERLEY, *Plain Dealer,* 1674

The great question . . . which I have not been able to answer, despite my thirty years in research into the feminine soul, is "What does a woman want?"
SIGMUND FREUD, quoted in Ernest Jones, *The Life and Work of Sigmund Freud,* vol. 2, 1955

No woman ever looks exactly what she is; if she did, she'd at once try to be different.
G. B. BURGIN, quoted in *New York Times,* June 9, 1968

Why can't a woman be more like a man?
ALAN J. LERNER, *My Fair Lady* (musical), 1956

The ability to have our own way, and at the same time convince others they are having their own way, is a rare thing among men. Among women it is as common as eyebrows.

> THOMAS BAILEY ALDRICH, quoted in *New York Daily News*, July 27, 1969

Women make much better soldiers than men. They always know where the real enemy is hidden.

> JOSÉ YGLESIAS, *The Kill Price*, 1976

For years they have been using the role of "sex object" as a cover while they spied out the land.

> ANATOLE BROYARD, *New York Times*, Apr. 10, 1975

The trouble with women in love is that they are too generous; give too much. Men don't really like this. On the other hand if a woman is off-hand they don't like that either. There is no answer.

> OMAR SHARIF, *Quote*, Apr. 30, 1967

When I have one foot in the grave I will tell the truth about women. I shall tell it, jump into my coffin, pull the lid over me and say, "Do what you like now."

> LEO TOLSTOY, quoted in Louis B. Nizer, *Thinking on Your Feet*, 1963

There will always be a battle between the sexes because men and women want different things. Men want women and women want men.

> GEORGE BURNS, *Quote*, May 15, 1977

SHORTNESS also see TALLNESS

If you're small, you better be a winner.

> BILLIE JEAN KING, 5'4½", quoted in *New York Times*, Jan. 14, 1976

Like a dime among pennies.

> FIORELLO H. LA GUARDIA, 5'2", on how it feels to be the smallest man in a group, quoted in *Village Voice* (New York), Nov. 21, 1968

I hope she can hear me.

> ABRAHAM BEAME, 5'0", when presenting gift to Queen Margarethe II of Denmark, 6'0", May 17, 1976

SHOW BIZ also see ACTORS/ACTING; HOLLYWOOD; MOVIES; THEATER

Art is okay, but give me a hot audience every time.
> MARVIN FLACK, press agent, quoted in *New York Times,* July 9, 1975

If you learn to be a perfect singer, you'll end up in the Mormon Tabernacle Choir—with your hands folded.
> DEAN MARTIN TO DAUGHTER, quoted in *Newsweek,* Mar. 18, 1968

You risk your life in this business every six months or you die.
> ELIA KAZAN, quoted in *New York Times,* Mar. 24, 1974

The prima donna's dressing room is the one nearest the exit.
> THELMA VOTIPKA, Metropolitan Opera soprano, obituary in *New York Times,* Oct. 27, 1972

A show is like having a climax. It's like having an incredible, natural climax. And then suddenly it's all finished, and you don't know what to do next.
> ROD STEWART, interview in *Newsweek,* Sept. 11, 1972

In show business you're a fruit picker. You go where the work is.
> ORSON WELLES, interview in *Newsweek,* Feb. 27, 1967

The first four cities, it's OK. You're light-hearted—la-lee-la. But after 30 you start going mad. Your face starts to look different. A strange feeling comes over you; it's really awful.
> MICK JAGGER, interview in *Newsweek,* Aug. 7, 1972

New York is surrounded on all sides by Bridgeport.
> SHOW-BIZ MAXIM

SICKNESS also see DOCTORS; HEALTH; HOSPITALS; MEDICAL CARE

We are sick because our cells are sick.
> DR. CHRISTIAN DE DUVE, quoted in *New York Times,* Oct. 11, 1975

In a sense sickness is a place, more instructive than a long trip to Europe, and it's always a place where there's no company, where nobody can follow.
> FLANNERY O'CONNOR IN 1956 LETTER TO "A," quoted in *The Habit of Being,* Sally Fitzgerald, ed., 1979

Many illnesses are promoted from the third-rate to the first-rate by the anxious mind.
ERIC PARTRIDGE, interview in *New York Times*, Nov. 7, 1974

No one on a sinking ship has ever been reported sick.
HARRY GOLDEN, *You're Entitle'*, 1962

SIMPLICITY

The simple man everywhere is apt to see whatever differs from himself as an affront, a challenge and a menace.
W. J. CASH, *The Mind of the South*, 1941

There is more simplicity in the man who eats caviar on impulse than in the man who eats Grapenuts on principle.
G. K. CHESTERTON, quoted in *New York Times*, Nov. 26, 1967

All simple statements are wrong.
FRANK KNIGHT, quoted in *New York Times*, Oct. 17, 1976

Everything should be made as simple as possible, but not simpler.
ALBERT EINSTEIN, quoted in *Newsweek*, Apr. 16, 1979

Keep it simple, stupid.
AXIOM OF ISRAELI AIR FORCE, 1969

SIN also see EVIL; GUILT

Original sin is that thing about man which makes him capable of conceiving of his own perfection and incapable of achieving it.
REINHOLD NIEBUHR, obituary in *Newsweek*, June 14, 1972

History offers some consolation by reminding us that sin has flourished in every age. Man has never reconciled himself to the Ten Commandments.
WILL AND ARIEL DURANT, *The Lessons of History*, 1968

It may or may not be debatable whether a man can live without God; but, if it were possible, we should pass a law forbidding a man to live without a sense of sin.
MURRAY KEMPTON, quoted in *New York Times*, Apr. 2, 1976

Every sin is the result of a collaboration.
STEPHEN CRANE, quoted in Eric Solomon, *Stephen Crane,* 1966

The Anglo-Saxon conscience does not prevent the Anglo-Saxon from sinning. It merely prevents him from enjoying it.
SALVADOR DE MADARIAGA, quoted in David Frost and Antony Jay, *The English,* 1968

There are three sorts of sin: little sins, bigger ones, AND TAKING OFF YOUR SHOES WITHOUT UNDOING THE LACES.
BRITISH NANNY'S WARNING, quoted in Jonathan Gathorne-Hardy, *The Unnatural History of the Nanny,* 1973

SINGERS see MUSIC: SINGERS

SKYSCRAPERS also see ARCHITECTURE; CITY; HOUSES

Cathedral of commerce.
REV. S. PARKES CADMEN AT DEDICATION OF WOOLWORTH BUILDING, Apr. 24, 1913

The most democratic building in the world, with its windows of uniform size dwarfing the downtown churches.
HANNAH TILLICH, *From Time to Time,* 1973

A hubristic tower of babel.
REINHOLD NIEBUHR, quoted in *University* (Princeton), Summer 1974

A high-rise building is like a 747. I can't think of any advantages.
C. ALLIN CORNELL, conference on high-rise buildings, Lehigh University, Aug. 24, 1972

The criticisms being offered about the high-rise buildings today were voiced in ancient Rome—lack of community, alienation, exploitation of the poor, hazard of fire, muggers, drunken bullies, noise from vehicles and crowding.
DOUGLAS D. FEAVER, conference on high-rise buildings, Lehigh University, Aug. 24, 1972

SLANG see LANGUAGE: SLANG

SLAVERY also see BLACKS

The Man That Was a Thing.
> HARRIET BEECHER STOWE'S ORIGINAL SUBTITLE FOR *Uncle Tom's Cabin: Life Among the Lowly*

Indeed, I tremble for my country when I remember that God is just.
> THOMAS JEFFERSON ON THE CONTRADICTION BETWEEN SLAVERY AND DEMOCRACY, speech to Virginia House of Delegates

No wonder that the Negroes become lazy. They never benefit from their own work.
> LOUIS PHILIPPE, DUKE OF ORLÉANS, 1797, *Diary of My Travels in America*, 1977

It was not that the slaves did not act like men. Rather, it was that they could not grasp their collective strength as a people and act like political men.
> EUGENE D. GENOVESE, *Roll, Jordan, Roll,* 1974

SLEEP also see DREAMS

Th' wan great object iv ivry man's life is to get tired enough to sleep.
> FINLEY PETER DUNNE, *Observations of Mr. Dooley,* 1902

No small art is it to sleep, it is necessary to keep awake all day for that purpose.
> FRIEDRICH NIETZSCHE, quoted in Hilary Rubenstein, *Insomniacs of the World, Goodnight,* 1974

Sleep is the most moronic fraternity in the world, with the heaviest dues and the crudest rituals.
> VLADIMIR NABOKOV, quoted in *New York Times,* Dec. 15, 1974

It's an eight-hour peep show of infantile erotica.
> J. G. BALLARD, *The Best Short Stories of J. G. Ballard,* 1978

SMALL TOWNS see TOWNS, SMALL

SNOBS/SNOBBERY

The most compelling of all temptations is the temptation to the inner circle. Men will lie, betray their wives for admission to the circle.
C. S. LEWIS, quoted in *New York Times,* May 3, 1974

There is no rationale that defends it and no attack that dissolves it.
MAYA ANGELOU, *New York Times,* May 25, 1975

I have never known a snob who was not also a damned liar.
PAUL THEROUX, *New York Times,* Apr. 24, 1977

Oh, so you're a Catholic. That's what my cook does on Sundays.
SOUTHAMPTON, N.Y., MATRON TO MRS. THOMAS E. MURRAY, quoted in Stephen Birmingham, *Real Lace,* 1973

SOCIAL CLASS see CLASS: SOCIAL

SOCIALISM also see CAPITALISM; COMMUNISM

Socialism is an attractive goal, but concentration of power is as dangerous as concentration of capital.
ASOKA MEHTA, Indian socialist, quoted in *Time,* Mar. 13, 1978

Socialism, or any other alternative to private enterprise, would inevitably mean a vast expansion of federal government. General Motors would not disappear; it would simply be lumped with Ford, Chrysler, Boeing, Pan American and so on in a vast Ministry of Transportation. And bureaucracy would conquer all.
JOHN W. GARDNER

A boring way to speed up the mess.
R. BUCKMINSTER FULLER, quoted in E. J. Applewhite, *Cosmic Fishing,* 1977

Logically socialism comes after capitalism—and that fundamental tenet of Marxism has not been disproved by history.
BERTRAND DE JOUVENEL, speech to Club of Rome, Philadelphia, Apr. 13, 1976

Whoever attempts to achieve socialism by any other route than that of political democracy will inevitably arrive at the most absurd and reactionary results.
NIKOLAI LENIN, quoted in Bertram D. Wolfe, *An Ideology in Power,* 1969

SOCIETY: THE CULTURE

Modern society is like a Calder mobile: disturb it here and it jiggles over there, too.
GEORGE F. WILL, *Newsweek,* May 2, 1977

The trouble with this society is that it is pop-culture oriented. Some people can only dig stage center. They need a martyr to kill every month.
ANONYMOUS, quoted in *New York Times,* Mar. 1, 1971

This is a youth-oriented society, and the joke is on them because youth is a disease from which we all recover.
DOROTHY FULDHEIM, *A Thousand Friends,* 1974

The society which scorns excellence in plumbing because plumbing is a humble activity, and tolerates shoddiness in philosophy because philosophy is an exalted activity, will have neither good plumbing nor good philosophy. Neither its pipes nor its theories will hold water.
JOHN W. GARDNER, *Saturday Evening Post,* Dec. 1, 1962

A society's greatest illusions are expressed in its morals.
RICHARD SENNETT, *The Fall of Public Man,* 1977

Is a society which frequently takes five to ten years to dispose of a single criminal case entitled to call itself an "organized" society?
CHIEF JUSTICE WARREN E. BURGER, speech at Ripon College, July 1967

You can measure a society by who shows up on skid row.
JEROME HANNAMAN, quoted in *Newsweek,* Sept. 23, 1974

It has been said that a society can be judged by the way it treats its children.
RICHARD N. GOTTFRIED, N.Y. State assemblyman, *New York Times,* May 11, 1976

Social progress can be measured with precision by the social position of the female sex.
> KARL MARX, quoted in *Columbia Forum,* Summer 1972

My own test is this: How does that society treat its old people and, indeed, all its members who are not useful and productive in the narrowest sense?
> KENNETH D. KAUNDA, *A Humanist in Africa,* Colin M. Morris, ed., 1968

People never see their environments. They never know them. They always know the preceding one.
> MARSHALL MCLUHAN, *Quote,* Oct. 8, 1967

We have changed our environment more quickly than we know how to change ourselves.
> WALTER LIPPMANN, *Drift and Mastery,* 1914

Anthropologists may go all over the world, only to discover that the most bizarre culture is the one they started from.
> LAURA NADER, quoted in *Newsweek,* July 20, 1970

If the whole society should come to an end, it would take me fifteen minutes to regain my composure.
> ST. IGNATIUS LOYOLA, quoted in *Newsweek,* Jan. 27, 1975

SOCIETY: THE SET

There are only about four hundred people in New York society.
> WARD MCALLISTER, interview in *New York Herald,* 1888

The 400 has been marked down to 3.98
> ANONYMOUS, quoted in *New York Times,* Nov. 2, 1975

Social life is a form of do-it-yourself theater.
> MURIEL OXENBERG MURPHY, interview in *New York Times,* July 23, 1976

Cocktails are society's most enduring invention.
> ELSA MAXWELL, quoted in Stephen Birmingham, *The Right People,* 1968

SOCIOLOGY

The illumination of experience.
PAUL STARR, *New York Times,* Oct. 31, 1976

Sociology, the guilty science, functions best by alarm.
HORTENSE CALISHER, *New York Times,* Sept. 19, 1977

It is *lower* middle-class, as shown by its use of big words and bad language.
SOCIOLOGIST, quoted in *Newsweek,* Oct. 7, 1974

Those academic accountants who think that truth can be shaken from an abacus.
PETER S. PRESCOTT, *Newsweek,* Apr. 14, 1972

Novels, when well-written, tell you more about life than the most sophisticated computerized sociology.
ROSMARIE WITTMAN LAMB, *New York Times,* June 22, 1975

There seems to be a touching belief among certain Ph.D.s in sociology that Ph.D.s in sociology will never be corrupted by power. Like Sir Galahad's, their strength is as the strength of ten because their heart is pure; and their heart is pure because they are scientists and have taken six thousand hours of social studies.
ALDOUS HUXLEY, *Brave New World Revisited,* 1959

SOLITUDE see ALONENESS

THE SOUTH/SOUTHERNERS

So many inconsistent Souths—the lazy South and the fighting South; the segregationist South and the liberal South; the booster South and the populist South; the rapacious urban South and the land-worshiping rural South; the black South and the white South.
ELI EVANS, *New York Times,* Jan. 16, 1977

Many southern states have political totems: tobacco in North Carolina, textiles in South Carolina, cotton in Mississippi, and oil in Louisiana and Texas. So long as an incumbent politician is faithful to the totem of his state, evil spirits seldom touch him.
ROBERT SHERRILL, *New York Times,* Nov. 7, 1971

They are great politicians. They are just more clever than the others. Just more clever.
RICHARD M. NIXON, "White House Tapes," Feb. 8, 1973

I always suspected the carpetbaggers were learners down here. They didn't bring it with them; they were taking lessons.
T. HARRY WILLIAMS, quoted in Jack Bass and Walter De Vries, *The Transformation of Southern Politics,* 1976

You know what ruined the country? The war. First World War. The bigwigs in Washington sent all the damn Yankees south and sent all the Southern people north and we haven't gotten it straightened out yet.
MATTIE WHITE, 100-year-old Texan, quoted in *Newsweek,* July 4, 1976

The South has produced writers as the Dark Ages produced saints.
ALFRED KAZIN, *Bright Book of Life,* 1973

Anything [written] that comes out of the South is going to be called grotesque by the Northern reader, unless it is grotesque, in which case it will be called realistic.
FLANNERY O'CONNOR

The Southern belle . . . is frigid, passionate, sweet, bitchy and scatter-brained—all at the same time.
FLORENCE KING, *Southern Ladies and Gentlemen,* 1975

You step on one of those magnolia blossoms and you'll break your foot.
MISSISSIPPIAN ON THE SOUTHERN BELLE, quoted in *New York Times,* June 2, 1976

Southerners are probably not more hospitable than New Englanders are; they are simply more willing to remind you of the fact that they are being hospitable.
RAY L. BIRDWHISTELL, interview in Israel Shenker, *Words and Their Masters,* 1974

An Easterner solicits the name of your school. A Northerner wants to know what business you're in. The first question most of us Southerners ask you, however, is, "Who was your grandmother, dear?"
MARILYN M. MICHAELSON, letter to *Newsweek,* July 18, 1977

Do you want a portrait of a New Southerner? He is Billy Graham on Sunday and Richard Nixon the rest of the week.
WALKER PERCY, *Lancelot*, 1977

We've been the butt of every bad joke for a hundred years. Don't let the Washington politicians keep one of *us* out of the White House.
SOUTHERN RADIO AD FOR JIMMY CARTER'S CAMPAIGN, 1976

SOVIET UNION/THE RUSSIANS

One of the reasons it's very, very hard to get pro-Russian for more than a few weeks is that we keep coming face to face with the fact that the Soviet Union must probably be the most boring country in the history of nations.
NORMAN MAILER, speech at "Theater of Ideas," N.Y.C., May 1968

If one did not know better it would seem the whole place is some gigantic post office and everyone its employee.
ARTHUR MILLER, *Harper's Magazine,* Sept. 1969

Russia scares me. The people on buses are so serious, they look like they're going to the electric chair.
MUHAMMAD ALI, quoted in *Newsweek,* June 26, 1978

The whole country has a fixation on shoes. Moscow is the only city where, if Marilyn Monroe walked down the street with nothing on but a pair of shoes, people would stare at her feet first.
JOHN GUNTHER, *Inside Russia Today,* 1962

I think the only advantage of their form of government is that it stops graffiti.
JOHN LINDSAY, quoted in Leonard Lyons' column, May 21, 1973

The Soviet Union exports violinists almost the way the United States does wheat.
RAYMOND ERICSON, *New York Times,* Oct. 30, 1975

Dealing with the Russians is like trying to play music through an ultrasonic dog whistle.
YUGOSLAV DIPLOMAT, quoted in C. L. Sulzberger, *The Last of the Giants,* 1970

The average Russian is no more interested in communism than the average American is interested in God.
ERICH FROMM, quoted in Richard I. Evans, *Dialogue with Erich Fromm*, 1966

PROSECUTOR: Do you know whom we were fighting [in World War II]?
BORIS KOCHUBIEVSKY: Fascism.
P: What were we fighting for? Was it freedom?
K: Yes.
P: Did we win?
K: Yes.
P: Well, there we are then; so we have freedom.
KIEV REGIONAL COURT RECORD, May 1969, quoted in Soviet underground bulletin, *Chronicle of Current Events, No. 8*

This is something you should bear in mind about the Russian. The better things go for him, the more arrogant he is. When we are successful, keep out of our way.
SOVIET DIPLOMAT, 1944, quoted in George F. Kennan, *Memoirs 1925–1950*, 1967

If we and the Soviet Union escape war in the next 30 years, we'll both wind up practically with the same economic system. I emphasize the word *economic*. It will be the welfare state writ large. I hope we won't lose our democracy, and I hope Russia will get more.
NORMAN THOMAS, 1959

SPAIN/THE SPANISH

This most cohesive and mutually abrasive nationality.
RICHARD EDER, *New York Times*, May 26, 1975

Since Spain has not had long periods of notably healthy government for nearly 500 years, Spanish culture may be said to have had a long history of existing in spite of official Spain.
BARBARA PROBST SOLOMON, *New York Times*, Sept. 18, 1977

A Catalan right-of-center party would be left of center anywhere else in Spain.
JAMES M. MARKHAM, *New York Times*, Nov. 7, 1976

Spain imports tourists and exports chambermaids.
CARLOS FUENTES, *New York Times*, May 5, 1974

The Spaniard is so proud he will fight and lose; a Portuguese is so vain he cannot bear to lose face and would avoid it rather than risk that.
PORTUGUESE BUSINESSMAN, quoted in *New York Times,* Oct. 12, 1975

SPORTS also see BASEBALL; BOWLING; FOOTBALL; GOLF; HOCKEY; TENNIS

I always turn to the sports page first. The sports page records people's accomplishments; the front page nothing but man's failure.
CHIEF JUSTICE EARL WARREN, quoted in Marabel Morgan, *Total Joy,* 1976

Professional sports should be reported on the entertainment pages along with circuses and vaudeville.
AVERY BRUNDAGE, obituary in *New York Times,* May 9, 1975

Sportsworld is a state of mind in which the winner becomes good because he won.
ROBERT LIPSYTE, *SportsWorld,* 1975

People don't want to see touch football. They want to see two guys knock the crap out of each other.
MIKE ANDERSON, contact karate promoter, quoted in *Newsweek,* July 14, 1975

Sports is like a war without the killing.
TED TURNER, "60 Minutes," CBS-TV, July 24, 1977

Baseball happens to be a game of cumulative tension. . . . Football, basketball and hockey are played with hand grenades and machine guns.
JOHN LEONARD, *New York Times,* Nov. 2, 1975

A professional football team warms up grimly and disparately, like an army on maneuvers: the ground troops here, the tanks there, the artillery and air force over there. Basketball teams, after the perfunctory lay-up drill, fall into the crowded isolation and personal style of ten city kids shooting at the same basket or playing one-on-one. A baseball team horses around the batting cage, leisurely shags flies, romps across the outfield, chats with the other team; the atmosphere is as frisky and relaxed as a country fair.
TED SOLOTAROFF, *New York Times,* June 11, 1972

A sportswriter is entombed in a prolonged boyhood.
JIMMY CANNON, *No Cheering in the Press Box,* Jerome Holtzman, ed., 1974

The toy department.
CITY-ROOM REPORTERS' TERM FOR THE SPORTS DEPARTMENT

STANDARD OF LIVING

What is called a high standard of living consists, in considerable measure, in arrangements for avoiding muscular energy, increasing sensual pleasure and for enhancing caloric intake above any conceivable nutritional requirement.
JOHN KENNETH GALBRAITH, *The Affluent Society,* 1958

We boast the highest standard of living when it's only the biggest.
FRANK LLOYD WRIGHT, quoted in Leonard Lyons' column, May 31, 1969

STATE DEPARTMENT also see BUREAUCRACY/BUREAUCRATS; DIPLOMACY; FOREIGN POLICY

Dealing with the State Department is like watching an elephant become pregnant.
FRANKLIN D. ROOSEVELT, quoted in H. R. Haldeman, *The Ends of Power,* 1978

A bowl of jelly.
JOHN F. KENNEDY, quoted in John Franklin Campbell, *The Foreign Affairs Fudge Factory,* 1971

STATISTICS also see AVERAGES; POLLS

Statistics are like alienists—they will testify for either side.
FIORELLO H. LA GUARDIA, *Liberty,* May 1933

The most exact of false sciences.
JEAN CAU, interview in Israel Shenker, *Words and Their Masters,* 1974

He uses statistics as a drunken man uses lamp posts—for support rather than illumination.
ATTRIBUTED TO ANDREW LANG

With seasonally adjusted temperatures, you could eliminate winter in Canada.
ROBERT L. STANSFIELD, on Canadian government announcement of a "seasonally adjusted" decline in unemployment, quoted in *New York Times,* Feb. 21, 1971

Statistics, which first secured prestige here by a supposedly impartial utterance of stark fact, have enlarged their dominion over the American consciousness by becoming the most powerful statement of the "ought"—displacers of moral imperatives, personal ideals, and unfulfilled objectives.
DANIEL J. BOORSTIN, *The Decline of Radicalism,* 1969

It does not follow that because something *can* be counted it therefore *should* be counted.
HAROLD L. ENARSON, speech to Society for College and University Planning, Sept. 1975

Because there weren't any balance-of-payments statistics.
JAMES CALLAGHAN WHEN ASKED WHY THERE WERE NO BALANCE-OF-PAYMENT CRISES IN QUEEN VICTORIA'S REIGN, quoted in *Wall Street Journal,* Jan. 12, 1966

STEALING also see CRIME

The number-one rule of thieves is that nothing is too small to steal.
JIMMY BRESLIN, "Evening News," NBC-TV, May 15, 1974

When you buy dog food, everybody trusts you.
GARRETT TRAPNELL, supermarket check "skinner," quoted in Eliot Asinof, *The Fox Is Crazy Too,* 1976

It seems they do it for money.
PETER ANDREWS ON SOCIOLOGICAL STUDY OF WHY GYPSIES STEAL, *New York Times,* Nov. 9, 1975

Is forbidden to steal towels, please. If you are not person to do such is please not to read notice.
SIGN IN TOKYO HOTEL ROOM, quoted in *Holiday,* May 5, 1969

STEREOTYPES also see PREJUDICES

Those who believe the tags—that they are "middle-aged," "adolescent," "Jewish," "member of a fraternity," as though this were predictive of their behavior—are foolish. In a society which has substituted the bell curve for the cross, to take a concept which is useful for a census-taker or statistician and apply it to oneself is the mark of a fool.
RAY L. BIRDWHISTELL, interview in *New York Times,* Apr. 1, 1969

We categorize people, call them names like "culturally disadvantaged" or "white racists," names that say something all right but not enough—because those declared "culturally disadvantaged" so often are at the same time shrewd, sensitive and in possession of their own culture, just as those called "white racists" have other sides to themselves, can be generous and decent, can take note of and be responsive to the black man's situation.
ROBERT COLES, *The South Goes North,* 1972

Tolerably early in life I discovered that one of the unpardonable sins, in the eyes of most people, is for a man to go about unlabelled. The world regards such a person as the police do an unleashed dog.
T. H. HUXLEY, *Quote,* Nov. 6, 1966

STOCK MARKET

There is a way to make a lot of money in the market; unfortunately it is the same way to lose a lot of money in the market.
PETER PASSELL AND LEONARD ROSE, *The Best,* 1974

October, this is one of the peculiarly dangerous months to speculate in stocks. The others are: July, January, September, April, November, May, March, June, December, August and February.
MARK TWAIN

In Wall Street the only thing that's hard to explain is—next week.
LOUIS RUKEYSER, "Wall Street Week," PBS, Oct. 1, 1976

The more money you have, the harder it is to outperform the market, because the law of averages will mug you in the next alley.
AXIOM OF PORTFOLIO MANAGEMENT, quoted in *Business Week,* Nov. 17, 1973

Once to accommodate a sick friend, I ghost-wrote his brokerage letter for a spell; no one noticed the difference even though I purposely engaged in double-talk, cliché, and empty tautology. Indeed, to tell the immodest truth, his fan mail swelled a bit.
PAUL A. SAMUELSON, *Newsweek*, Aug. 21, 1978

The stock market has called nine of the last five recessions.
PAUL A. SAMUELSON, lecture at M.I.T., 1960

STUPIDITY also see INTELLECT/INTELLIGENCE

Stupidity is more difficult to control than evil.
LORD GOODMAN, *The Sack of Bath*, 1973

I am patient with stupidity, but not with those who are proud of it.
EDITH SITWELL, quoted in Elizabeth Salter, *The Last Years of a Rebel*, 1967

The good Lord set definite limits to man's wisdom, but set no limits on his stupidity—and that's just not fair.
KONRAD ADENAUER, quoted in *Forbes*, Mar. 15, 1975

The quickest of us walk well-wadded with stupidity.
GEORGE ELIOT, *Middlemarch*, 1872

SUBURBS also see CITY; TOWNS, SMALL

Suburbia lives imaginatively in Bonanza-Land.
MARSHALL MCLUHAN AND QUENTIN FIORE, *The Medium Is the Massage*, 1967

The rich are moving out of your cities two yards a day, including weekends.
CONSTANTINOS DOXIADIS, quoted in *New York Times*, July 8, 1969

They conceive of the city's problems as something you can run away from. But there isn't a far enough place to run.
JOHN W. GARDNER, quoted in *New York Times*, June 7, 1969

The contrived homogeneity of many suburbs, in violation of the American tradition of pluralism, has produced a kind of cultural dehydration.
REPORT, President's Task Force on Suburban Problems, Dec. 14, 1968

The people would talk about their lawns and the stock market like it was their sex lives.
STEPHEN MacDONALD, former suburbanite, quoted in *New York Times*, Apr. 14, 1968

On weekends, everybody plays tennis, and it's very competitive. The last thing it's for is laughs and fun.
SUBURBANITE, quoted in Alex Shoumatoff, *Westchester*, 1979

The great advantage of suburban tract housing is that it is junk and we can throw it away without losing anything. The only bad things are the permanent basements and the monumental barbecues.
PETER BRABHAM, speech at Aspen International Design Conference, 1965

SUBWAYS also see CITY; TRANSPORTATION

The crisis in human dignity. . . . I've been spat on, vomited on, pushed and shoved, delayed three hours in a fire, and wound up on a D train which became an F train in midflight.
HAROLD M. PROSHANSKY, interview in *New York Times*, Apr. 3, 1971

When you ride the subway twice a day, it's difficult to think of the immortal soul.
ANONYMOUS

It is 3:30 in the morning and I am the only one in this subway station and I'm scared.
GRAFFITO, N.Y.C. subway station, 1970

SUCCESS also see FAILURE; LOSING; MAKING IT

In America, it's the big nickel or nothing; in between, nothing but tundra.
SAUL MALOFF, *New York Times*, Mar. 23, 1975

FIX THE FLIVVER AND BUY A WILD EASTER HAT.
CARL SANDBURG'S TELEGRAM TO HIS WIFE AFTER SELLING RIGHTS TO HIS LINCOLN BIOGRAPHY, quoted in Helga Sandburg, *A Great and Glorious Romance*, 1978

Everybody agrees that success has not changed me at all, but I see that everybody around me has changed.
MILOS FORMAN, "Dick Cavett Show," PBS, July 2, 1979

In my 20s, young ladies turned away from me nobly; now they smile at me with all their teeth.

JAMES ENSOR, nineteenth-century artist, quoted in *Newsweek*, Jan. 31, 1977

Now that I'm here, where am I?

JANIS JOPLIN, quoted in *Newsweek*, Mar. 28, 1977

There is an obvious cure for Failure—and that is Success. But what is the cure for Success?

DANIEL J. BOORSTIN, *Democracy and Its Discontents*, 1974

Is anyone who's successful universally beloved? America was built on the fact that if you get your head and shoulders above the crowd, someone's there to shoot you down.

TOM SNYDER, interview in *TV Guide*, May 8, 1976

Every time a friend succeeds I die a little.

GORE VIDAL, quoted in *New York Times*, Feb. 4, 1973

Success is the sole earthly judge of right and wrong.

ADOLF HITLER, *Mein Kampf*, 1924

The bitch-goddess.

WILLIAM JAMES, letter to H. G. Wells, Sept. 11, 1906

SUFFERING

Suffering exists in order to make people think.

EZRA POUND, quoted in Mary de Rachewiltz, *Discretions*, 1971

Suffering is the swiftest beast that bears us to perfection.

QUOTED WITHOUT ATTRIBUTION IN LETTER OF THOMAS MANN

I do not believe that sheer suffering teaches. If suffering alone taught, all the world would be wise. To suffering must be added mourning, understanding, patience, love, openness and the willingness to remain vulnerable.

ANNE MORROW LINDBERGH, *Hour of Gold, Hour of Lead*, 1973

SUICIDE also see DEATH

Like divorce, suicide is a confession of failure. And like divorce, it is shrouded in excuses and rationalizations.
A. ALVAREZ, *The Savage God,* 1972

If the rate of cancer or TB or anything else was up like suicide, we'd hear about it and the government would be allocating money to study it and wipe it out.
FRANCINE KLAGSBRUN, *Too Young to Die,* 1976

The right to choose death when life no longer holds meaning is not only the next liberation but the last human right.
MARYA MANNES, *Last Rights,* 1974

Is the best life the longest life?
DR. SEYMOUR PERLIN, speech at International Congress on Suicide Prevention, Jerusalem, Oct. 24, 1975

SUN also see MOON

The sun, with all those planets revolving around it and dependent upon it, can still ripen a bunch of grapes as if it had nothing else in the universe to do.
GALILEO GALILEI, quoted in *Reader's Digest,* Oct. 1968

The sun is pure communism everywhere except in the cities, where it's private property.
MALCOLM DE CHAZAL, *Plastic Sense,* 1971

SUPERMARKETS also see MERCHANDISING

Go into one of those vast sepulchral markets, where people hardly talk to one another, and where self-service prevails, and you quit it more wormy than Lazarus.
EDWARD DAHLBERG, *New York Times,* Mar. 5, 1967

To shop in a supermarket is rather like shopping with Kafka.
JOHN KEATS, *What Ever Happened to Mom's Apple Pie?,* 1976

If you ask for something you want but do not see, the store manager will put you in your place, for he is a *gauleiter*.
KEATS, *What Ever Happened to Mom's Apple Pie?*

The store managers start as bag boys and keep going until they're the ruler of the Queen's Navy.
ROY BEASLEY, quoted in *Newsweek,* Jan. 16, 1978

SURVIVAL/SURVIVORS also see FAILURE; MAKING IT; SUCCESS

Who speaks of victory? Survival is the issue.
ATTRIBUTED TO RAINER MARIA RILKE

Of the thirty-six ways of avoiding disaster, running away is best.
CHINESE PROVERB

When the water reaches the upper decks, follow the rats.
FRANK KENT, quoted in *Newsweek,* Jan. 20, 1969

Women make better survivors than men.
TERENCE DES PRES, *The Survivor,* 1976

Of the ancient past, only the crab and cockroach are with us now.
Kaiser News, no. 3, 1967

SWITZERLAND/THE SWISS

The real good fortune of belonging to a small country is that in it patriotism is not at odds with humanity.
MAX FRISCH, *Sketchbook 1946–1949,* 1977

If Switzerland didn't exist, the financial world would have to invent it.
FINANCIAL AXIOM

This country will never produce any great ideas or great achievements because the people don't like or trust anyone who rises above the ordinary. But it is a very agreeable place to live, people are so polite and helpful.
FRANÇOIS BONDY, quoted in *New York Times,* Sept. 7, 1976

The only interesting thing that can happen in a Swiss bedroom is suffocation by feather mattress.
>DALTON TRUMBO, *Additional Dialogue: Letters of Dalton Trumbo, 1942–1962*, Helen Manfull, ed., 1970

THE SYSTEM

A president doesn't make the system. The system makes the president.
>MICHAEL DANN, former president of CBS, quoted in David Halberstam, *The Powers That Be*, 1979

Stay in the system. Don't get mad—get even.
>JIMMY BRESLIN, interview in Peter Joseph, *Good Times*, 1973

TALENT also see GENIUS

The excitable gift.
>ANNE SEXTON, "Live" in *Live or Die*, 1966

Thousands of people have talent. I might just as well congratulate you on having eyes in your head. The one and only thing that counts is: Do you have staying power?
>NOËL COWARD, quoted in Lilli Palmer, *Change Lobsters—and Dance*, 1975

Whom the gods wish to destroy they first call promising.
>CYRIL CONNOLLY, quoted in *New York Times*, Apr. 10, 1977

Nothing could be easier than to compile lists of novelists, poets, playwrights, critics, who can manipulate words and ideas with the skill of poolplayers.
>ALAN PRYCE-JONES ON TALENT VS. GENIUS, *New York Post*, Mar. 10, 1969

TALLNESS also see SHORTNESS

Because I'm tall, people notice me on the street. I have to be respectable. I can't dress like a bum except around the house.
>LARUE MARTIN, 6'11", interview in *New York Times*, June 8, 1976

About the only thing I can buy easily is a tie clip.
LARRY MELILLO, 6'8", quoted in *New York Times,* May 5, 1971

Some tall people act like it's a special talent.
ANONYMOUS

Horizontally, it doesn't make any difference.
ANNE MEARA ON BEING A HEAD TALLER THAN HER HUSBAND, quoted in
Newsweek, Mar. 3, 1975

TAPE RECORDERS

The tape recorder is to blame for lumpen-sincerity and honking books.
JOHN LEONARD, *New York Times,* May 1, 1977

A monster with the appetite of a tapeworm. . . . through its creature,
oral history, [it engenders] an artificial survival of trivia of appalling
proportions.
BARBARA TUCHMAN, interview in *Newsweek,* Aug. 5, 1974

People forget that it takes two years to listen to two years of tapes.
H. R. HALDEMAN, *The Ends of Power,* 1978

TAXES

People hate taxes the way children hate brushing their teeth—and in
the same shortsighted way.
PAUL A. SAMUELSON, *Newsweek,* Mar. 6, 1972

Taxes are what we pay for civilized society.
OLIVER WENDELL HOLMES, JR., quoted in Gerald Carson, *The Golden
Egg,* 1977

It looks as if the tax laws are a conspiracy in restraint of understanding.
TAX COURT CHIEF JUDGE HOWARD A. DAWSON, JR., quoted in *Newsweek,* Apr. 4, 1977

Tax reform means don't tax you, don't tax me, tax that fellow behind
the tree.
RUSSELL B. LONG, Senate debate, 1976

TEACHERS/TEACHING   also   see   COLLEGES/UNIVERSI-
TIES; EDUCATION; SCHOOLS

There is no use trying to make ideas safe for students. You have to
make students safe for ideas.
      ALEXANDER HEARD, quoted in *Newsweek*, May 25, 1970

When I transfer my knowledge, I teach. When I transfer my beliefs, I
indoctrinate.
      ARTHUR DANTO, *Analytic Philosophy of Knowledge*, 1968

Teachers should unmask themselves, admit into consciousness the idea
that one does not need to know everything there is to know and one
does not have to pretend to know everything there is to know.
      ESTHER P. ROTHMAN, *Troubled Teachers*, 1977

A neurotic does not teach, he infects.
      CRAIG W. JAMES, *Social Studies*, Oct. 1968

Professors are the only people who never listen.
      GÜNTER GRASS, interview in *New York Times*, Mar. 19, 1970

They simply can't discuss a thing. Habit compels them to deliver a lecture.
      HAL BOYLE, *Quote*, July 21, 1968

When the man who knows all about the fruit fly chromosomes finds
himself sitting next to an authority on Beowulf . . . there may be an
uneasy silence.
      BRAND BLANSHARD, *The Uses of a Liberal Education*, Eugene Free-
man, ed., 1974

The ambitious teacher can only rise in the academic bureaucracy by
writing at complicated length about writing that has already been
much written about.
      GORE VIDAL, *Matters of Fact and of Fiction*, 1977

In much academic writing, clarity runs a poor second to invulnerabil-
ity.
      RICHARD HUGO, *The Triggering Town*, 1979

Almost every major professor has administrative experience equal to
that of the head of a small corporation.
      GEOFFREY HARTMAN, quoted in *Newsweek*, Jan. 2, 1978

Compared with the college politician, the real article seems like an amateur.
Woodrow Wilson, quoted in Henry Wilkinson Bragdon, *Wilson: The Academic Years,* 1967

If a university faculty were to unionize and then use the strike to achieve its objectives, it might find that college teachers are not taken as seriously as sanitation workers.
Albert H. Bowker, quoted in *Wall Street Journal,* Dec. 16, 1968

TECHNOLOGY also see MODERN TIMES

Technological society has succeeded in multiplying the opportunities for pleasure, but it has great difficulty in generating joy.
Pope Paul VI, apostolic exhortation, *Gaudete in Domino,* May 16, 1975

It is ... the modern version of original sin, tempting us beyond the limits of moral judgment and intelligence.
W. H. Ferry, speech at Dartmouth College, June 1976

The continuing increases in purchasing power and leisure time that have made Americans the envy of working people everywhere have not come from working ever harder—but from working ever smarter.
William C. Freund, *Newsweek,* Jan. 29, 1979

One consequence of postwar technology has been the acceleration of change in our society, so that we seem to produce a new generation about every five years.
Ross Macdonald, *New York Times,* Apr. 25, 1971

The characteristic of the exploding technological society is that changes sooner or later *must* take place in a fraction of the time necessary even to assess the situation.
John Wilkinson, *John Wilkinson on the Quantitative Society,* 1964

In guessing the direction of technology it is wise to ask who is in the best position to profit most.
Ben H. Bagdikian, *The Information Machines,* 1971

It would appear that national ambitions and technological progress go hand in hand with the tonic-dominant harmonies of the Sousa march.
Yehudi Menuhin, *Theme and Variations,* 1972

If we continue in the direction we are going today, we will make this world uninhabitable—not because we want to, but because we don't care.
ROBERT THEOBOLD, quoted in *New York Times*, Mar. 3, 1968

It was naive of the 19th century optimists to expect paradise from technology—and it is equally naive of the 20th century pessimists to make technology the scapegoat for such old shortcomings as man's blindness, cruelty, immaturity, greed, and sinful pride.
PETER F. DRUCKER, *Technology, Management and Society,* 1970

Just the other day I listened to a young fellow sing a very passionate song about how technology is killing us and all that. But before he started, he bent down and plugged his electric guitar into the wall socket.
PAUL GOODMAN, quoted at American Marketing Association Congress, June 16, 1969

Today technology has a bad name. Young people believe it is irrelevant. If they continue to believe this, we, and particularly they, will soon be irrelevant.
EDWARD TELLER, speech at Conference of Governors, N.Y.C., May 12, 1973

TELEPHONES

The one thing that can interrupt intercourse.
EDMUND CARPENTER, *Oh, What a Blow That Phantom Gave Me!*, 1973

Prolonged adolescence was invented in the 20th century so that there would be somebody to use the phone in the afternoon. . . . Before the telephone, there were no teenagers.
JOHN LEONARD, *New York Times*, Aug. 25, 1976

Instead of belles-lettres we have Ma Bell.
DONAL HENAHAN, *New York Times*, Nov. 6, 1977

In Britain it will connect you to all sorts of people you had no intention of speaking to in the first place.
ROBERT B. SEMPLE, JR., on London's confused phone connections, *New York Times,* Aug. 6, 1976

No greater instrument for counterrevolution and conspiracy can be imagined.
> JOSEPH STALIN, opposing Trotsky's plan for a modern telephone system in the Soviet Union, *The Social Impact of the Telephone,* Ithiel da Sola Pool, ed., 1977

TELEVISION see TV

TEMPER

It was my daughter who first suggested to me that bad temper is a form of public littering, and indicated that she would as soon have a casual acquaintance drop her dirty Kleenex on her as her foul language and ill-humor.
> DR. WILLARD GAYLIN, *Feelings,* 1979

The worst tempered people I've met were people who knew they were wrong.
> WILSON MIZNER, quoted in Richard O'Connor, *Rogue's Progress,* 1975

TENNIS also see SPORTS

A perfect combination of violent action taking place in an atmosphere of total tranquility.
> BILLIE JEAN KING, *Billie Jean,* 1974

I can't subscribe to that old cliché that it is not whether you win or lose, but how you play the game. In that case, why keep score?
> DONALD DELL, quoted in *Newsweek,* June 24, 1968

People don't seem to understand that it's a damn war out there.
> JIMMY CONNORS, quoted in Thomas Tutko and William Bruns, *Winning Is Everything and Other American Myths,* 1976

Hit at the girl whenever possible.
> BILL TILDEN ON MIXED DOUBLES, quoted in Phil Pepe and Zander Hollander, *The Book of Sports Lists,* 1979

IF YOU CAN CONQUER YOUR MIND, YOU CAN CONQUER TENNIS AND LIFE.
> HEADLINE, *New York Times,* Feb. 13, 1977

If God had meant Wimbledon to be played in great weather, he would have put it in Acapulco.
BRITISH TENNIS OFFICIAL, quoted in *Newsweek*, July 4, 1977

TERRORISM

Propaganda by deed.
WALTER LAQUEUR, *Terrorism*, 1977

The success of a terrorist operation depends almost entirely on the amount of publicity it receives. This was one of the main reasons for the shift from rural guerilla to urban terror in the 1960s; in the cities the terrorist could always count on the presence of journalists and TV cameras.
LAQUEUR, *Terrorism*

The terrorists are most dangerous not when they act like the crazies of the '60s, but when they begin to act as sovereign states. That is when people start to die.
DR. FREDERICK HACKER, quoted in *Newsweek*, Feb. 25, 1974

Nobody really knows what kind of society they envision.
KURT SONTHEIMER, quoted in *Time*, Oct. 31, 1977

Terrorism, a set of tactics intended to further a group's goals, may itself become an ideology . . . terrorism for the sake of terrorism.
BRIAN JENKINS, report for State Department, Mar. 26, 1976

If you want an open society you have to put up with the chaos.
J. BOWYER BELL, quoted in *Newsweek*, Dec. 26, 1977

TEXAS also see HOUSTON

In Texas you can look farther and see less than in any other place.
APHORISM

That overgrown sandbox.
KATHARINE SWAN, letter to *Newsweek*, Oct. 30, 1978

Home of the shoot-out and divorce-by-pistol.
Time, Apr. 19, 1968

When a Texas Ranger tells you to stop doing what you're doing and you don't stop, that's suicide.
CORONER RULING AS SUICIDES TWO CONVICTS KILLED WHILE ATTEMPTING TO ESCAPE FROM PRISON, quoted in *Newsweek,* Dec. 12, 1977

In west Texas, the higher a man rises in worldly affairs, the more likely he will be given a lowly and even earthy nickname by his admiring and envious fellow citizens.
H. ALLEN SMITH, *Return of the Virginian,* 1974

Texas is annexed. I think I'll expatriate myself.
GEORGE TEMPLETON STRONG, Dec. 30, 1845, *The Diary of George Templeton Strong,* Allan Nevins and Milton H. Thomas, eds., 1952

THEATER also see ACTORS/ACTING; HOLLYWOOD; MOVIES; SHOW BIZ

In the theater you work very, very hard right up to the curtain, here we go, bang, and adrenalin does the rest. In the movies the curtain never goes up. It's like a loose rubber band—no tension.
VERA ZORINA, interview in *Newsweek,* Oct. 9, 1967

The stage is actor's country. You have to get your passport stamped every so often or they take away your citizenship.
VANESSA REDGRAVE, interview in *Newsweek,* Feb. 10, 1975

The terrible thing about acting in the theater is that you have to do it at night.
KATHARINE HEPBURN, interview in *New York Times,* Jan. 16, 1976

There is something about seeing *real people* on a stage that makes a bad play more intimately, more personally offensive than any other art form.
ANATOLE BROYARD, *New York Times,* Feb. 6, 1976

In Broadway jargon, any play that's not a hit is a flop.
PAUL GARDNER, *New York Times,* Jan. 16, 1977

You know what the most remarkable moment in the theater is? It's the moment after the last performance. There's been that explosion of energy from the audience, and then there's the striking of the set. People come and take the nails out. Something's happened and it's finished. The theater is built on sand—it's like castles in the sand.
ANDREI SERBAN, interview in *Newsweek,* Feb. 28, 1977

THINNESS see FATNESS/THINNESS

THIRD WORLD

Some countries are going through their period of Richard III for the moment. No reason to scoff at them. We were there ourselves.
PETER USTINOV, interview in *Bookviews,* Nov. 1977

Watch the developing nations. It's a trillion dollar race.
HERMAN KAHN, quoted in *New Yorker,* Nov. 13, 1978

One illusion is that you can industrialize a country by building factories. You don't. You industrialize it by building markets.
PAUL G. HOFFMAN, obituary in *New York Times,* Oct. 9, 1974

What else do the banks do—walk in and turn off the lights in the country?
WILLIAM SLEE, London banker, on extending credit to heavily indebted underdeveloped countries, quoted in *Newsweek,* Feb. 27, 1978

TIME

Time is a slippery thing.
SHERWOOD ANDERSON, *Sherwood Anderson's Memoirs,* Ray Lewis White, ed., 1969

Time crumbs all ramparts.
W. H. AUDEN, "The Garrison" in *Epistle to a Godson and Other Poems,* 1972

Time is what keeps everything from happening all at once.
GRAFFITO, Bethel, Alaska, quoted in *New York Times,* Aug. 20, 1975

A measure of civilization is the degree that men perceive the use of time to be a problem.
ROBERT S. KLEEMEIER, *Aging and Leisure,* 1961

For so it is, oh Lord, my God, I measure it, but what it is I measure I do not know.
ST. AUGUSTINE, quoted in *New York Times,* Aug. 30, 1975

TOWNS, SMALL also see CITY; SUBURBS

I never thought of Plains as a sleepy little town. The ladies are always busy planting flowers, sewing, cooking. There are two garden clubs.
> A. L. BLANTON, mayor, Plains, Ga., quoted in *Newsweek,* May 3, 1976

It was the kind of place where on Saturday night everybody lined up in front of the barbershop to watch the haircuts.
> RODERICK LANKLER ON HIS NATIVE COURTLAND, N.Y., interview in *New York Post,* Oct. 28, 1976

Anyone needs me, they just sit down on the curb and I'll be by presently.
> RUSTY RUSTAD, one-man police force, Sacred Heart, Minn., quoted in *New York Times,* July 23, 1973

I'm so bored in the town where I live. I know all the vending machines by name.
> DAVID LEWIS, McMinnville, Ore., "Saturday Night Live," NBC-TV, Nov. 27, 1977

Even in small towns, everybody talks about Dubuque, Iowa.
> A. D. ANDERSON, quoted in *Princeton Alumni Weekly,* Nov. 20, 1973

TRADITION

Tradition means giving votes to that obscurest of classes, our ancestors. It is the democracy of the dead.
> W. H. AUDEN, *Columbia Forum,* Winter 1970

It's like this, when you live in a place you've always lived in, where your family has always lived. You get to see things not only in space but in time.
> SHIRLEY ANN GRAU, *Keepers of the House,* 1964

This is the only country I know which can create tradition by having a ball game a second time.
> RAY L. BIRDWHISTELL, interview in *New York Times*

TRAGEDY also see COMEDY/COMEDIANS; LAUGHTER

Comedies make comments, but tragedy reflects man's destiny.
> HERBERT LIEBERMAN, interview in *New York Post,* July 17, 1976

Tragedy has been debased by the squandering of the word on what is merely pathetic. Tragedy should be reserved for the disasters that strike down the high and the mighty because fortune or the gods have frowned on pride or ambition.
HUBERT SAAL, *Newsweek*, July 31, 1972

TRANSPORTATION also see AIRPLANES; AUTOMOBILES; SUBWAYS

Many people advocate mass transit for the other person so they themselves will be able to enjoy riding on congestion-free expressways.
ERIC SEVAREID, "Evening News," CBS-TV, 1970

Mass transportation is doomed to failure in North America because a person's car is the only place where he can be alone and think.
MARSHALL MCLUHAN, quoted in *Newsweek*, Sept. 22, 1975

When I was asked to come to the [Transportation] Department, I was asked that old saw: "If we can go to the moon, why can't we get across town?" Well the reason, I learned, is that it's tougher. There are people in the way getting across town, and there aren't any people on the way to the moon.
JAMES M. BEGGS, Under Secretary of Transportation, speech at Urban Technology Conference, N.Y.C., May 25, 1971

The train, the automobile, and the airplane long since have turned political subdivisions such as counties, states and municipalities into governmental fossils.
Kaiser News, no. 1, 1970

TRAVEL

Americans speak of "going to Europe" as though Europe were a place one could arrive at, like Columbus Circle.
BRITISH VISITOR, quoted in *New York Times*, June 19, 1977

Americans say they want to meet natives. But only as long as they never have to leave their Hilton bubble.
SKIP SKIPWORTH, travel agent, quoted in *Newsweek*, Jan. 17, 1977

I wish I weren't locked in my own language.
CAROL BURDICK HUDSON, *New York Times*, Dec. 22, 1974

What a magnificent banquet room this would make.
CÉSAR RITZ IN ST. PETER'S CATHEDRAL, quoted in *New York Times*, Dec. 26, 1968

It's my color—beige.
ELSIE DE WOLFE AT THE PARTHENON, quoted in *Fortune*, Mar. 1966

People in bus terminals look tired even before they start the trip.
JIMMY CANNON, *Nobody Asked Me, But...*, Jack and Tom Cannon, eds., 1978

I don't mind going someplace just so long as I can be home for lunch.
CHARLES SCHULZ, "Dick Cavett Show," PBS, Jan. 30, 1978

TRUTH also see **LIES/LIARS**

Truth is the baby of the world. It never gets old.
DICK GREGORY, "Wide World Special," ABC-TV, Nov. 14, 1975

The simple truth is never commonplace unless it is spoken by a commonplace mind.
ALLEN TATE, *Memoirs and Opinions 1926–1974*, 1975

I speak the truth, not so much as I would, but as much as I dare; and I dare a little more, as I grow older.
CATHERINE DRINKER BOWEN, *Family Portrait*, 1970

Believe those who are seeking the truth; doubt those who find it.
ANDRÉ GIDE, *So Be It*, 1959

No statement is so absurd that it doesn't contain some truth.
FRANK KNIGHT, quoted in *New York Times*, Oct. 17, 1976

TV also see **RADIO**

Television is simply automated day-dreaming.
LEE LOVINGER, *Quote*, July 30, 1967

Chewing gum for the eyes.
FRED ALLEN, quoted in *Newsweek*, Jan. 10, 1977

The whole message of American society—television—is you do not have to bear any discomfort.
EVELYN HANSEN, interview in *Newsweek,* May 15, 1978

It has spread the habit of instant reaction and stimulated the hope of instant results.
ARTHUR M. SCHLESINGER, JR., *Newsweek,* July 6, 1970

The Plug-In Drug.
TITLE OF BOOK BY MARIE WINN, 1977

Nothing is "really" real unless it happens on television.
DANIEL J. BOORSTIN, *New York Times,* Feb. 19, 1978

It's the menace that everyone loves to hate but can't seem to live without.
PADDY CHAYEFSKY, quoted in *Newsweek,* Nov. 22, 1976

I have come to feel about television the way I do about hamburgers: I eat a lot of hamburgers and I don't remember a single one of them.
JOHN BARROW, *New York Times,* Aug. 5, 1973

They say that 90 per cent of TV is junk. But 90 per cent of *everything* is junk.
GENE RODDENBERRY, TV producer, interview in *TV Guide,* Apr. 27, 1974

I've never seen it chiselled on stone tablets that TV must be uplifting.
JOHNNY CARSON, interview in *New Yorker,* Feb. 20, 1978

Television is a golden goose that lays scrambled eggs, and it is futile and probably fatal to beat it for not laying caviar.
LEE LOVINGER, quoted in *Public Utilities Fortnightly,* Sept. 8, 1966

In some ways television is more sophisticated and literate than the people who watch it.
LEO ROSTEN, "David Susskind Show," Metromedia, Feb. 19, 1978

Whatever its faults, it's a well-recognized godsend for people who are more or less housebound. No other period has ever had anything remotely like that.
ROBERT C. ALBERTS, *New York Times,* Nov. 17, 1974

People who deny themselves television deny themselves participation in life today. They are self-exiled from the world.
JOHN MASON BROWN, quoted in *Kaiser News,* no. 3, 1966

TV: COMMERCIALS also see ADVERTISING

Television is the business of gathering you and selling you like cattle to the advertisers.
NICHOLAS JOHNSON, speech at N.Y. Consumer Assembly, Mar. 4, 1972

How do you put on a meaningful drama or documentary that is adult, incisive, probing, when every fifteen minutes the proceedings are interrupted by twelve dancing rabbits with toilet paper?
ROD SERLING, speech at School of Communications, Ithaca College, 1974

You've got to bring on a couple of copulating elephants or something to stop people from tuning out.
DAVID OGILVY, advertising executive, quoted in *Newsweek,* Aug. 18, 1969

Commercials have become the most pervasive music in the history of—er, civilization.
JACK KROLL, *Newsweek,* Mar. 31, 1975

I think in TV jingle terms often.
JOYCE MAYNARD, *Looking Back,* 1973

The nostalgia buffs of the next century will collect tapes of the commercials we are hearing today, and they will make fun of them.
ANONYMOUS

TV: MOVIES/DRAMA also see MOVIES

America, on one level, is a great old-movie museum.
ANTHONY BURGESS, "David Susskind Show," Metromedia, Jan. 4, 1976

This is summer stock with 20 million people watching.
RICHARD CARLSON ON MADE-FOR-TV DRAMA, obituary in *New York Times,* Nov. 27, 1977

It takes you ten weeks to make a piece of crap. It takes me four days.
CAROL BURNETT WHEN WALTER MATTHAU ASKED WHY SHE MADE "THAT
TV CRAP," quoted in *Newsweek,* Sept. 25, 1978

TV: NEWS also see NEWS/NEWSPAPERS

Electronic journalism, like print journalism, is essentially a process of
trolling for information.
SHELDON ZALAZNICK, *Fortune,* May 1969

As professionals strive to capture the world in a few exciting words
and pictures there emerges a new semblance of the truth, a kind of al-
legory of events.
DANIEL SCHORR, *Clearing the Air,* 1977

Television has a real problem. They have no page two. Consequently
every story gets the same play and comes across to the viewer as a
really big, scary one.
ART BUCHWALD, quoted in *Public Utilities Fortnightly,* Sept. 25, 1969

The superficial symptoms are those most easily dramatized. So a
bloody head shocks the eye, while the challenge of the anti-intellectual
brain passes without a report.
KINGMAN BREWSTER, speech at American Association for Advancement of Science, Boston, Dec. 19, 1969

We perform the function of responsible gossips, and shouldn't pretend
that we do more.
JOHN HART, *TV Guide,* Mar. 25, 1972

Television is show business and thus TV news is a part of show business.
AV WESTIN, quoted in *Newsweek,* Oct. 11, 1976

Everywhere I went, I saw anchorpersons—men and women—devoting
the crucial 30 minutes immediately before air time not to gathering
and writing the news, but to applying makeup on their faces and
spraying their hair into immobility.
RON NESSEN, *TV Guide,* Dec. 2, 1978

The *Times* can't show you Nixon pushing Ziegler. It can't show you
beads of perspiration.
JOHN CHANCELLOR, quoted in *Newsweek,* Oct. 11, 1976

If we had seen a telecast of Flanders there might never have been another war.
> DON SAFRAN, *Dallas Times-Herald,* 1970

TV: PROGRAMMING

Program makers are supposed to devise and produce shows that will attract mass audiences without unduly offending ... or too deeply moving them. . . . Such ruffling, it is thought, will interfere with their ability to receive, recall, and respond to the commercial messages.
> BOB SHANKS, *The Cool Fire,* 1976

If minority views were aired regularly on prime time, it would cease to be prime time.
> REPORT, National Commission on the Causes and Prevention of Violence, Jan. 13, 1970

We don't even consider a program unless it can pull an audience of 80 million.
> CBS EXECUTIVE, quoted in *New York Post,* Nov. 27, 1976

It's ... the sort of go-for-broke daring that gave France the Maginot Line.
> HARRY F. WATERS, *Newsweek,* Dec. 15, 1975

In 1927 Philo T. Farnsworth transmitted television images without wires. . . . Farnsworth used the dollar sign as a test pattern.
> BEN H. BAGDIKIAN, *The Information Machines,* 1971

Television is the first truly democratic culture—the first culture available to everyone and entirely governed by what the people want. The most terrifying thing is what people do want.
> CLIVE BARNES, *New York Times,* Dec. 30, 1969

The amount of good programming on television in one year would fill Broadway theaters for twenty years.
> ROBERT WOOD, president, CBS-TV, quoted in *Newsweek,* Feb. 16, 1976

You can learn more about America by watching one half hour of "Let's Make a Deal" than you can get from watching Walter Cronkite for a month.
> MONTY HALL, program host, quoted in *Newsweek,* July 7, 1975

TV: TALK SHOWS

They're quite Puritan. You're not supposed to frighten people.
PETER USTINOV, interview in *Bookviews,* Nov. 1977

Being interviewed demands very little from a celebrity but time and canned opinions.
JOHN LEONARD, *New York Times,* Mar. 20, 1977

What we have is a chatterbox-equipped nightlight.
TERRY GALANOY ON JOHNNY CARSON, *Tonight!* 1972

Doing the show was like painting the George Washington Bridge. As soon as you finished one end, you started right in on the other.
JACK PAAR, interview in *Newsweek,* Aug. 14, 1972

Television is an invention that permits you to be entertained in your living room by people you wouldn't have in your home.
DAVID FROST, "David Frost Revue," CBS-TV, Sept. 19, 1971

TV: VIOLENCE also see VIOLENCE

Death has been tidied up, cleansed of harmful ingredients and repackaged in prime-time segments that pander to baser appetites but leave no unpleasant aftertaste. . . . The Caesars of network television permit no mess on the living room floor.
DONALD GODDARD, *New York Times,* Feb. 27, 1977

Why are sex and violence always linked? I'm afraid they'll blur together in people's minds—sexandviolence—until we can't tell them apart. I expect to hear a newscaster say, "The mob became unruly and the police were forced to resort to sex."
DICK CAVETT, *TV Guide,* July 22, 1978

TV: THE YOUNG

Most young people emerge from the darkened living room wearing television tubes for eyes and they will never see anything except what the "sponsor" puts on. These are the people who will mind the store and keep things going.
Kaiser News, no. 1, 1969

The average 16-year-old has clocked more time watching television than he has spent in school. *TV Guide* outsells every other magazine on the nation's newsstands. That's more serious than venereal disease.
JOHN LEONARD, *New York Times*, Apr. 17, 1977

One reason that children are inclined to learn from television is that it ... is never too busy to talk to them, and it never has to brush them aside while it does household chores.... Television seems to want their attention at any time, and goes to considerable lengths to attract it.
REPORT, National Commission on Causes and Prevention of Violence, Sept. 25, 1969

The Third Parent.
R. BUCKMINSTER FULLER, quoted in *Think*, 1969

TYPEWRITER/TYPING

Two-finger typists do terrible things to their muscles.
LEON EDEL, *New York Times*, Feb. 6, 1972

The electric typewriter ... is too brainy for me; it hits a letter if I breathe too hard.
ANN DICKINSON, *Writer's Digest*, July 1978

I believe that composing on the typewriter has probably done more than anything else to deteriorate English prose.
EDMUND WILSON, quoted in *New York Times*, Nov. 10, 1976

UNEMPLOYMENT

The hardest work in the world is being out of work.
WHITNEY M. YOUNG, JR., *Quote*, Dec. 3, 1967

There are times when I wonder not whether I will ever have a job again, but whether if I do, I will be able to function.
UNEMPLOYED EXECUTIVE, *New York Times*, May 31, 1977

It's not that your friends desert you, it's that they don't know what to do with you.
UNEMPLOYED BROKERAGE HOUSE RESEARCHER, quoted in "Adam Smith" (George Goodman), *Supermoney*, 1972

UNITED NATIONS

The United Nations is the psychoanalyst's couch of the world.
BRAZILIAN DIPLOMAT, quoted in *New York Times,* Oct. 14, 1974

Other countries regard it as a convenient spot for throwing tantrums.
ERIC REDMAN, *New York Times,* Oct. 6, 1974

The Security Council can't really bite, but if you're a small country they can gum you to death.
ISRAELI DIPLOMAT, quoted in *Newsweek,* July 3, 1967

One of the difficulties of the United Nations is that the smaller countries send their best men and the large countries send the men they can spare.
PETER USTINOV, "Dick Cavett Show," PBS, Mar. 28, 1979

UNIVERSE

You sit out at night and watch the stars and your eye consciously spans that distance and you wonder if you're sitting on an electron that revolves around a proton in a series of infinite universes.
JAMES JONES, *From Here to Eternity,* 1951

We step out of our solar system into the universe seeking only peace and friendship, to teach if we are called upon; to be taught if we are fortunate.
U.N. SEC. GEN. KURT WALDHEIM, U.N. message in *Voyager I,* launched toward outer space, Sept. 5, 1977

VICE PRESIDENTS also see PRESIDENTS

All that Hubert needs over there is a gal to answer the phone and a pencil with an eraser on it.
LYNDON B. JOHNSON ON HUBERT H. HUMPHREY, L.B.J. obituary in *New York Times,* Jan. 26, 1973

The best part of being Vice President is presiding over the Senate. Where else could I have Barry Goldwater addressing me as Mr. President?
NELSON D. ROCKEFELLER, quoted in *Wall Street Journal,* Sept. 19, 1975

There is absolutely no circumstance whatever under which I would accept that spot. Even if they tied and gagged me, I would find a way to signal by wiggling my ears.

> RONALD REAGAN AT PRESS CONFERENCE, 1968 Republican National Convention, Aug. 5, 1968

VIETNAM: BEFORE

If we have to fight, we will fight. You will kill ten of our men, and we will kill one of yours, and in the end it will be you who will tire of it.

> HO CHI MINH TO JEAN SAINTENY SHORTLY BEFORE THE WAR WITH FRANCE, 1945, quoted in *New York Times,* July 13, 1975

A year ago none of us could see victory. . . . Now we see it clearly—like light at the end of the tunnel.

> FRENCH GEN. HENRI EUGÈNE NAVARRE SIX MONTHS BEFORE THE DIEN-BIENPHU DEFEAT

Let every nation know, whether it wishes us well or ill, that we shall pay any price, bear any burden, meet any hardship, support any friend, oppose any foe to assure the survival and the success of liberty.

> JOHN F. KENNEDY, inaugural speech, Jan. 20, 1961

I predict that you will sink step by step into a bottomless military and political quagmire, however much you spend in men and money.

> CHARLES DE GAULLE TO JOHN F. KENNEDY, May 31, 1961, *Memoirs of Hope, 1958–1962,* 1971

We don't see the end of the tunnel, but I must say I don't think it's darker than it was a year ago, and in some ways lighter.

> JOHN F. KENNEDY, Dec. 12, 1962, quoted in Clyde Edwin Pettit, *The Experts,* 1975

I feel like I just grabbed a big juicy worm with a right sharp hook in the middle of it.

> LYNDON B. JOHNSON TO BILL MOYERS FOLLOWING VIETNAM BRIEFING, Nov. 24, 1963, TWO DAYS AFTER BECOMING PRESIDENT, quoted in *Newsweek,* Feb. 10, 1975

My solution? Tell the Vietnamese they've got to draw in their horns . . . or we're going to bomb them back into the Stone Age.

> GEN. CURTIS E. LeMAY, Air Force Chief of Staff, May 6, 1964, quoted in Clyde Edwin Pettit, *The Experts,* 1975

But we are not about to send American boys nine or ten thousand miles away from home to do what Asian boys ought to be doing for themselves.
LYNDON B. JOHNSON, campaigning, Akron, Ohio, Oct. 21, 1964

VIETNAM: THE WAR

Nail the coonskin to the wall.
LYNDON B. JOHNSON TO U.S. COMMANDERS, Cam Ranh Bay, Oct. 25, 1966

When we add divisions can't the enemy add divisions? If so, where does it all end?
LYNDON B. JOHNSON TO GEN. WILLIAM C. WESTMORELAND SEEKING MORE TROOPS, Apr. 27, 1967, *Pentagon Papers,* 1971

How do you win a war in a peasant country on the side of the land-lords?
I. F. STONE, quoted in "Recollections of I. F. Stone's Weekly," PBS, Jan. 10, 1977

I see light at the end of the tunnel.
WALT W. ROSTOW, *Look,* Dec. 1967

It became necessary to destroy the town in order to save it.
MAJOR WHO DIRECTED FIRE INTO BEN TRE, Feb. 7, 1968, quoted by Associated Press, Feb. 9, 1968

It looks like the world caught smallpox and died.
MARINE OFFICER ON THE BOMB-POCKED KHE SANH PERIMETER, quoted in *New York Times,* Mar. 28, 1968

Well, I'm happy to say that the Army's casualties finally caught up with the Marines' last week.
GENERAL AT VIETNAM PRESS BRIEFING, quoted in *New York Times,* Mar. 3, 1968

It's like some giant corporation where you can't quit and everybody has gone crazy.
U.S. SOLDIER, quoted in *Newsweek,* Mar. 21, 1970

I thought you knew. You sent me there.
LT. COL. WALLEN SUMMERS, whenever asked why he went to Vietnam, quoted in *Newsweek,* May 24, 1971

You always write it's bombing, bombing, bombing. It's not bombing. It's air support.
> COL. DAVID H. E. OPFER, air attaché, U.S. Embassy, Cambodia, 1973, quoted in *New York Times,* Nov. 28, 1974

I would like to ask a question. Would this sort of war or savage bombing which has taken place in Vietnam have been tolerated for so long, had the people been European?
> INDIRA GANDHI, quoted in *Newsweek,* Feb. 19, 1973

Peace is a continuation of war by other means.
> GEN. VO NGUYEN GIAP AFTER PARIS CEASE-FIRE AGREEMENT, quoted in *Newsweek,* Feb. 5, 1973

VIETNAM: AFTER

Wrong and morally wrong in its conduct and consequences, it was nevertheless not evil in intent or origin. What propelled us into this war was a corruption of the generous, idealistic, liberal impulse.
> ALEXANDER M. BICKEL, *The Morality of Consent,* 1975

Conceived, promoted and directed by intellectuals fascinated with power and eager to prove their toughness and resolve.
> RONALD STEEL, *Imperialists and Other Heroes,* 1971

I have heard every political and technical explanation there is for the failure of our ten-year-long adventure in Southeast Asia. But I think there is one that takes precedence over them all. Quite simply, we didn't know who the Vietnamese were.
> MEG GREENFIELD, *Newsweek,* Feb. 2, 1976

We were a world power with a half-world knowledge. We knew only Europe.
> HUBERT H. HUMPHREY, "Bill Moyers' Journal," PBS, Apr. 11, 1976

If we had won in Vietnam what is it that we would have won?
> FATHER OF BOY KILLED IN VIETNAM, quoted in Gloria Emerson, *Winners and Losers,* 1977

VIOLENCE also see TV: VIOLENCE

Men seeking to seize, hold, or realign the levers of power have continually engaged in collective violence as part of their struggles. The oppressed have struck in the name of justice, the privileged in the name of order, those in between in the name of power.
REPORT, National Commission on Causes and Prevention of Violence, June 6, 1969

Deeds of violence in our society are performed largely by those trying to establish their self-image, to defend their self-image, and to demonstrate that they, too, are significant.
ROLLO MAY, *Power and Innocence,* 1972

Ethnic, religious and racial mixture—above all the last of these—are the fundamental determinants of American violence.
RICHARD H. HOFSTADTER, *American Violence,* 1970

Nonviolence is a big flop. The only worse flop is violence.
JOAN BAEZ, *Quote,* Sept. 10, 1967

VIRGINITY see SEX

VIRTUE also see EVIL

If the necessity for virtue could tell us how to practice it, we should be virtuous overnight.
ALLEN TATE, *Memoirs and Opinions 1926–1974,* 1975

I know myself too well to believe in pure virtue.
ALBERT CAMUS, quoted in Dick Dabney, *A Good Man,* 1976

VOTING also see POLITICS: THE ELECTION

Laws are written at the ballot box.
LAWYER, quoted in *Public Relations Journal,* May 1965

Can anyone remember voting for the metric system or the Albany Mall?
WILFRID SHEED, *New York Times,* Oct. 9, 1977

Voters do not decide issues, they decide *who* will decide issues.
GEORGE F. WILL, *Newsweek,* Mar. 8, 1976

Whereas in depression or during great bursts of economic reform people vote for what they think are their economic interests, in times of prosperity they feel free to vote their prejudices.
RICHARD H. HOFSTADTER, *Columbia Forum,* Fall 1965

Disillusionment in the voting process comes not from having your candidate beaten but from having him elected.
NICHOLAS VON HOFFMAN, "Bill Moyers' Journal," PBS, Feb. 2, 1979

Many times I wished that I could vote "Maybe."
MAURINE NEUBERGER, *Quote,* Nov. 13, 1966

I don't vote. It just encourages them.
MAINE COUNTRYWOMAN, quoted on "Dick Cavett Show," ABC-TV, May 16, 1972

WAR also see PEACE; VIETNAM; WORLD WAR I; WORLD WAR II

War is the unfolding of miscalculations.
BARBARA TUCHMAN, *The Guns of August,* 1962

War is fear cloaked in courage.
GEN. WILLIAM C. WESTMORELAND, *McCall's,* Dec. 1966

A highly cooperative method and form of theft.
JACOB BRONOWSKI, "The Ascent of Man," PBS, Jan. 14, 1975

Blood is the currency of war. It's just like money really. You try to invest yours—to get as high a return as possible. And you try to spend the enemy's.
CHARLES COE, *Young Man in Vietnam,* 1968

Only the winners get away with their lies, as only the winners decide what were war crimes.
GARRY WILLS, *New York Times,* July 10, 1975

Had not innumerable soldiers shed their blood, there would have been no Hellenism, no Roman civilization, no Christianity, no Rights of Man and no modern developments.
CHARLES DE GAULLE, *The Edge of the Sword,* 1960

There is an invisible but real wall between the man who has been there and the man who has not; and the man who has been there is likely to feel closer to the men on the side of the line across from him than he does to his compatriots back home.

IRWIN SHAW, *New York Times,* June 12, 1977

This year you're a hero. Next year you'll be a disabled veteran. And after that you'll just be a cripple.

DOCTOR TO WORLD WAR II WOUNDED AT ARMY REHABILITATION CENTER, 1945

Sometime they'll give a war and nobody will come.

SMALL GIRL, Carl Sandburg, *The People, Yes,* 1936

WAR OF THE SEXES see SEXES, WAR OF THE

WASHINGTON, D.C. also see POLITICS: THE POL

Washington is a crazy quilt of people who have each other by their vulnerable parts.

DOUGLAS CATER, "David Frost Show," CBS, Sept. 17, 1970

Washington is an endless series of mock palaces clearly built for clerks.

ADA LOUISE HUXTABLE, *New York Times,* Sept. 22, 1968

A place where men praise courage and act on elaborate personal cost-benefit calculation.

JOHN KENNETH GALBRAITH, *New York Times,* Apr. 25, 1971

A city with southern efficiency and northern charm.

JOHN F. KENNEDY, quoted on "Evening News," ABC-TV, July 19, 1973

Washington is a Democratic company town. When Democrats come here, they have nowhere better to go back to, so they stay. When Republicans come, they're regarded as a temporary occupying army. They'll go away.

WASHINGTON SOCIAL LEADER, quoted in *Newsweek,* Aug. 2, 1969

The majority who come to do good end up, as the saying goes, panting to do well, or simply to survive.

MAX FRANKEL, *Columbia Forum,* Winter 1973

The real trick in Washington is to keep as unobligated as you can while piling up as many IOU's as possible.
DAN H. FENN, JR., *Harvard Business Review,* Jan.–Feb. 1967

Success and prominence are Washington's true transients.
LAURENCE LEAMER, *Playing for Keeps in Washington,* 1977

Washington, under Democrats and Republicans, has a profoundly neurotic attitude toward "the people." It is built on equal parts of suspicion, loathing, fear, respect and dependence.
MEG GREENFIELD, *Newsweek,* June 19, 1978

The further you get away from Washington, the more you think things are under control there.
ART BUCHWALD, *New York Times,* 1968

WATERGATE

HALDEMAN: Now, on . . . the Democratic break-in thing, we're back in the problem area, because the FBI is not under control . . . their investigation is now leading into some productive areas. . . . Mitchell . . . came up with yesterday, and John Dean . . . concurs now . . . that the only way to solve this . . . is for us to have Walters [CIA deputy director] call Pat Gray [FBI acting director] and just say, "Stay the hell out of this . . . we don't want you to go any further."
NIXON: You call them in . . . play it tough.
WHITE HOUSE TAPE, June 23, 1972, six days after the break-in; this was the "smoking pistol," the proof that "national security" would be used as a ruse to persuade the FBI, through the CIA, to drop its investigation

DEAN TO NIXON: We have made it this far and I am convinced we are going to make it the whole road and put this thing in the funny pages of the history books.
WHITE HOUSE TAPE, Feb. 28, 1973, the day after Nixon assigned Dean to give full attention to Watergate

NIXON: I think we have to find a way to make statements . . . just so somebody can say that—a statement has been made through the President . . . to the effect that he has confidence in his staff—I didn't do this, I didn't do that, da da da da da da da da da da da da da da da. Haldeman didn't do this, Ehrlichman didn't do that. Colson didn't do that.
HALDEMAN: I wouldn't say that this is the whole truth.
WHITE HOUSE TAPE, Mar. 20, 1973

DEAN TO NIXON: I can give a show we can sell them, just like we were selling Wheaties.
WHITE HOUSE TAPE, Mar. 21, 1973

NIXON TO DEAN: Just be damned sure you say I don't remember, I can't recall, I can't give any honest—an answer to that that I can recall.
WHITE HOUSE TAPE, Mar. 21, 1973, before Dean's grand jury appearance

NIXON TO DEAN: Well, for Christ's sake, get it.
WHITE HOUSE TAPE, Mar. 21, 1973, on Howard Hunt's demand for $120,000

The problem is not Watergate or the cover-up. It's that he hasn't been telling the truth to the American people. The tape makes it evident that he hasn't leveled with the country for probably 18 months. And the President can't lead a country he has deliberately misled for a year and a half.
PATRICK BUCHANAN TO NIXON'S DAUGHTERS, Aug. 3, 1974, quoted in Bob Woodward and Carl Bernstein, *The Final Days,* 1976

Our long national nightmare is over.
GERALD R. FORD, swearing-in speech, Aug. 9, 1974, the day Nixon resigned

So now we know everything about the Watergate affair except why it happened.
ANATOLE BROYARD, *New York Times,* May 12, 1975

WELFARE

Welfare is hated by those who administer it, mistrusted by those who pay for it and held in contempt by those who receive it.
PETER C. GOLDMARK, JR., N.Y. State budget director, quoted in *New York Times,* May 24, 1977

When hundreds of millions of dollars are given to bankrupt railroads, failing defense manufacturers, shipping interests and the like, the words "welfare" or "relief" are not used. Instead, such things are done to "strengthen the economy." Perhaps welfare to needy individuals can someday be discussed with the same particularity and with the same equanimity.
CHIEF JUSTICE EARL WARREN, *A Republic, If You Can Keep It,* 1972

Social security took welfare out of politics and put it in the bureaucracy, and that, by the way, is the last time anyone understood it.
ANONYMOUS, quoted on "The Others," PBS, Nov. 19, 1976

WHITE HOUSE also see PRESIDENTS

Living over the shop.
LADY BIRD JOHNSON, "David Frost Show," CBS, Nov. 2, 1970

The White House is one of the few places in downtown Washington where you can get something to eat after 11 o'clock at night.
ROSALIND RUSSELL, obituary in *New York Times*, Dec. 5, 1976

The White House is not a healthy place.
JOHN MITCHELL, advising John Dean not to accept appointment as counsel to the president, quoted in John Dean, *Blind Ambition*, 1976

The White House doesn't try to restrict me—I don't think they even claim to know me any more.
BILLY CARTER, quoted in *Newsweek*, Oct. 31, 1977

Have you seen this—this so-called White House? The way the Garfields left it? I will not live in a house looking that way.
CHESTER A. ARTHUR, quoted in *Show*, Nov. 1964

WIDOWS

I don't feel like a survivor. I feel left behind.
HELEN BEVINGTON, *Along Came the Witch*, 1976

I don't even have an autographed ball. You don't ask your husband for an autographed ball. He'd probably think you were nuts.
CLAIRE RUTH (MRS. BABE RUTH), interview in *New York Times*, Aug. 12, 1973

People want widows to marry, but not to date.
DR. NORMAN I. BARR

WIT also see COMEDY/COMEDIANS; HUMOR/HUMORISTS; LAUGHTER; SATIRE

Wit has truth to it. Wisecracking is simply calisthenics with words.
DOROTHY PARKER, obituary in *New York Times*, June 8, 1967

Wit is social criticism, and its object is to *deflate.*
NOËL COWARD, quoted in William Marchant, *The Privilege of His Company,* 1975

Impropriety is the soul of wit.
W. SOMERSET MAUGHAM, *The Moon and Sixpence,* 1919

Wit is the epitaph of an emotion.
FRIEDRICH NIETZSCHE, quoted in *Newsweek,* Apr. 21, 1975

WIVES also see MARRIAGE; SEXES, WAR OF THE

If the value of a wife's services in a home were included in the U.S. gross national income, that figure would double in a year.
JULIA MONTGOMERY WALSH, *Quote,* Jan. 1, 1967

I am on trial every time they sit down to eat, every time they put on a white shirt.
CONSUELO SAAH BAEHR, *Report from the Heart,* 1976

Damn, damn, damn. I am sick of being this handmaid to the Lord.
ANNE MORROW LINDBERGH, *Locked Rooms and Open Doors,* 1974

You're running France. I'm running the house.
MME CHARLES DE GAULLE TO THE PRESIDENT, quoted in Alain de Gaulle, *The Secret Life of My Uncle Charlie,* 1969

Who in the world ever saw a retired housewife?
ANONYMOUS, *Quote,* Nov. 13, 1966

Certainly if housewifery lacks the appeal of astro-physics or consumer-protection litigation, it is no more tedious than insurance sales, real-estate development, or product-package design. Why then is it the object of derision?
WEST VIRGINIA SUPREME COURT JUSTICE RICHARD NEELY, *New York Times,* May 18, 1975

Each [of my wives] was jealous and resentful of my preoccupation with business. Yet none showed any visible aversion to sharing in the proceeds.
J. PAUL GETTY, *As I See It,* 1976

A female will almost never set fire to her own bed, but you can always tell when a woman's done it; she first piles her husband's clothes on it.
JOHN BARRACATO, deputy chief fire marshal, N.Y.C., speech at International Congress of Crime Writers, Mar. 15, 1978

WOMEN also see MALE CHAUVINISM; MEN; SEXES, WAR OF THE

Women are smarter than men because they listen.
PHIL DONAHUE, interview in *Newsweek,* Mar. 13, 1978

Woman is a constipated biped with a backache.
J. P. GREENHILL, *Office Gynecology,* 1965

The strongest evidence to prove that God exists is a beautiful woman.
GIOVANNI LEONE, PRESIDENT OF ITALY, interview in Rizzoli Press Service—Europo, Apr. 1973

Nothing so stirs a man's conscience or excites his curiosity as a woman's complete silence.
Services and Industry, 1966

After an acquaintance of ten minutes many women will exchange confidences that a man would not reveal to a lifelong friend.
PAGE SMITH, *Daughters of the Promised Land,* 1970

One of the mistakes women have made is to romanticize life in the rose-covered cottage and then, discovering their error, proceed to romanticize life in the working world.
JUANITA M. KREPS, *Secretary,* June–July 1970

Women are most fascinating during their 30's after they have run a few races and know how to pace themselves.
CHRISTIAN DIOR, quoted in *New York Post,* Sept. 29, 1972

From 35 to 45 women are old, and at 45 the devil takes over, and they're beautiful, splendid, maternal, proud. The acidities are gone, and in their place reigns calm. They are worth going out to find, and because of them some men never grow old. When I see them my mouth waters.
JEAN-BAPTISTE TROISGROS, obituary in *New York Times,* Oct. 24, 1974

Fortunately for women, her body is still a trap—if no longer a baby trap, a man trap.
> CLARE BOOTHE LUCE, quoted in *New York Times,* Mar. 2, 1969

I do not believe in using women in combat, because females are too fierce.
> MARGARET MEAD, *Quote,* Jan. 15, 1967

A woman will buy anything she thinks a store is losing money on.
> ATTRIBUTED TO KIN HUBBARD (FRANK MCKINNEY HUBBARD).

To call a woman pleasant is to imply that her underwear is made of linoleum.
> FREDERICK LONSDALE, *The Last of Mrs. Cheyney* (drama), 1925

How does it feel to be a woman minister? I don't know; I've never been a man minister.
> GOLDA MEIR, ISRAELI PRIME MINISTER, interview in *New York Post,* Mar. 8, 1969

WOMEN'S LIBERATION

We are refusing to be trivialized.
> LETTY COTTIN POGREBIN, speech at Douglass College commencement, June 1973

Not only am I angry, but I'm also angry at all the years I wasn't angry.
> CAROL KLEIMAN, *Ms.,* Apr. 1978

Today's youth seem finally to have understood that only by freeing woman from her exclusively sexual role can man free himself from his ordained role in the rat-race: that of the rat.
> CAROLYN G. HEILBRUN, *New York Times,* Nov. 17, 1968

The women's liberation warriors think they have something new, but it's just their armies coming out of the guerrilla hills. Sweet women ambushed men always: at their cradles, in the kitchen, the bedroom . . .
> MARIO PUZO, *Fools Die,* 1978

Scratch most feminists and underneath there is a woman who longs to be a sex object. The difference is that is not *all* she longs to be.
> BETTY ROLLIN, *First, You Cry,* 1976

Despite a lifetime of service to the cause of sexual liberation, I have never caught venereal disease, which makes me feel rather like an Arctic explorer who has never had frostbite.
GERMAINE GREER, *Times* (London), Feb. 3, 1973

Many books today suggest that the mass of women lead lives of noisy desperation.
PETER S. PRESCOTT, *Newsweek*, May 30, 1977

The people I'm furious with are the women's liberationists. They keep getting up on soapboxes and proclaiming women are brighter than men. That's true, but it should be kept quiet or it ruins the whole racket.
ANITA LOOS, interview in *New York Times*, 1973

The women's movement . . . would probably run more smoothly if men were running it.
BOB MELVIN, quoted in Earl Wilson's column, Mar. 24, 1977

WORDS also see LANGUAGE

Words are all we have.
SAMUEL BECKETT, quoted in *New York Times*, Sept. 15, 1974

You can taste a word.
PEARL BAILEY, interview in *Newsweek*, Dec. 4, 1967

Words are loaded pistols.
JEAN-PAUL SARTRE, quoted in Geoffrey Wolff, *Inklings*, 1978

Each day the human mouth expels so many words that inevitably a percentage will emerge as irrelevant, embarrassingly egotistical, meaningless, shocking, inane or just appallingly dumb.
LEWIS GROSSBERGER, *New York Post*, Mar. 23, 1974

Scientists who refer to people as *subjects*, businessmen who refer to people as *personnel*, teachers who refer to people as *culturally disadvantaged* are not merely describing; they are committing themselves to a point of view.
NEIL POSTMAN, *Crazy Talk, Stupid Talk*, 1976

For millions of people today, words like communism, capitalism, imperialism, peace, freedom, democracy, have ceased to be words the meaning of which can be inquired into and discussed, and have become right and wrong noises to which the response is as involuntary as a knee-reflex.
> W. H. AUDEN, speech accepting National Medal for Literature, May 1, 1967

As far as I'm concerned, the most beautiful word in the English language is cellar-door.
> DOROTHY PARKER, obituary in *New York Times,* June 8, 1967

I always wanted to write a book that ended with the word mayonnaise.
> RICHARD BRAUTIGAN, *In Watermelon Sugar,* 1969

WORK also see BLUE-COLLAR BLUES; THE JOB; SECRETARIES

One of the saddest things is that the thing a man can do for eight hours a day, day after day, is work. You can't eat eight hours a day nor drink for eight hours a day nor make love for eight hours—all you can do for eight hours is work.
> WILLIAM FAULKNER, *Lion in the Garden,* James B. Meriwether and Michael Millgate, eds., 1968

Work is less boring than pleasure.
> J. PIEPER, *Leisure, the Basis of Culture,* 1963

If it were not for the demands made upon me by my business, I would provide living proof that a man can live quite happily for decades without ever doing any work.
> J. PAUL GETTY, quoted in *Forbes,* June 1, 1967

There's a big difference between busy and real work.
> TOM McGREAL, Iowa farmer, interview in *Newsweek,* May 15, 1978

THE WORLD

Impure and unjust and totally unfit for the weak.
> MIKHAIL DYOMIN, *The Day Is Born of Darkness,* 1976

The world just doesn't work. It's an idea whose time is gone.
> JOSEPH HELLER, *Something Happened,* 1974

The whole world is for sale these days; all you need is the down payment.
AL LAPIN, JR., president, International Industries, quoted in *Business Week,* June 21, 1969

The world is changing and anyone who thinks he can live alone is sleeping through a revolution.
MARTIN LUTHER KING, JR., speech in Memphis, Tenn., Mar. 31, 1968

The world is always in crisis; the unspeakable has always been occurring; the end of the world has always been at hand, because man is appallingly wicked.
MARTIN GREEN, *The Challenge of the Mahatmas,* 1978

For all its shame, drudgery and broken dreams, the world is still a beautiful place.
PIERRE ELLIOTT TRUDEAU, quoted in *Newsweek,* June 4, 1979

Enjoy the world gently, enjoy the world gently; if the world is spoiled, no one can repair it, enjoy the world gently.
BABALOWOS SONG, Nigeria

WORLD WAR I also see WAR

The First World War was a war of no tactics, no strategy, no mind. Just slaughter.
PAUL FUSSELL, *The Great War and Modern Memory,* 1975

When man first faced the full weight of the profusely distributed metal of heavy industry.
FRANK KERMODE, *New York Times,* Aug. 31, 1975

Plugging shellholes with live soldiers.
SANCHE DE GRAMONT, *The Strong Brown God,* 1975

Man is fighting against matériel with the sensation of striking out at empty air.
CÉSAR MÉLÉRA, French sgt. major, at Verdun, quoted in *New York Times,* Feb. 20, 1966

Not armies but whole nations broke and ran.
WINSTON CHURCHILL, *World Crisis,* 1929

All my beautiful lovely safe world blew itself up.
> F. Scott Fitzgerald, *Tender Is the Night,* 1934

Oh why was I born for this time? Before one is 30 to know more dead than living people.
> Lady Cynthia Asquith, *Diaries 1915–1918,* 1968

This war—as the next war—was called the war to end wars.
> David Lloyd George, quoted on "World War I," PBS, Mar. 28, 1976

WORLD WAR II also see THE BOMB; THE HOLOCAUST; WAR

And while I am talking to you mothers and fathers, I give you one more assurance. I have said this before, but I say it again and again and again: Your boys are not going to be sent into any foreign wars.
> Franklin D. Roosevelt, campaigning, Boston, Oct. 30, 1940, 13 months before Pearl Harbor

We shall fight in France, we shall fight on the seas and oceans, we shall fight with growing confidence and growing strength in the air, we shall defend our island, whatever the cost may be, we shall fight on the beaches, we shall fight on the landing grounds, we shall fight in the fields and in the streets, we shall fight in the hills; we shall never surrender.
> Winston Churchill, speech to House of Commons, June 4, 1940, on completion of the Dunkirk evacuation

But if we fail, then the whole world, including the United States, including all that we have known and cared for, will sink into the abyss of a new Dark Age more sinister, perhaps more protracted, by the lights of perverted science.
> Winston Churchill, speech to House of Commons, June 18, 1940

This war no longer bears the characteristics of former inter-European conflicts. It is one of those elemental conflicts which usher in a new millennium and which shake the world once in a thousand years.
> Adolf Hitler, speech at Reichstag, Apr. 26, 1942

I want 1,000 [Italian] dead to be able to sit at the conference table.
> Benito Mussolini, quoted on "World at War," PBS, Nov. 11, 1973

For the Allies, as well as for Germany, it will be the longest day.
> Field Marshal Erwin Rommel predicting the first 24 hours of the coming Allied invasion would be decisive, quoted in Cornelius Ryan, *The Longest Day,* 1959

Is Paris burning?
> Adolf Hitler when told the Allies had liberated Paris, Aug. 25, 1944, quoted in Larry Collins and Dominique Lapierre, *Is Paris Burning?,* 1965

I peed in the Rhine.
> Lt. Gen. George S. Patton, Jr., marginal note on operations report when U.S. Third Army reached the Rhine, Mar. 1945

How the Great Democracies Triumphed and so Were Able to Resume the Follies Which Had so Nearly Cost Them Their Life.
> Winston Churchill, subtitle of final volume of his World War II history, *Triumph and Tragedy,* 1953

WRITERS/WRITING also see BOOKS; LITERATURE; READING

Unless one is a genius, it is best to aim at being intelligible.
> Anthony Hope Hawkins, quoted in *Personnel,* Nov. 12, 1969

Real seriousness in regard to writing is one of the two absolute necessities. The other, unfortunately, is talent.
> Ernest Hemingway, *By-Line,* William White, ed., 1967

Each story teaches me how to write *it,* but not the one afterwards.
> Eudora Welty, "The Originals," PBS, May 18, 1978

My family can always tell when I'm well into a novel because the meals get very crummy.
> Anne Tyler, interview in *New York Times,* May 8, 1977

She would write eight or ten words, then draw her gun and shoot them down.
> E. B. White on his wife, Katharine S. White, introduction to Katharine White, *Onward and Upward in the Garden,* 1979

First of all, you must have an agent, and in order to get a good one, you must have sold a considerable amount of material. And in order to sell a considerable amount of material, you must have an agent. Well, you get the idea.
> Steve McNeil, *TV Guide,* Dec. 12, 1970

YACHTING

It's quite easy to simulate the joys of yachting in your own home. All you have to do is stand in a very cold shower and tear up twenty-dollar bills.
YACHTSMEN'S AXIOM

If the America's Cup is lost, its place will be taken by the head of the man who loses it.
MOTTO OF N.Y. YACHT CLUB, WHICH HAS HELD THE CUP SINCE 1851

YOUTH also see ADOLESCENCE; CHILDHOOD; CHILDREN

I have something to say but I don't know what it is.
PARIS GRAFFITO, quoted in New York Times, June 18, 1968

I'm not even sure what I want, but that's not the point—it's that I want it now.
ELVIS COSTELLO, interview in Newsweek, May 8, 1978

The young have no depth perception in time. Ten years back or 10 years forward is an eternity.
ROBERT C. ALBERTS, New York Times, Nov. 17, 1974

Their intolerance is breath-taking. Do your thing means do their thing.
PAUL GOODMAN, New Reformation, 1970

They pick the rhetoric they want to hear right off the top of an issue and never finish reading to the bottom.
MARTHA MITCHELL

Kids get in trouble, but it's human nature to get as close to the hot stove as you can—and sometimes you touch it.
JOHN WAYNE, interview in Newsweek, Mar. 19, 1973

To assume that the young will inevitably be both wiser and better than their elders is a forlorn hope, hardly justified by historic experience.
HAROLD BLAKE WALKER, Prairie Farmer, Jan. 3, 1970

Every new generation of Americans is assured that it is the smartest, the best educated, the most idealistic ever.
KENNETH CRAWFORD, Newsweek, Mar. 30, 1970

The words *you know* and *I mean* are strewn like loose gravel through ordinary conversation, causing slippage in meaning.
NORMAN COUSINS, *Saturday Review,* Mar. 23, 1974

The only premarital experience they seem to deny themselves is cooking.
DAVID FROST AND ANTONY JAY, *The English,* 1968

Today's younger generation is no worse than my own. We were just as ignorant and repulsive as they are, but nobody listened to us.
AL CAPP, quoted in *Education Digest,* Sept. 1968

ZEN also see THE MEDITATION KICK

The noisy sleepwalkers on the Open Road.
PETER HYUN ON BEAT ZEN, *New York Times,* May 18, 1972

INDEX

ACKNOWLEDGMENTS

Grateful acknowledgment is made to the following for permission to reprint selections included in this book:

Columbia Journalism Review, (New York) *Daily News,* Dow Jones & Company, Inc., Publishers, *Forbes* Magazine, *Kaiser Aluminum News, Life,* NBC, *Newsweek, The New Yorker, Princeton Alumni Weekly, Public Relations Journal, Public Utilities Fortnightly, Saturday Review, Time, TV Guide, University: A Princeton Quarterly, Writer's Digest.*

GEORGE ALLEN & UNWIN: quotation from *Autobiography of Bertrand Russell* by Bertrand Russell.

AMERICAN BROADCASTING COMPANY: quotations from ABC News and entertainment programs. © American Broadcasting Companies, Inc., 1979. Reprinted by permission.

ATHENEUM PUBLISHERS, INC.: quotations from *Who Pushed Humpty Dumpty?* by Donald Barr. Copyright © 1971 by Donald Barr. Reprinted by permission of Atheneum Publishers.

BUSINESS WEEK AND MCGRAW-HILL, INC.: quotations from *Business Week* by special permission.

COLUMBIA FORUM: quotations from *Columbia Forum.* Reprinted by permission of The Trustees of Columbia University in the City of New York.

DELACORTE PRESS: quotation from "The Pill Versus the Springhill Mine Disaster," excerpted from *The Pill Versus the Springhill Mine Disaster* by Richard Brautigan. Copyright © 1968 by Richard Brautigan. Reprinted by permission of Delacorte Press/Seymour Lawrence.

DODD, MEAD & COMPANY, INC.: quotation from "A Little Night Music," music and lyrics by Stephen Sondheim, book by Hugh Wheeler. Copyright © 1973 by Hugh Wheeler, Stephen Sondheim and Harold S. Prince. Lyrics copyright © 1973 by Revelation Music Publishing Corporation/Beautiful Music, Inc. Reprinted by permission of the authors and publisher, Dodd, Mead & Company, Inc.

FARRAR, STRAUS & GIROUX, INC.: quotation from *Carrying the Fire* by Michael Collins. Copyright © 1974 by Michael Collins. Reprinted by permission of Farrar, Straus & Giroux, Inc.

FIELD NEWSPAPER SYNDICATE: quotations of Earl Wilson and Leonard Lyons.

FORTUNE MAGAZINE: Courtesy of *Fortune* Magazine.

HARCOURT BRACE JOVANOVICH, INC.: quotations from *Two Cheers for Democracy* by E. M. Forster; *Locked Rooms and Open Doors* by Anne Morrow Lindbergh; *Four Quartets* by T. S. Eliot; and *The Philosophy of Andy Warhol* by Andy Warhol.

HAPRPER & ROW, PUBLISHERS, INC.: quotation from "Letter to E.S.P. Haynes" from *Letters of Aldous Huxley*, edited by Grover Smith. Copyright © 1969 by Laura Huxley. Copyright © 1969 by Grover Smith.

ALAN JAY LERNER: quotation from "My Fair Lady."

LITTLE, BROWN AND COMPANY: quotation from *Children of Crisis, Vol. III: The South Goes North* by Robert Coles. Copyright © 1972 by Robert Coles. Reprinted by permission of Little, Brown and Co. in association with the Atlantic Monthly Press.

MACMILLAN PUBLISHING CO., INC.: quotations from *The Screwtape Letters* by C. S. Lewis. Copyright © 1942 by C. S. Lewis; *For Colored Girls Who Have Considered Suicide/When the Rainbow Is Enuf* by Ntozake Shange. Copyright © 1975, 1976, 1977 by Ntozake Shange; and *A Thief's Primer* by Bruce Jackson. Copyright © 1969 by Bruce Jackson.

MCGRAW-HILL, INC.: quotations from *How to Get Along with Automation* by Donald and Eleanor Laird.

NEW DIRECTIONS PUBLISHING CORP.: quotation from *Personae* by Ezra Pound. Copyright © 1926 by Ezra Pound. Reprinted by permission of New Directions.

NEW STATESMAN: quotations from *New Statesman*. Reprinted from New Statesman, London, by permission.

NEW YORK POST. Reprinted by permission of the New York Post, New York Post Corporation.

THE NEW YORK TIMES: quotations from *The New York Times*. Copyright © 1979 by The New York Times Company. Reprinted by permission.

RANDOM HOUSE, INC.: quotations of W. H. Auden from *Forewords And Afterwards*. Copyright © 1973 by W. H. Auden; *Another Time*, Copyright © 1940 by W. H. Auden, © renewed 1968 by W. H. Auden; *Epistle to a Godson and Other Poems*. Copyright © 1969, 1970, 1971, 1972 by W. H. Auden; *The English Auden* edited by Edward Mendelson. Copyright © 1978 by Edward Mendelson. Quotations of William Faulkner from *Selected Letters of William Faulkner*, edited by Joseph Blotner. Copyright © 1977 by Joseph Blotner; *Faulkner* by Joseph Blotner. Copyright © 1974 by Joseph Blotner. Quotation of Frank O'Hara from *Meditations in an Emergency* by Frank O'Hara. Copyright © 1954 by Maureen Granville-Smith, administratrix of the Estate of Frank O'Hara.

READER'S DIGEST: quotation by Arnold H. Glasgow. Reprinted with permission from the June 1974 Reader's Digest.

THE SATURDAY EVENING POST: quotation by Sir Denis Brogan from the June 5, 1963, issue. © 1963 The Curtis Publishing Company. Excerpt by Abraham Kaplan from the September 23, 1961, issue. © 1961 The Curtis Publishing Company. Excerpt by Paul Tillich from the June 14, 1958, issue. © 1958 The Curtis Publishing Company.

SIMON & SCHUSTER, INC.: quotations from *The B. S. Factor* by Arthur Herzog. Copyright © 1973 by Arthur Herzog; *The Final Days* by Bob Woodward and Carl Bernstein. Copyright © 1976 by Bob Woodward and Carl Bernstein; *Global Reach* by Richard J. Barnet and Ronald Müller. Copyright © 1975 by Richard J. Barnet and Ronald Müller. *Lessons of History* by Will and Ariel Durant. Copyright © 1968 by Will and Ariel Durant.